FUNCTIONALISM
AND WORLD POLITICS

FUNCTIONALISM AND WORLD POLITICS

A STUDY BASED ON UNITED NATIONS PROGRAMS FINANCING ECONOMIC DEVELOPMENT

BY JAMES PATRICK SEWELL

PRINCETON, NEW JERSEY
PRINCETON UNIVERSITY PRESS
1966

FOR MY PARENTS

Preface

SPEAKING AT dedication ceremonies for the University of Chicago Law School on 1 May 1960, the late Dag Hammarskjöld observed that "we are still in the transition between institutional systems of international coexistence and constitutional systems of international cooperation. It is natural that, at such a stage of transition, theory is still vague. . . ."

If theory to guide the statesman directly involved with United Nations matters is vague, it is no less so for the student of international organization. The latter would understand and explain that vast complex of activities known as the United Nations system. To do so he must grasp at straws of evidence borne by the turbulent and shifting winds of the modern world. The order of explanation often seems a far cry from the chaos of the real world.

The functionalist argument formulated by David Mitrany and others rises to this challenge.[1] In its explanatory role this thesis proffers a means toward understanding the relationship between international organization and international community; within the interstices of its explanatory scheme an interpretation of international politics appears.

Nor do the functionalists pause with the explanation of relationships. As Inis L. Claude, Jr. puts it, the functionalist thesis "is not merely a recipe to be studied, but also a dish to be tasted. . . ."[2] In its role as prescription the functionalist argument suggests a pathway for mankind to work its way toward peace and plenty. "Peace by Pieces"—Lyman C. White's fitting appellation[3]—would

[1] Especially Mitrany's *A Working Peace System: An Argument for the Functional Development of International Organization* (London: The Royal Institute of International Affairs, 1943).

[2] Inis L. Claude, Jr., *Swords Into Plowshares* (rev. ed.; New York: Random House, 1959), p. 387.

[3] Lyman C. White, "Peace by Pieces," *Free World*, XI (January 1946), pp. 66-68.

offer both a solace from potential dangers and deliverance from some present ones. World community shall be sought through international cooperation in activities which make this cooperation both plausible and fruitful. International negativism will be wiped from the face of the earth by an interlinked series of small efforts which accentuate the positive in terms of immediate objectives and ultimate consequences alike. Along the way, the ubiquitous totalitarian tendency of our day will be circumvented by shunting aside its vital force.

This is a report on the success of the functionalists in both their explanatory and prescriptive attempts. The functionalist recipe is studied, prepared, and then tasted, insofar as the present agenda may serve to test an argument which is notably shy of verbal standards, notably fond of the proverbial proof of the pudding.

The inquiry is both an endeavor to evaluate a "theory" and to analyze several programs operating as part of the United Nations system. These tasks are complementary. Full evaluation of the theory will require other cases, so selected as to encompass many variables and yet to satisfy the conditions set by the functionalist argument; full understanding of the present cases will never be achieved, although different approaches and studies by other investigators will help. These limitations are readily acknowledged, but the worthiness of both goals is affirmed. The first aim provides the framework for this project. The second is not insignificant simply because it is pursued within this framework: economic development, its instruments no less than its other aspects, hardly needs justification today as a focus for study.

In Part I the functionalist thesis is laid out for examination. What is the argument, what are its assumptions, what apparent weaknesses does it display? To what segment of the universe of experience is it addressed, and how may it be applied in a systematic analysis and interpretation of concrete events?

Part II sets a challenge for the functionalist argument by introducing several programs in the United Nations system involved in the financing of economic development. The International Bank for Reconstruction and Development (IBRD), the International Finance Corporation (IFC), the International Development Association (IDA), the United Nations Special Fund (abbreviated here as SF) are surveyed; other proposals are considered. Has the functionalist thesis been borne out in these activities? In what respects and to what extent?

The answers to these questions provide a point of departure for Part III, where the central query involves the interpretative capacity of the functionalist argument as demonstrated in this particular application. Does it yield insights as to *why* these programs developed and why they operate as they do? Are other explanations needed? Finally, how well is the functionalist normative claim substantiated, given the limitations of scope, methods, and execution of this study? How justifiable do the functionalist contentions appear to be with regard to building the Great Community?

Each portion of the undertaking introduces itself, but a few points of reference for the whole must be set forth here.

"Functionalism" is perhaps newer to the social sciences than to biology, psychology, and philosophy; certainly it has a familiar ring to the student in any of these disciplines. The several strands within the more general functionalist tradition have surprisingly little in common, but it might be said that all hold "function," however defined, to be preeminent in an explanatory, a chronological, or a normative sense. Thus, the slogan "form follows function" carries a somewhat ambiguous meaning, even though it affords a handy principle for lumping together functionalists of all varieties. Similarly, the functionalist rubric overarches a loose family of concerns with *relationships*—relationships, for instance, between organs, attitudes, concepts, variables, institutions, processes; between these and organisms, theories, systems; between these and their environments, concrete or analytically defined. The functional approach to international organization moves with the broader tradition in several instances, but these confluences will be treated only as seems appropriate to the present inquiry. Here the concern is with the species, not the genus.

Even "species" is misleading. Throughout the study "functionalists" are referred to as though they constituted a distinct school of interpretation and prescription within the field of international relations. This has seemed more desirable than fencing in each reference with a score of qualifications. But "functionalist" in these pages refers to an argument, not a school. President John F. Kennedy said in his first State of the Union message: "Where nature makes natural allies of us all, we can demonstrate that beneficial relations are possible, even with those with whom we most deeply disagree, and this must someday be the basis of world peace and world law." At that moment he was a functionalist, for purposes of this study.

The student of international relations who is drawn to study the functional approach is almost certain to assume an intellectual debt to those who preceded him. So it is with this inquiry. Besides the argument's major exponents, subsequently acknowledged, the present study owes much to the work of Curtis W. Martin and Harold E. Engle. Claude's excellent chapter provides both a lucid exposition and a searching critique of the functional approach.[4] This study attempts something a little different, but it has been nourished by their efforts.

[4] Curtis W. Martin, "The History and Theory of the Functional Approach to International Organization," unpublished Ph.D. dissertation, Department of Government, Harvard University, 1950; Harold E. Engle, "A Critical Study of the Functional Approach to International Organization," unpublished Ph.D. dissertation, Department of Public Law and Government, Columbia University, 1957; Claude, *op.cit.*, pp. 373-402.

During its dissertation phase, the inquiry profited from the guidance of Richard E. Caves, John H. Schaar, and especially Ernst B. Haas, whose learning, intellectual curiosity, and innovative prowess contributed more than the printed word can readily acknowledge. To the staff of the Bureau of International Relations Library of the University of California (Berkeley) I extend a belated vote of thanks for unfailing helpfulness and unflagging patience. I am grateful to the Carnegie Foundation for sustenance while bringing forth the initial draft, to the Rockefeller Foundation for enabling me to gain the distance and perspective afforded by a year of teaching and research in Africa before revising it, and to Berkeley (N.J., R.B., S.M.L., E.B.H., R.A.S.) for its role in both opportunities. A Brookings Institution summer seminar on the United Nations shaped and tempered my judgment on at least one matter. I am grateful, and for good reason, to staff members of the International Bank for Reconstruction and Development, who read a portion of the manuscript. Charles K. Derber reviewed the graphic data in Chapter IV. They have made this book more accurate in both a narrow and a broad sense, but of course the responsibility for what is said and not said between these covers rests with me alone. The book would have been far more difficult to read without the suggestions of brothers and sisters in my extended family, and Princeton University Press. Remaining difficulties are a measure of their task, not their qualifications or their labors. There would have been no book without my wife, who helped in ways much more fundamental and important than those exercises which might appear to reflect the sum total of this endeavor.

A final point of reference was Robert A. Dahl's timely warning that "the quest for empirical data can turn into an absorbing search for mere trivialities unless it is guided by some sense of the difference between an explanation that would not matter much even if [it] could be shown to be valid by the most advanced methods now available, and one that would matter a great deal if it should turn out to be a little more or a little less plausible than before, even if it remained in some considerable doubt."[5] There is a need to have continuously at hand the question "is that really correct?" But the most devastating question of all is "so what?"

[5] Robert A. Dahl, "The Behavioral Approach in Political Science: Epitaph for a Monument to a Successful Protest," *American Political Science Review*, LV (December 1961), p. 772.

Contents

List of Figures

PART I. FUNCTIONAL APPROACH, FUNCTIONALIST ARGUMENT

Humpty Dumpty sat on a wall;
Humpty Dumpty had a great fall.
All the king's horses,
And all the king's men,
Couldn't put Humpty together again.

—English version of a common nursery rhyme

Steam shall work melodiously,
Brotherhood increase.
You'll see the world and all it holds
For fifty cents apiece.

—Vachel Lindsay's Kallyope

. . . so would I enjoy the contemplation of that
which interests me above all things: namely, Life:
the force that ever strives to attain greater power
of contemplating itself. What made this brain of
mine, do you think? Not the need to move my limbs;
for a rat with half my brain moves as well as I.
Not merely the need to do, but the need to know what
I do, lest in my blind efforts to live I should be
slaying myself.

—G. B. Shaw's Don Juan

I

An Introductory Exposition

THE ARGUMENT for a "functional approach" to international organization holds that the most desirable route to international community-building proceeds gradually from initial transnational cooperation in the solution of common problems. Ben Bella's words[1] readily convey the functionalist thought: "We think that genuine unity, which would be crowned with firm and permanent structural ties, should above all be the outcome of common, patient and serious work in all fields in which complete identity of views already exists."

While the "functions" encompassed by this argument ultimately include governance and security, both the approach and the "functional sector" of international activities have come to be associated either with those areas customarily designated "social," "humanitarian," or "economic," in accordance with their substance, or with the labels "technical," "non-controversial," or "non-political," in reference to the procedure by which problems in these areas are ostensibly defined and their solutions found and applied. Is peace the aim? Its foundation must be laid by piecemeal international efforts in commonly recognized transnational problem areas which are readily adaptable to procedures shaped and accepted by modern man. This is the functionalist plea. Stretching beyond it, the functionalist thesis purports to explain the dynamics and products of international undertakings such as these and, inferentially, to explain the status of other international activities and their relationship to the functional sector.[2]

---

[1] Uttered shortly before the African summit meeting which launched the Organization of African Unity. Reported by TANJUG (Yugoslavia) News Agency in *Daily News*, published by Imperial Ethiopian Government, Ministry of Information, 17 May 1963.

[2] The terms "functionalist" and "functionalists" will be employed

I

Taken in a broad sense, this approach can be traced far back in time. The earliest foreshadowing of the modern argument known to the present writer is by Aristophanes. In his comedy *The Peace*, Aristophanes has Trygaeus (who is a farmer or "harvester") set out for Heaven on a huge dung beetle to rescue the goddess Peace. Having landed, Trygaeus finds that she lies at the bottom of a well, imprisoned by heavy stones. Since he is unable to free her by himself, Trygaeus calls for help—not to those representing the commercial interests from Athens and Sparta, many of whom have vested interests in the protracted conflict by virtue of their connections with the arms industry, but to the farmers from various warring city-states. Theirs is a common interest in peaceful settlement: their farmlands on the outskirts have known the ravages of invaders time and again. They pool their experience and blend their efforts to solve the common problem at hand. Peace is freed to return earthward and join with the others in the ensuing festivities. It might be noted that in Aristophanes' play the delegates from some warring city-states are considerably more interested in freeing Peace than are the dawdlers and obstructionists from others. But this raises a thought which must be saved for a later chapter.

To a much more substantial degree, functionalism is exemplified by the growth of the public international unions and private international associations which appeared in the nineteenth century, and by the commentaries of those who later undertook an interpretation of

---

as shorthand references to those who espouse a functional approach to international organization, whether the espousal is set forth in systematic or ad hoc fashion; "functionalist argument" or "functionalist thesis" will be applied to the substance of their contentions; and "functional approach" will refer to its literal embodiment in practice. "Functionalism" embraces thesis and practice.

their appearance.[3] Chief among these agencies were the International Telegraphic Union (1865) and the Universal Postal Union (1874). Some commentary has viewed them as a new genus in the evolution of social institutions, virtually blind to the intervention of human will. Inis L. Claude, Jr. emphasizes this aspect of their growth but implies also the role of "social invention," to borrow Graham Wallas' phrase. "This trend," writes Claude, "was not the product so much of proposals as of facts, conditions, and needs. It represented adaptation, not innovation. . . ." Yet ideas there were, for it was "the imaginative initiative of individuals and groups [which] sparked a process of conscious social contrivance to meet the requirements formulated by circumstances."[4]

Regardless of the relative weight to be assigned conscious inventiveness and environmental conditioning, these agencies were generally extolled in their day for the specific services they provided rather than the collateral value of international cooperation.

World War I sparked cooperative efforts on the part of the Allies in organizing and administering their transAtlantic supply line. J. A. Salter, Secretary to the Allied Maritime Transport Council and Chairman of its Executive, later recounted this experience and systematized his own conclusions.[5]

Necessity rather than foresight seemed the chief impulse behind the development of the League of Nations' economic and social system. When postwar ills pressed home the need for new organs, League actors looked to the only models they could find—the Universal Postal

[3] See especially Paul S. Reinsch, *Public International Unions* (Boston: Ginn and Company, 1911), *passim*; Simeon E. Baldwin, "The International Congresses and Conferences of the Last Century as Forces Working Toward the Solidarity of the World," *American Journal of International Law*, I (July 1907), pp. 565-78.

[4] Claude, *op.cit.*, pp. 35-36.

[5] J. A. Salter, *Allied Shipping Control* (Oxford: Clarendon Press, 1921).

Union, for instance, and the Allied Maritime Transport Council. Secretary-General Sir Eric Drummond created an economic section of the Secretariat in 1919. This section's studies of needs led to the Brussels Financial Conference in 1920, which in turn recommended establishment of a permanent economic and financial organization. The League Council approved plans for a Provisional Economic and Financial Committee the same year. Technical organs were directed to request the approval of the political League Council before undertaking "any communication of . . . proposals . . . to the Members." Experience seems to have suggested a division of labor, for shortly thereafter the economic and financial functions were organizationally separated, and later yet, as committees, these two were joined by the Fiscal Committee, Committee of Statistical Experts, and a Coordination Committee. The last named was established years later, in 1938, to furnish "more continuous supervision and coordination of the Economic and Financial Organization's work than could be provided by either the Council, Assembly or occasional conferences."[6]

One other League organ demands inclusion in this brief survey, even though it never passed the blueprint stage. In 1939, faced with serious and continuing economic and social problems, increasing difficulty in coordinating the various committees, and a need for collaboration with important non-League members, the League Council estab-

[6] Daniel S. Cheever and H. Field Haviland, Jr., *Organizing for Peace* (Cambridge: Harvard University Press, 1954), pp. 162-67. See also L. Larry Leonard, *International Organization* (New York: McGraw-Hill Book Company, Inc., 1951), pp. 332ff.; F. P. Walters, *A History of the League of Nations* (London: Oxford University Press, 1952), I, 175ff.; Martin Hill, *The Economic and Financial Organization of the League of Nations* (Washington: Carnegie Endowment for International Peace, 1946), especially pp. 106ff.; H. R. G. Greaves, *The League Committees and World Order* (London: Humphrey Milford, 1931), pp. 35ff., 69ff.; Egon F. Ranshofen-Wertheimer, *The International Secretariat* (Washington: Carnegie Endowment for International Peace, 1945), pp. 157-61.

lished the Bruce Committee and assigned it the study of these problems. This Committee's report recommended a new central organ to assume the major burden of supervision over functional bodies and activities. Before it could be established, the war intervened. The importance of this groundwork is that with the presentation of the Bruce Committee report "a seed had been sown which was to grow eventually into the United Nations Economic and Social Council."[7]

These events, like the public and private international institutions of the nineteenth century and the wartime consultative machinery, prompted commentaries on the direct and indirect values of international cooperation through common endeavors.[8] World War II precipitated other formulations. We turn now to an examination of the findings and recommendations of these several genera-

[7] Cheever and Haviland, *op.cit.*, p. 166. See also Walters, *op.cit.*, II, 761-62; Ranshofen-Wertheimer, *op.cit.*, pp. 163-66. The latter sees the permanent significance of the Bruce Report "not in the concrete proposals it contains but in its underlying idea, namely the desirability of granting the technical organs a greater degree of autonomy than they possessed from 1919 to 1940." *Ibid.*, pp. 165-66.

[8] In addition to the sources cited above, see, e.g., C. Delisle Burns, *A Short History of International Intercourse* (London: George Allen & Unwin Ltd., 1924), pp. 151-54; Burns, "International Administration," *British Year Book of International Law*, 1926 (London: Humphrey Milford, n.d.), especially pp. 68-72; Francis Delaisi, *Political Myths and Economic Realities* (New York: The Viking Press, 1927), especially pp. 409ff., 427ff.; William E. Rappard, "The Evolution of the League of Nations," *American Political Science Review*, XXI (November 1927), especially 792-94, 809-19; Rappard, *The Geneva Experiment* (London: Humphrey Milford, 1931), pp. 58-65; C. Howard-Ellis, *The Origin and Working of the League of Nations* (Boston: Houghton Mifflin Company, 1928), pp. 476ff.; Pitman B. Potter, *This World of Nations* (New York: The Macmillan Company, 1929), pp. 188-99; Potter, *An Introduction to the Study of International Organization* (4th ed. rev.; New York: D. Appleton-Century Company, 1935), pp. 484-85; Potter, "Note on the Distinction Between Political and Technical Questions," *Political Science Quarterly*, L (June 1935), 264-71; S. H. Bailey, "Devolution in the Conduct of International Relations," *Economica*, X (November 1930), 259-74; David Mitrany, *The Progress of International Government* (New Haven: Yale University Press, 1933).

tions of commentators, with special emphasis on the work of David Mitrany, who named the "functional way."[9]

I I

The functional way is the way of "action itself."[10] Writing in the sunset of nineteenth-century optimism, Paul Reinsch characterized his age as "realistic and practical; its concepts [as] positive and concrete. The high ideals which it is conceiving are viewed not as cloud castles but as mountain tops soaring aloft in untarnished beauty, yet resting upon an immovable and massive foundation. . . . The positive ideal of our day is undoubtedly that the whole earth shall become a field of action open to every man. . . ."[11]

One generation and two world wars later, Mitrany plays the pragmatic chords in a minor key. "It seems to be the fate of all periods of transition that reformers are more ready to fight over a theory than to pull together on a problem," he says. "I do not represent a theory. I represent an anxiety." Invoking Edmund Burke, he cautions the

[9] Mitrany may well have drawn on the writings of H. G. Wells for the word "function." In *Anticipations of the Reaction of Mechanical and Scientific Progress Upon Human Life and Thought* (New York: Harper and Brothers, 1902), *The World of William Clissold* (London: Benn, 1926), *The Open Conspiracy* (London: Victor Gollancz, 1928), and other works, Wells had outlined a plan for depriving states of their significance "by replacing their functions," as Clissold explained. Wells' active factor—rather more than a catalyst, this—was a self-acknowledged international "conspiracy of 'functional' men with interests and responsibilities transcending national frontiers, pledged to work for the supersedure of the established political order by a unified system of scientifically managed world controls. . . ." W. Warren Wagar, *H. G. Wells and the World State* (New Haven: Yale University Press, 1961), pp. 43-44. By contrast, Mitrany's scheme places far less emphasis upon world-minded, creative individual actors conscious of their bonds to a collective mind and collective will.

[10] Mitrany, *A Working Peace System* (London: The Royal Institute of International Affairs, 1943), p. 55. Except where otherwise indicated this edition is used.

[11] Reinsch, *op.cit.*, pp. 2, 3.

reader that " 'Government is a practical thing' . . . and we should beware of elaborating political forms 'for the gratification of visionaries.' "[12] The real, the solid, the living; practicality, activity, achievement—this is the language of the functionalist argument.

The functional approach to international organization would proceed by means of the "functional selection and organization of international relations," as Mitrany puts it. This is the way of "natural selection," the "binding together [of] those interests which are common, where they are common, and to the extent . . . they are common."[13] George Catlin, observing that this was largely the official British post-World War II view of international organization, speaks of it as cooperation "along technical and economic lines, now christened by the word 'functions.' "[14]

Following the selection of an area of common interest or concern comes the organization of international will and effort. In much of the literature this organizational step is treated as a residual consideration, secondary to discussion of both initial needs and ultimate results. Mitrany does bring this phase of the process to the surface, explicitly (though rather summarily) referring to the functional approach as a "political device." "[L]ike other forms of union, it too links together a number—any number— of political units, but for one purpose at a time. . . . One

[12] Mitrany, "The Functional Approach to World Organization," *International Affairs*, XXIV (July 1948), 350. Cf. Mitrany's introduction to James A. Joyce (ed.), *World Organization—Federal or Functional?* (London: C. A. Watts and Co., Ltd., 1945); Lyman C. White, "Peace by Pieces," *One World*, II (August-September 1948), 165; Mitrany, "Problems of International Administration," *Public Administration*, XXIII (Spring 1945), 11; Mitrany, "International Consequences of National Planning," *Yale Review*, XXXVII (September 1947), 29.
[13] Mitrany, *A Working Peace System*, p. 32. Cf. Mitrany, "Functional Unity and Political Discord," in *World Unity and the Nations* (London: National Peace Council, n.d.), p. 5.
[14] George Catlin, in Joyce, *op.cit.*, p. 13.

might put it, that [it] is a form of limited liability association between political units."[15]

What will be the structural offspring of these unions?
A survey of descriptive phrases from the functionalist
literature, while suggestive, is hardly sufficient to develop
a picture. These writings abound in such general designations as "functional organizations,"[16] "joint international
agencies,"[17] "international cooperative functional committees,"[18] and "special commissions."[19] However, two common themes suggest the composition and procedural
character of functional bodies, by whatever name graced.
They are to be *representative*, and they are to be *expert*.
These themes will be explored in the following chapter.

Functionalists would consider impertinent the question
of structure. With certain exceptions[20] requisite organizational attributes of a functional effort are treated as
the flexible emanations of the need in question, inte-
grally and uniquely related to the status of that need over
time. "No fixed rule is needed, and no rigid pattern is
desirable for the organization of [the] functional strata."
Each functional sector is to be organized "according to its

[15] Mitrany, "International Cooperation in Action," *International
Associations*, XI (September 1959), 646.

[16] David Thomson *et al.*, *Patterns of Peacemaking* (New York:
Oxford University Press, 1945), p. 319.

[17] Mitrany, introduction to W. Friedmann, *International Public
Corporations as Agencies of Reconstruction* (London: Herbert
Joseph, Ltd., 1946), p. 3.

[18] Harrop Freeman, "This Is Victory," in Freeman (ed.), *Peace
is the Victory* (New York: Harper and Brothers, 1944), p. 250.

[19] H. G. Wells, "Renvoi," in Joyce, *op.cit.*, p. 47.

[20] Mitrany, A *Working Peace System*, p. 34: "A certain degree
of fixity would not be out of place . . . in regard to the more *negative* functions, especially those related to 'law and order,' but also
to any others of a more formal nature, . . . which are likely to
remain fairly static. Security, for instance, could be organized on an
interlocking regional basis; and the judicial function likewise, with a
hierarchy of courts. . . . Yet even in regard to security, and in
addition to regional arrangements, the elasticity inherent in functional organization may prove practicable and desirable, if only in
a period of transition." The emphasis is Mitrany's.

nature, to the conditions under which it has to operate, and to the needs of the moment." All necessary freedom should be allowed "for practical variation in the organization of the several functions. . . ."[21]

Mitrany is true to the formula implicit in the more general functionalist tradition—"form follows function." His argument implies the immanence of structure *within* function. "The functional dimensions . . . determine themselves. In a like manner the function determines its appropriate organs."[22]

Mitrany suggests a few additional specifications for a functional beginning. Each component in a functional system should be given a specific task. Its jurisdiction should be "no wider than the most effective working limits of the function. . . ." Finally, these functional elements should be "largely autonomous," both in terms of each other and in relation to any existing political authority.[23]

I I I

Less functionalist attention is devoted to the conditions for these undertakings than to their development and ramifications. The "creation of functional bodies . . . handling world social and economic problems is not an end in itself, but a step towards the achievement of a larger objective"[24]—at least as viewed by some of its proponents.

In Mitrany's argument, as noted, the organizational component of each functional unit is intimately related

[21] Mitrany, *A Working Peace System*, pp. 34, 33. On page 35 Mitrany adds: "Not only is there . . . no need for any fixed constitutional division of authority and power, prescribed in advance, but anything beyond the most general formal rules would embarrass the working of these arrangements." Cf. Thomson, *op.cit.*, p. 326.

[22] Mitrany, *A Working Peace System*, p. 35. Emphasis omitted.

[23] *Ibid.*, pp. 21, 33, 38; Mitrany, "The Functional Approach to World Organization," *op.cit.*, p. 360. Cf. Friedmann, *op.cit.*, p. 38.

[24] "Functional Approach to International Co-operation," *Nature* editorial, CLIV (22 July 1944), p. 98.

to the need which it is to satisfy. The development of each functional unit, however, does not depend solely on the status of that need which is its *raison d'être*. This developmental process relies upon "a cardinal virtue of the functional method—what one might call the virtue of technical self-determination."[25] Mitrany's concept is offered to explain what he calls the "autonomous development"[26] of functional units. Sometimes "function" connotes the same operation; it demonstrates "through practice the nature of the action required under the given conditions, and in that way the *powers* needed by the respective authority. The function, one might say, determines the executive instrument suitable for its proper activity. . . ."[27]

Given the initial need and an operation of technical self-determination, the individual functional units will develop. But there is more. Along with growth goes a certain reproductive tendency. With the New Deal as his model for functional illustration, Mitrany describes the self-propelled expansion of programing. "Every function was left to generate others gradually, like the functional subdivision of organic cells. . . ."[28]

Here, then, is a course of events which begins with the modest institution of functional programs concerned with specific needs and develops by means of technical self-determination and organizational mitosis. In a world populated with an increasing number of functional units, is there not apt to arise a new kind of problem, necessitating a super-function to assure the proper sphere for the exercise of each function? The possibility does not

[25] Mitrany, A *Working Peace System*, p. 35.
[26] Mitrany, "The Functional Approach to World Organization," p. 357.
[27] Mitrany, A *Working Peace System*, p. 35. Emphasis in original. Cf. Carl J. Friedrich's comment: "Function is intimately related to process; it is in terms of function that a process is molded." Friedrich, *Constitutional Government and Democracy* (rev. ed.; Boston: Ginn and Company, 1950), p. 123.
[28] Mitrany, A *Working Peace System*, p. 21.

seem a major difficulty to Mitrany. He stresses that "it
would be out of place to lay down in advance some formal
plan" and suggests that the next development would itself "have to come about functionally." Notwithstanding
this uncertainty, "certain needs and possibilities can be
foreseen . . . , though some are probable and others only
likely. . . ."[29] Mitrany's developmental progression goes
thus:

"1. *Within the same group* of functions probably
there would have to be co-ordination either simply for
technical purposes or for wider functional ends, and
this would be the first stage towards a wider integration.
. . .

"2. The next degree or stage might be, if found desirable, the co-ordination of *several groups* of functional
agencies. . . .

"3. The co-ordination of such working functional
agencies with any *international planning* agencies would
present a third stage, and one that brings out some interesting possibilities, should the ideas for an International Investment Board or an International Development Commission, as an advisory organ, come to
fruition. . . . Co-ordination of such a general kind may in
some cases amount almost to arbitration of differences
between functional agencies. . . .

"4. Beyond this there remains the habitual assumption . . . that international action must have some over-
all *political authority* above it."[30]

Last on this list of needs and developments is the problem of security, "in fact a separate function like the others,
not something that stands in stern isolation, overriding
all the others."[31] The ultimate achievement of security is
directly related to the downgrading of state sovereignty.

[29] *Ibid.*, p. 35.
[30] *Ibid.*, pp. 35, 36, 37. Emphasis in original.
[31] *Ibid.*, p. 38.

In some functionalist writings this treatment of sovereignty is hardly obvious; for instance, Mitrany at one
point pleads not for a surrender of sovereignty, but for a
"pooling" of it.[32] Elsewhere Mitrany's advance on sovereignty becomes somewhat more open. Its "content and
working . . . could be modified by . . . inconspicuous and
partial transfers of authority to international functional
organs," he writes, and thus "that most disruptive and
intractable of international principles, the principle of
state equality, may well be tamed by specific functional
arrangements which would not steal the crown of sovereignty while they would promise something for the purse
of necessity."[33]

Other writers, too, argue that sovereignty is more apt
to be weakened by transformation than delegation. Stanley
Hoffmann, who foresees a possible "decentralization of alle-
giance" via "the establishment of functional institutions
based on trans-national interests," holds that under certain
conditions such an arrangement would catch the nation-
state "in a variety of nets," thus causing a gradual and
perhaps unobtrusive shift in power. "The most effective
attack on sovereignty is not a frontal one—it is one which
slowly but clearly deprives sovereignty of its substance,
and consequently of its prestige."[34]

J. L. Brierly has written of much the same process,
labeling it "the method of attacking sovereignty by erosion," although his suggestions are offered in a more general proposal not necessarily tied to specific functional
units. In Brierly's view, the way to engineer sovereignty's
erosion is simply by "doing everything we can to make it
easy for States to work together and so gradually develop
a sense of community which will make it psychologically

[32] One is reminded of Wendell Willkie's admonition that sovereignty is not something to be hoarded, but something to be used.

[33] Mitrany, *A Working Peace System*, p. 29.

[34] Stanley Hoffmann, "The Role of International Organization:
Limits and Possibilities," *International Organization*, X (August
1956), 365-66.

more difficult to press the claims of sovereignty in ways
that are anti-social. . . . For our hopes for the United
Nations we must look, I think, to the General Assembly,
and more especially to the Economic and Social Council
which in effect is one of its committees."[35]

In his introduction to the fourth printing of A *Working
Peace System*, Mitrany gives more extended consideration
to the transmigration of sovereignty. Having suggested
the need for a certain "sacrifice" of state sovereignty in
order to preserve the peace, he outlines a brief natural
history of sovereignty, and offers a projection. "In any
normal evolution the change [in status of sovereignty]
has been gradual," he writes; human history has witnessed
"a gradual transfer of sovereignty from the ruler to the
people, the people in their turn gradually entrusting its
exercise to a central authority. Therefore the democratic
tests have all along been expressed in a selection of policy
and of ultimate control of its execution, and not in any
grandiose juridical gesture. Sovereignty cannot . . . be
transferred effectively through a formula, only through a
function. By entrusting an authority with a certain task,
carrying with it command over the requisite powers and
means, a slice of sovereignty is transferred from the old
authority to the new; and the accumulation of such partial
transfers in time brings about a translation of the true seat
of authority. If that has been the considered process in
the domestic sphere, is it not still more relevant in the
international sphere, where even the elements of unity
have to be built up laboriously by this very process of
patient change?"[36]

Mitrany suggests that a new system of sanctions for
assuring security will eventually replace territorially ori-

[35] J. L. Brierly, *The Covenant and the Charter* (Cambridge:
Cambridge University Press, 1947), p. 26.

[36] Mitrany, *A Working Peace System* (London: National Peace
Council, 1946), p. 9. Cf. Harold J. Laski, *Socialism as Internationalism* (London: Fabian Publications Ltd., 1949), pp. 14, 15.

ented force, presently symbolized by the principle of state
sovereignty. The functional units will come to have a
veto on use of the means of war-making. "Economic
technical agencies would be preventive, by their very nature, in a way in which military agencies never can be.
Just as it would be their function to give service wherever
it was needed, so it would clearly be their duty to deny
service where it was not obviously needed and might be
abused. And they would have the means to do so without
using force." The functional units could even stop a conflict once it had begun: they "would be able, if aggression
should occur, effectively to check it simply by withholding
their services at a moment's notice."[37]

But the new security would not find its deepest meaning
and support in such negative considerations. "The joining
of service with . . . punishment through the work of technical economic agencies shows how such arrangements
would at last give a new and . . . real sense to the whole
idea of security. The absence of violence is not enough for
peaceful life, let alone for a good life. Government has
never and nowhere been merely a matter of policing; and
any scheme of international security which tries to confine
itself to police work will soon be in difficulty. That has
been the chief weakness of all our past efforts."[38]

Peace is more than the absence of violence. Though
peace be the goal, the quest for peace proceeds through
the growth of community: to build peace by functionalist
means is to build community. The relationship between
community and its components is spelled out in its defini-

[37] Mitrany, *The Road to Security* (London: National Peace
Council, 1944), pp. 16ff. Mitrany's scheme for a functional veto on
massive violence brings to mind another Aristophanes play, *Lysi-
strata,* and H. G. Wells' more recent proposal that international
bankers withdraw credit to governments or industries bent on expanding their production of arms. "Has the Money-Credit System
a Mind?" *The Banker,* VI (1928), 221-33, also in *The Saturday
Evening Post,* 5 May 1928, pp. 14-15, as cited by Wagar, *op.cit.,*
p. 185.
[38] Mitrany, *Road to Security,* pp. 18-19.

tion: " 'a community may be regarded as the sum of the functions performed by its members.' "[39] To nurture community is thus to strive for "the performance of a variety of common functions"; to gain community is to provide a sense of purpose for all of that community's human parts, and thereby to escape the "totalitarian pattern" which is the mark of the present-day world.[40] So goes the functionalist argument. "Function" is both community building-block and lodestar for the individual: man finds himself and his place in the universe as he realizes his purpose in his own community.

Finally, the functional approach would bring a governmental system for its world community. As Mitrany has indicated, this would be a sequential capstone to the functional edifice.[41] "We cannot have a world government before we have a world community," as Mitrany puts it elsewhere; "we can begin to build up the parts of a world community before we get the acceptance for full world government."[42] Nor can the significance of a world governmental system be regarded as overwhelming in Mitrany's scheme: "a political authority without active social functions would remain an empty temple,"[43] even if such an arrangement were more than hypothetically possible. Furthermore, the virtues of world community postulated

[39] Mitrany, quoting Leonard T. Hobhouse, "the most distinguished sociologist England has produced so far," in International Congress on Mental Health, *Proceedings of the International Conference on Mental Hygiene* (London: H. K. Lewis & Co. Ltd., 1948), IV, 84. Cf. G. D. H. Cole, *Social Theory* (London: Methuen & Co., Ltd., 1920), p. 50.

[40] Mitrany in *Proceedings*, p. 84; Mitrany, *A Working Peace System*, p. 31. In G. D. H. Cole's words: "Due performance by each association of its social function . . . not only leads to smooth working and coherence in social organisation, but also removes the removable social hindrances to the 'good life' of the individual. In short, function is the key not only to 'social,' but also to communal and personal well-being." *Social Theory*, p. 62.

[41] Mitrany, *A Working Peace System*, p. 37.

[42] Mitrany in *Proceedings*, p. 84.

[43] Mitrany, *A Working Peace System*, p. 54.

by the functionalists include virtually all the benefits seemingly obtainable at present only through governmental systems. "World law," similarly, is not a *sine qua non* of peace, but a formal embellishment upon the global community—an index of the efficacy of a functional approach, after the fact. In short, to observe that government and law come last in Mitrany's sequence is not to deny that for him they may also be of least importance.

I V

Having introduced the functionalist argument, we turn to a consideration of two alternative approaches to international organization. These approaches might, with some latitude, be taken also as interpretations of the process by which existing international organizations have come about and been modified in the course of their existence. The purpose in presenting them is twofold. First, a backlog of interpretative approaches may aid later in plying the selected cases for insights. In a sense the inquiry's foundation is being broadened so as to provide for the eventuality that the functionalist analysis will fail to aid the understanding of certain aspects of the phenomena to be observed.

The second purpose is more modest and yet probably more important. This brief exposition of two other views should lend clarity to the explication of the functionalist argument itself. The basic objective is to prepare the way for a more systematic consideration of the functionalist argument in the next chapter. But rigor must be preceded by understanding, and understanding is sharpened by the comparison and contrast of alternatives—even alternative *emphases* in the explanation of complex phenomena.

Elihu Root, formerly Secretary of War, Secretary of State, and U.S. Senator, President of the Carnegie Endowment for International Peace, and, as a Republican, a key potential supporter for Woodrow Wilson's postwar plans, attended a dinner party on the evening of April 11, 1918, with former President William H. Taft, the Archbishop of York, and Colonel Edward M. House. Conversation turned to the nature of a desirable arrangement to preserve the peace. Root let his views be known, and was asked to develop them in a memorandum to be given Colonel House. This he did. Wilson carried it to Paris, and in modified form it provided the substance of Article XI of the League of Nations Covenant. Here are the relevant portions of the manuscript, excerpted from Sir Alfred Zimmern's book, *The League of Nations and the Rule of Law*:

"The first requisite for any durable concert of peaceable nations to prevent war is a fundamental change in the principle to be applied to international breaches of the peace. . . .

"At the basis of every community lies the idea of organisation to preserve the peace. Without that idea really active and controlling there can be no community of individuals or of nations. It is the gradual growth and substitution of this idea of community interest in preventing and punishing breaches of the peace which has done away with private war among civilised peoples. . . .

"When you have got this principle accepted openly, expressly, distinctly, unequivocally by the whole civilised world, you will for the first time have a Community of Nations, and the practical results which will naturally develop will be as different from those which have come from the old view of national responsibility as are the results which flow from the American Declaration of Independence compared with the results which flow from the Divine Right of Kings."[44]

The memorandum illustrates a view of international organization, as Zimmern proceeds to demonstrate. This

[44] Alfred Zimmern, *The League of Nations and the Rule of Law*, 1918-1935 (London: Macmillan and Co., Limited, 1936), pp. 230, 231.

view may better be understood by outlining some of Root's assumptions.

There is, first of all, an assertion that the key to ultimate peace lies in an initial enunciation of a legal precept. That precept's eventual embodiment is an "organisation to preserve the peace," but its interim existence is incorporeal, symbolized variously in the quotation by the words "idea" and "principle."

Second, there is implied a process by which the "growth and substitution of this idea of community interest in preventing and punishing breaches of the peace" comes about. The crucial change during this process appears to be a gradual realization and acceptance by international society of the practical significance of the legal principle.

Finally, the assurance of peace comes as an end product in this process. "When you have got this principle accepted openly, expressly, distinctly, unequivocally by the whole civilised world, you will for the first time have a Community of Nations. . . ."

This approach to international organization may be further exemplified by a similar example explored by Zimmern. Root is once again the protagonist, but this time the "form" to be followed by the development of an effective function is not a legal precept, but an international organization as such. As early as 1907 Root had been an advocate of a World Court. Zimmern suggests that such a proposal would sound paradoxical to the British mind; to it, a Court would seem to "go ill" with other rudimentary institutions at that phase in social development, and might better appear at a much later stage. Zimmern continues:

"But Mr Root would have a ready reply, drawn from the . . . outlook and habits of a forward-looking people. . . . The community of the world can be made . . . by the devising of suitable institutions with names pointing ahead to what they will ultimately become. . . . [F]or Mr Root there was nothing misleading or unreal in attaching the name of 'Court' to the project of a body which he must have known full well would not realise that high appellation for many years to come. The main thing, after all, he would say, is to have a *sense of direction*. If by speaking of 'institutions,' and by the names which we attach to them, we can give mankind a sense of the direction in which it is moving, we shall speed human progress and make regression more difficult. . . . Let us get [men] to recognise . . . words: words will set up associations, associations will lead to habits and habits will eventually issue in acts. Thus by calling a body a Court we are taking the first steps towards making it a Court."[45]

There is a point of view behind this interpretation of the development of international patterns; it shines more clearly yet through Arthur N. Holcombe's words of 1948:

"[T]he national state is highly charged with the dynamic purposes and the powerful sentiments which make the legal fiction of sovereign equality a potent factor in international politics. To try to promote respect for fundamental freedoms by framing an international bill of rights means the beginning of an audacious adventure in the development of the relations not only among individuals, but also between states and the general organization of mankind.

.   .   .   .

"What the United Nations under the present Charter can best do to promote respect for human rights among different peoples with their own peculiar notions and customs is to follow the example of our own people at the time of our Revolution. Something can be accomplished by proclaiming in a solemn state paper the general principles of good government and by setting forth good advice concerning the conduct of public affairs.

.   .   .   .

[45] *Ibid.,* 233-34. Emphasis in original.

"The most effective declaration of rights would . . . possess great inspirational value without committing all the members of the United Nations to uniform solutions of their domestic problems regardless of basic differences in the character and achievement of their respective peoples. It would constitute a standing invitation to all to advance as rapidly as possible toward a universally acceptable goal, but it would not involve the assumption of responsibilities by the United Nations for the adjustment of relations between individuals and their national governments, which were not assumed in the United States until the time of the Fourteenth Amendment. The peoples of the modern world are far from ready to add anything like the Fourteenth Amendment to the Charter of the United Nations.

. . . .

"An international declaration of rights, broadly conceived and limited to a few simple basic interests to which different peoples can give legal protection in their different ways as their several circumstances make it possible for them to do so, can do much to give a sense of direction and advancement toward the common goal to peoples in different stages of political development."[46]

[46] Arthur N. Holcombe, *Human Rights in the Modern World* (New York: New York University Press, 1948), pp. 121-22, 124, 125, 138-39. On its first page, *The United Nations and Human Rights* (New York: United Nations, 1963) explains that the Declaration of Human Rights "says how people in the world should live. It does not mean that everyone actually lives that way. Although . . . not a law, it has deeply influenced the laws of many countries. . . . The Declaration was written and adopted by the General Assembly as a standard by which people in every country should try to live." See also "Human Rights: Progress and Prospects," *United Nations Review*, IV (December 1957), 16-17; René Cassin, "How to Achieve a Better World: The Universal Declaration of Human Rights," *United Nations Review*, V (September 1958), 14-19. Cf., as a statement of principle, the International Labour Organisation's Philadelphia Declaration adopted by the ILO General Conference in 1944; ILO, *Lasting Peace the I.L.O. Way* (Geneva: International Labour Office, 1951), pp. 103-05.

If we abstract from these accounts and proposals the common elements relevant to our concern, we find that the basic formula involves the launching of a principle, a promissory instrument, a declaration, or a resolution, and the subsequent passage of an extended period of time during which attitudes change and the original ideal becomes actual practice.

Like the functionalist argument, this is a doctrine of community building—although here the community has as its chief component an ideal or cluster of ideals which are articulated at the outset and about which community coalesces. Like the functionalist argument, it purports to offer a "natural" approach to the development of institutions: "practical results . . . naturally develop," as Root phrases it. Finally, it too is a counsel of gradualism.

However, this argument—which might be called "in-principle gradualism"—differs from that of the functionalists on a key point. The functionalists argue that world community can best be built by a joint performance of those functions which together constitute such a community, letting form or structure take the hindmost. The in-principle gradualists seem to advance the thesis that functioning must necessarily follow form. They suggest that it is necessary to start with that form (or the ideal which is its interim embodiment) and thereby provide the first step toward an "active and controlling" acceptance of it by the embryonic community eventually to be born of this process. Functionalists stress the solution of common problems in the economic and social sectors by confronting those problems with cooperative international action directed at the specific need, and eschew the "wide and abstract terms"[47] of grand designs for future realization. The in-principle gradualists focus upon ideals. They stress the desirability of declarations and resolutions regarding such goals as higher world standards of health, education, and welfare.

[47] Mitrany in *Proceedings*, p. 82.

The third and final interpretation of how international institutions originate and develop is not very different from that of the in-principle gradualists. Its primary distinguishing characteristic is its temporal dimension.[48] The essence of this position is that efforts at international organization prove fruitful as soon as—but only when—potential constituents adopt constitutional elements or systems with real powers. "The awful spectacle of a world without a world government can be ended by means of plans which moderate and conciliatory politicians are capable of making."[49] Binding agreement is the test: with it, international organs are efficacious; without it, they are ineffectual. Likewise the *extent* to which a given international organ is effective would depend on the nature of the powers and sanctions granted it by the initial and subsequent agreements qua basic instruments and amendments. This is the explanatory emphasis within the third position.

This third approach, with its assumptions on display, is well exemplified by a passage from the introduction to that magistral plan for United Nations Charter revision set forth by Grenville Clark and Louis B. Sohn under the formula and title *World Peace Through World Law*:

"The fundamental premise of the book is identical with the pronouncement of the President of the United States on October 31, 1956: 'There can be no peace without law.' In this context the word 'law' necessarily implies the law of a world authority, i.e., law which would be uniformly applicable to all nations and all individuals in the world and which would definitely forbid violence or the threat of it as a means for dealing with any international dispute. This world law must also be law in the sense of law which

[48] Curiously, some commentators, having interpreted American history as a gradual evolution of institutions drawn forth by Constitutional leading-strings, then proceed to use this same historical model to show how world government can be achieved *now*.

[49] Holcombe, *Our More Perfect Union* (Cambridge: Harvard University Press, 1950), p. 428.

is capable of enforcement, as distinguished from a mere set of exhortations or injunctions which it is desirable to observe but for the enforcement of which there is no effective machinery."[50]

Clark and Sohn then bring in the domestic analogy to show the necessary (and presumably the sufficient) conditions for peace—as well as the procedure for its achievement. "The proposition 'no peace without law' . . . embodies the conception that peace cannot be ensured by a continued arms race, nor by an indefinite 'balance of terror,' nor by diplomatic maneuver, but only by universal and complete national disarmament together with the establishment of institutions corresponding in the world field to those which maintain law and order within local communities and nations."[51]

Most modern propositions of the world-government genre suggest international federation, whether Atlantic-centered or universal. A federation would seemingly be more palatable to potential constituents than a unitary scheme.[52] Furthermore, a federal arrangement could better make use of American experience.[53] Some comments go beyond the United States as *example*: Holcombe con-

[50] Grenville Clark and Louis B. Sohn, *World Peace Through World Law* (rev. ed.; Cambridge: Harvard University Press, 1960), p. xv.

[51] *Ibid.*, p. xv.

[52] Claude, *op.cit.*, pp. 422ff.; see also the argument advanced by Clark and Sohn, *op.cit.*, p. xvii.

[53] It is perhaps of some significance that Gladstone's too facile distinction—"As the British Constitution is the most subtle organism which has ever proceeded from progressive history, so the American Constitution is the most wonderful work ever struck off at a given time by the brain and purpose of man"—is further distorted by its customary American abbreviation to the second portion of Gladstone's comment. Cf. Carl Van Doren, *The Great Rehearsal* (New York: The Viking Press, 1948), p. viii; Holcombe, *Our More Perfect Union*, pp. 2, 428-29. The American incidence of these writings is striking. For further examples, see August O. Spain, "International Federalism in Recent American Thought," *The Southwestern Social Science Quarterly*, XXXIII (December 1952), 187-205.

tends that "The American people cannot perfect their own Federal Union without at the same time forming a more perfect Union of all mankind."[54] (This comment must, of course, be read in the context of Holcombe's entire presentation.) Less subtle is the reference by one group to the future role of the "Uniting States," a role implied by their further observation that "No number is prescribed to the stars on [our] flag."[55]

These are some examples of what might be called the "apocalyptic approach" to international organization. Inis Claude's introduction explains the designation: "Finding the nations in a state of nature which has become intolerable, it prescribes an apocalyptic leap out of anarchy. . . . [I]t postulates a flash of creativity which carries mankind into the era of order."[56]

The in-principle gradualists provide a mirror image of the functionalists' "form follows function" sequence; the apocalyptics display an antipodal temperament. To Mi-

[54] Holcombe, *Our More Perfect Union*, p. 428. Cf. Nelson A. Rockefeller, *The Future of Federalism* (New York: Atheneum, 1963), pp. 59-83. See also W. W. Rostow, *The United States in the World Arena* (New York: Harper & Brothers, 1960), pp. 549-50: "It is not easy or particularly useful to peer far beyond the time when [the] great human watershed is attained. Nevertheless, it can be said that the American regional interest would still continue to embrace elements from the long sweep of the past. Convergent and conflicting relationships of geography, of cultural connection, of economic interest would in substantial measure be simply transferred from a setting where military force enters the equation of negotiation to one of global domestic politics. When the great conference has ended and the freely moving inspectors take up their initial posts from one end of the world to the other and the nightmare passes, the agenda of international politics will look not unfamiliar. Much in the historic relation of the United States to the balance of affairs in Eurasia will remain. There will be, however, a special dimension to global politics with special meaning for Americans— the problem of so conducting the world's affairs as to avoid a dissolution of the federal machinery and civil war."

[55] *The City of Man, a Declaration on World Democracy* (New York: Viking, 1941), p. 72, as quoted by Claude, *op.cit.*, p. 410.

[56] Claude, *op.cit.*, p. 415. Claude's exposition and criticism of the "governmentalist" argument is excellent. See especially pp. 407-32.

trany's gibe about "feverish reformers who want to set up at once pre-fabricated Cities of God,"[57] the apocalyptics might well counter with the words of Charles G. Bell, contributor to *Common Cause*, journal of The Committee to Frame a World Constitution: "The noblest calling is always over the most treacherous defile. Creative spirit hovers in us like the force in a breaking wave, ready to leap at the moment of crashing foam from the vision-abandoned shards to other waves, other worlds."[58]

The aim of this discussion has been to suggest differing emphases. These approaches to international organization share a basic goal, even though their assumptions and prescriptions vary somewhat. Differing perspectives may aid the interpretation of actual international institutions and their programs. But that opportunity must await other quests, beginning with a more systematic examination of the functionalist argument.

[57] Mitrany in *Proceedings*, p. 84.

[58] Charles G. Bell, "Toward A New Organic," *Common Cause*, IV (June 1951), 600. An earlier contributor to the same journal writes that "the most acute and consistent functionalists (like Mitrany) are not federalists; in a logically flawless way they consider functionalism as the alternative to federalism. . . . Federalists should make their choice accordingly. One cannot serve God and Mammon. . . . [T]here are no steps toward world government; world government is the first step." Andrea Chiti-Batelli, "Functional Federalism," *idem*, III (April 1950), 475, 477. Emphasis omitted.

The Argument Examined: Criticism
and Operationalization

THE PREVIOUS chapter provided an introduction to the functionalist argument by way of a consideration of its temperament, its aims, and the sequence it foretells. That discussion concluded with a confrontation designed to clarify the basic functionalist position. Here we shall spell out the argument further in order to seek and examine its assumptions.

This study is even more concerned with an evaluation of the functional approach by empirical criteria. Thus, it will be necessary to provide somewhat sharper statements of the expectations of the functionalists. Given a propitious situation, *what* consequences do the functionalists foresee? *How* may this process be checked? And *why* will these consequences have occurred? The process of readying for this sort of quest has come to be called "operationalization"—the framing of propositions, derived from a general hypothesis or hypotheses, which have been shaped to fit empirical testing. Their manner of construction will be further considered later in this chapter.

I

A person often reveals his presuppositions as the backdrop fashioned for his argument. He may frame a perspective from which his proposal appears most appropriate. He may do so without acknowledgment of the special character of his brushwork. Mitrany, preparing to define the situation which will support his argument, states that he desires "not . . . to discuss whether the trend [of the day] is desirable or inevitable, but merely to establish . . . the conditions from which our international house-

building must start."[1] What are the presuppositions of
the functionalist argument—the setting with promise for
a functional approach?

The functionalist estimate revolves about the present
relationship between the world's static and dynamic elements or, to phrase it only slightly differently, between
state and society.[2] For Mitrany, the modern history of
political evolution can be read largely in the changing role
of the state since the birth of national consciousness.
Originally the nation-state was an instrument of order,
"protecting the social life of a community."[3] As such the

[1] Mitrany, "The Functional Approach to World Organization,"
p. 351. Leonard Woolf writes toward the end of his remarkable
treatise, *International Government*, "All I have tried to do is to
examine the facts and to see things in their right proportions."
(New York: Brentano's, 1916), p. 356.

[2] Mitrany's use of the terms "state" and "society" appears to
parallel that of Sir Ernest Barker, in the main. In his translator's
introduction to Gierke's *Natural Law and the Theory of Society,
1500 to 1800*, Barker introduces the concepts as follows: "Society,
or community, which in our modern life takes the form of national
society or community, is a naturally given fact of historical experience. Each national society is a unity; and each expresses its unity
in a common way of looking at life in the light of a common
tradition, and in the development of a common culture, or way of
life in all its various forms. But each society is also a plurality. It is
a rich web of contained groups . . . all dyed by the national colour,
and yet all (or most of them) with the capacity, and the instinct,
for associating themselves with similar groups in other national societies, and thus entering into some form of international connection. Such is society, at once one and many, but always, in itself,
the play of a voluntary life and the operation of the voluntary
activity of man. This is the material on which . . . is stamped the
form of the State. The State, we may say, is a national society which
has turned itself into a legal association, or a juridical organisation.
. . ." See further Otto Friedrich von Gierke, *Natural Law and the
Theory of Society, 1500 to 1800*, translated with an introduction by
Ernest Barker (Cambridge: University Press, 1934), I, xxii-xxiv.

For the functionalists, however, the word "community" is in most
cases reserved for references to society of a higher order. Thus,
"community" often follows "international" or "world"; the term's
usage further implies that a "community" has attained superior
attributes of a largely unspecified nature.

[3] Mitrany in *Proceedings*, p. 78.

state served an essentially negative (if necessary) purpose. It was the shield of the status quo, not the instrument of change: the guardian of rights, not the creator of positive benefits. And as long as the demands by society upon the state remained minimal, the state's assignment—to provide physical security—rendered its potential use of force a benign factor.

But today the state has become "too weak to secure us equality" and yet "too strong to allow us liberty."[4] The "widening circle of communal action" has been "broken abruptly at the limits of the national state"; now "all social life is subordinated to and risked for the [state's] defence." Means and ends have been transposed. "The preservation of the building has come to matter more than [that] of the people and . . . the life within it. . . ."[5]

Moreover, this condition eludes diagnosticians because of a pervasive " 'State fixation.' "[6] The state has assumed a malignant posture; it "organise[s] the nation-group on a basis of conformity" in order to assure the "cohesion, discipline and loyalty . . . vital for the survival of the state."[7] Far from mitigating the situation, human efforts, misguided as they are by virtue of the State fixation, exacerbate the tendency: the state assumes an increasingly anthropomorphic bearing in human perception even as it appears to struggle desperately for its self-preservation. Totalitarianism is not restricted to any "particular form of state or government"; the general malaise is such that rabid security activity is the pattern everywhere, and "under modern conditions of organisation for defence and war . . . , all states are driven to assume continuous and widening control of all aspects of economic and social life, including communications and freedom of expression." This control includes an inculcation of national

[4] Mitrany, *The Progress of International Government*, p. 141.
[5] Mitrany in *Proceedings*, p. 78.
[6] Mitrany, *The Progress of International Government*, p. 99.
[7] Mitrany in *Proceedings*, p. 80.

stereotypes. Individuals and groups are subjected to an intensive conditioning process. "Sporadic individual prejudices turn into systematic collective ideologies which permeate all spheres of social and mental life."[8]

The state has turned to prey on its own artificer. Society is being devoured.

To understand Mitrany's interpretation of the situation he defines, it is desirable to pursue the analysis beyond the state as a sign of the times. Another indicator is the changing substance of "nationalism," today radically different from what the term implied in nineteenth-century usage. Whereas "the earlier nationalism was liberal, the present nationalism is socialistic; the first had a negative aim, to limit and restrain the scope of public authority, through written constitutions; the present is pressing increasingly for the use of public authority for positive social action. . . . Perhaps one might sum it up politically by saying that the first was concerned essentially with establishing the national state, the present rather with changing the life within the state. . . ."[9]

In Mitrany's formulation, modern nationalism is best understood as a social phenomenon, even though the state apparatus has become intimately involved in nationalism's present design. "The central fact in all these issues is that, in the words of General [Jan C.] Smuts, this is the 'Social Century.' "[10] And "nationalism is now an instrument of the social revolution."[11]

An important implication derives from this difference between nineteenth-century nationalism and modern "so-

[8] Ibid., p. 80.
[9] Mitrany, "International Consequences of National Planning," pp. 26-27. See also Mitrany, "The Functional Approach to World Organization," p. 356.
[10] Ibid., p. 25; Mitrany, "Problems of International Administration," p. 10.
[11] Mitrany, "International Consequences of National Planning," p. 27.

cial nationalism."[12] The former "rested mainly on cultural
and other differentiating factors, so that the setting up of
national states inevitably meant division in the world. . . ."
But "the new nationalism rests essentially on social factors,
which are not only alike but cannot make good progress
in isolation."[13] In other words, cultural nationalism carried with it an ineluctable separatist tendency, whereas
social nationalism bears within it at least the seeds of a
community of interest. Present social reform programs at
the level of the nation-state manifest "a central interest
. . . which clamours for their being linked together in the
most suitable practical way, instead of hamstringing the
new goals by fidelity to outgrown administrative divisions
and instruments."[14]

The stage has now been set for the functionalist prescription: "We are favoured by the need and habit of
material co-operation, we are hampered by the general
clinging to political segregation. How to reconcile these
two trends, both of them natural and both of them active,
is the main problem of political architecture at present.
. . . [O]ur end will be difficult to achieve simply by changing the dimensions of traditional political instruments.

[12] *Ibid.*, p. 30; Mitrany, "The Functional Approach to World
Organization," p. 356.

[13] Mitrany, "Problems of International Administration," p. 10.
Cf. Clark Kerr, John T. Dunlop, Frederick Harbison, and Charles
A. Myers, "Industrialism and World Society," *Harvard Business
Review*, XXXIX (January-February 1961), 113-14: "From South-
east Asia to Western Europe and from Chile to the Congo, the
forces making for uniformity—especially uniformity in the all important relations between labor, management, and government—
tend surely to become stronger than the forces perpetuating diversity.
The imperatives of industrialization cause the controlling elites to
overcome certain constraints and to achieve objectives *which are
the same in all societies undergoing transformation.* . . . Thus, more
and more the questions before the ruling groups become *technical.*
How can the transition to industrialism best be made, given these
conditions? Increasingly, the bosses all appear to wear gray flannel
suits. They become aware of the similarity of many problems and
of the similarity of some solutions." Emphasis in original.

[14] Mitrany, "Problems of International Administration," p. 10.

That being so, we are bound to look for a new political device, and the device which seems to fit that framework [of need and desire] is the functional idea. . . ."[15]

To state the matter in somewhat different terms, the functionalist analysis traces the world's difficulties to a global pattern of overtaxed nation-state machinery. For the functionalists, society is innovator, but also society is a maker of claims. Expectations grow for the performance of services (functions), yet the state is no longer able to fulfill even its initially assigned function—the provision of security.[16] Along with the general breakdown in security, linked to it and given a special status by the functionalist thesis, the state has proved itself impotent to satisfy the expanding non-security needs pressed upon it by society.

Yet this increase in functional assignments is not to be taken as debilitating per se to the cause of humanity. The core of the general problem lies in the current relationship between functional assignments and "outgrown administrative divisions and instruments." The separation of functional needs into specific tasks and their reassignment to new structures will itself presumably ease the strain wrought by the present disparity. This the functionalist argument implies.

One question lingers. Would this rectification of the functional-structural imbalance render a change in kind, or only a change in scale? The functionalists allude to a better system as well as a different one, a more human as well as a more peaceful order. But there is little fullness to the glimpses they offer of that community which would "have to come about functionally." The functionalist vi-

[15] Mitrany, "The Functional Approach to World Organization," pp. 351, 354.
[16] For a perceptive analysis of the erosion of the nation-state's ability to provide security, see John H. Herz, *International Politics in the Atomic Age* (New York: Columbia University Press, 1959), pp. 43-61, 96-108, or Herz, "Rise and Demise of the Territorial State," *World Politics*, IX (July 1957), 473-93.

sion seems to vacillate between two conceptions: community as a vast production-line, and community as a congeries of voluntary associations held together only by the grace of common membership by free-floating individuals. Either would be a welcome relief from the situation so darkly painted by the functionalist brush. Both conceptions leave something wanting. Given the functionalist conception of "state" as a static and uncreative entity, it is hardly surprising that little attention is given the role of its successor in a projected global order. Whether this conceptual emphasis hinders the functionalist interpretation of the interim process of community-building remains to be seen.

The present functionalist-defined crisis can be approached from yet another perspective, a perspective which employs more specifically political notions. International relations literature abounds in the phrase "peaceful change." Both elements—"peaceful" and "change"— have a variable content in their usage, but generally "peaceful" has implied a relatively small exercise of violence (if not its threat) and "change" has referred to a modification of territorial status. To spell it out in the customary language, a state (defined as a territorial political entity) agrees to give up its sovereignty over a piece of territory without surrender of the sovereignty over its remaining territory. The effect is a transfer of jurisdiction to another state, now defined as old territory plus new. As such, "peaceful change" is a rare historical happenstance indeed.[17]

The functionalists, however, offer a different content for "peaceful change." Their touchstone is quite the opposite of traditional usage: the very *absence* of any transfer of territory, or for that matter the absence of any desire for such transfer. As Mitrany states his claim, "the func-

[17] Cf. Lincoln P. Bloomfield, *Evolution or Revolution?* (Cambridge: Harvard University Press, 1957), especially chs. 2-5, 7.

tional method by implication denies that there is much progress to be made through changes of frontiers. The only sound sense of peaceful change is to do internationally what it does nationally: to make changes of frontiers unnecessary. . . ."[18]

Peaceful this may be, the reader may admit, but in what way is it "change"? And how is the territorial element to be extracted? Mitrany's answer is brief: the change is a change in human attitude; the means, functional activity. To his thinking, "the true task of peaceful change is to remove the need and the wish for changes of frontiers. The functional approach may be justifiably expected to do precisely that: it would help the growth of such positive and constructive common work, of common habits and interests, [as would make] frontier lines meaningless by overlaying them with a natural growth of common activities and common administrative agencies."[19]

The functionalist contention leaves a great deal unsaid in its formulation of the concept of peaceful change. Patently, much more is implied than attitude change. The contention probably relies in large measure upon a continuation or speeding-up of certain secular developments during modern economic history. One such trend is the decline of land as a factor of production relative to capital, labor, and that "new" factor subsumed under the catchall "know-how." Another is the rise in value of interregional trade, along with its related division of labor.

The functionalists say naught of another apparent objective corollary of a territorial status quo mediated by functional peaceful change: a process of distribution or redistribution of (non-territorial) wealth which could appropriately be characterized as both "peaceful" and "change."[20] The process is presumably covered by Mi-

[18] Mitrany, *A Working Peace System,* p. 26.

[19] *Ibid.,* pp. 26-27.

[20] For a brief consideration of redistributive economic policies as correlate and indicator of community-in-the-making, see Karl W.

trany's reference to "common activities and common administrative agencies," augmented by the Mitranian dictum that sovereignty cannot be transferred "through a formula, only through a function."[21] Yet to avoid the more painful implications of a redefinition of peaceful change is to beg significant questions about modifying national and subnational attitudes, some wedded to the preeminence of peacefulness and others to change at any cost.

"Peaceful change" as defined by the functionalists is laden with implied manifestations which would signal the progress—or regress—of functional development. These would include a radically different role for the state, an abandonment of the principle of state equality in international organs,[22] the demise of sovereignty both as legal principle and (more rapidly) description of reality, and a transubstantiation of jurisdiction from a territorial to a functional locus. Authority would attach to the specific task, and, being "conditioned by it,"[23] would grow with that task's growth. Even law, formal and static though its inherent nature makes it, would undergo significant transformation. Its instrumental attributes might well be seen by the terms of reference offered by Roscoe Pound.[24] Law's ultimate end would lie beyond the structuring of a framework of order. It would become an instrument maximizing social utility by balancing the various claims of societal segments. And those societal segments with interests fructified in the balance would, in a functionalist world, be *transnational* as well as—perhaps more than—subnational and national.

Deutsch, "The Price of Integration," in Philip E. Jacob and James V. Toscano (eds.), *The Integration of Political Communities* (Philadelphia: J. P. Lippincott Co., 1964), esp. pp. 146ff.

[21] Mitrany, A *Working Peace System,* 1946 edition, p. 9.

[22] *Ibid.,* 1943 edition, pp. 27ff.

[23] *Ibid.,* p. 44.

[24] Roscoe Pound, *An Introduction to the Philosophy of Law* (rev. ed.; New Haven: Yale University Press, 1954), pp. 42-47.

II

Here we digress somewhat to consider several apparent weaknesses which lie near the heart of the functionalist argument itself.

The first difficulty might best be introduced through an examination of that chief justification for the launching of functional enterprise and the major battle in the war for a more peaceful world: the *solution of problems*. What is a "problem" in international relations? How is it recognized as such? How is it "solved," and why accepted as having been solved? Above all, how do both "problem" and "solution" differ from problems and solutions in other fields?

These are not easy questions to answer, and it is the view here that the functionalists treat them all too lightly. "Problems" in the field of international relations would seem to display at least those facets which can be tentatively grouped under the categories "external" and "internal." That is, a problem (*any* problem) implies both a situation observed and the observer who designates that situation "problem." The problem's "solution" implies some change in the relationship between observer and observed, subject and object. This change involves a modification either of the actual situation observed or of the manner in which it is perceived—for instance, the application of an engineering solution, or simply the reaching of that solution in the first place.

Problem-definition and problem-solution become more complex when other variables are grafted onto the basic formula. For instance, there may be more than one observer, and these observers may differ as to the existence of a problem, not to mention the means to its solution. Furthermore, the "object" defined as part of a problem may itself consist, in part, of actors (*engagé* individuals or groups of various kinds) who regard *themselves* observers of a problem even as they are, from the original perspective, seen as the source of the original problem and the roadblock to its solution. The problem of winning a game between two teams is perhaps an adequate example here, though it oversimplifies another aspect of the problems with which we are apt to be concerned: in a game, the problem is at least defined, and the lines drawn.

Most current problems in international relations are inadequately symbolized by the sketch offered here. For one thing, those political factors which exaggerate the complexities of most current international problem-solving have not been injected into the model. There will be occasion to consider these additional factors when the empirical bases of the study are brought to bear. At that time there will also be opportunity for more specificity. Here the point is to consider the functionalist argument itself at the level of problem-solving *without* politics as a conditioning factor. A functionalist weakness thus revealed must be suspected, *a fortiori*, of being a weakness in the face of additional buffeting by the winds of international politics.

Briefly, the weakness of the functionalist argument on problem-solving is that it emphasizes the material aspects of problems and their solutions while soft-pedaling the human aspects involved. Certainly the functionalist retort to this criticism would be that an emphasis on the material side of problems—the shift of attention "from power to problem and purpose," as Mitrany puts it—is precisely the *strength* of the functional approach. At any rate, if that approach is viewed in terms of some of its synonyms —"technical," for instance—the accentuation of the material aspect of problems comes very near to being identical with the functional approach, by definition. The difficulty arises as soon as we remember that the areas of functionalist attention necessarily have a human as well as a material dimension.

The functionalists are compelled to address this human aspect; Mitrany strives to make a virtue of the necessity, it would seem. Whereas the material aspect made its auspicious debut through such concepts as "technical self-determination," the human element enters in the guise of the "felt common need."[25] Problems, in Mitrany's scheme, are readily identifiable precisely because they are widely felt by human beings. Here the contention sounds rather more like a vindication of democracy by way of A. D. Lindsay's shoe-pinching argument than the justification of a technocracy managed by Platonic guardians. But elsewhere, when the functionalists return to their dominant emphasis, the assumption switches accordingly: the problem, now assumed to have been defined to everyone's satisfaction, takes on a purely material cast, and hence requires little more than an application of "technical self-determination."

This difficulty can be considered at the level of mechanism—the functionalist transmission belt by which needs commonly felt ("problems") are conveyed to the functional unit which must satisfy these needs (solve these problems). The concept of representation provides an opportunity, for it is at one and the same time the hub around which most modern discussion of this phase has revolved and the functionalists' own focus. Thus the overloading of the state structure by societal demands is, for Mitrany, epitomized by a breakdown in the system of representation based on territorial units.

"What are the chief difficulties which the planned State brings into the working of the representative system? Three, above all:

"i) the extension, without any obvious way of limiting them, of the functions and powers of central government;

"ii) consequent upon this, the loss of parliamentary initiative and control; and

[25] Mitrany, "International Cooperation in Action," p. 646. Emphasis omitted.

"iii) likewise, the loss of contact between government and electorate."[26]

Mitrany's ideas for unburdening the overtaxed state have already been discussed. To remedy the representative breakdown, he proposes for each problem-area "a functional assembly, composed of people who really know something about the task in hand and at the same time the relevant non-governmental organisations" which would, by implication, "provide an informed electorate, when the mass electorates in our own countries have lost all democratic virtue." Just so will functional unions "help to bridge the contradictions between our old democratic principles and the somewhat domineering way of the new State planning."[27]

Yet we may ask if the external and internal elements involved in problem-solving are bridged by the functionalist answer. A functional representative system, formal or informal, may be a desirable, even a necessary part of the communications network linking needs or problems to functional agencies. But is it a sufficient provision even for need- or problem-reportage? Does the functionalist reliance on "common" problems not paper over certain

[26] *Ibid.*, p. 647.

[27] *Ibid.*, p. 647. See also Mitrany's comments on ILO, following an address delivered at Chatham House on 4 March 1948, as reported in the summary of the discussion following "The Functional Approach to World Organization," p. 361; Mitrany, "An Advance in Democratic Representation," *International Associations*, VI (March 1954), 136-38. Cf. Reinsch's earlier observation that "the organization of economic and social activities of the world is being based upon the representation of interests in definite organs. While the parliamentary systems of the national states are still based on the abstract quantitative idea, the more natural system of interest representation is being used in international affairs. . . . If . . . world organization spontaneously takes this form from the beginning, it will profit by the combined energies which all these interests represent." Paul S. Reinsch, "International Administrative Law and National Sovereignty," *American Journal of International Law*, III (January 1909), 16; quoted by Engle, *op.cit.*, p. 71. See also Woolf, *op.cit.*, especially pp. 171ff., 352ff.

difficulties which may exist in the world of deeds and motives? Can we assume there is a perfect correspondence between the interests represented in a functional assembly and those actually implicated in the problems which it purports to treat?[28]

To raise these questions is not to answer them, of course. The subsequent investigation may well reveal that Mitrany's notion serves admirably as an interpretative spring-board, regardless of its efficacy as a surrogate for lost democratic virtue.

There are difficulties of another order. Effective problem-solving—including the ready acceptance of solutions by the respective publics involved—would seem to depend partly upon a clear, accepted ambit for each functional unit's operations. Mitrany apparently would agree; one of his criticisms of state planning, as already noted, is "the extension, without any obvious way of limiting them, of the functions and powers of central government[s]." What arrangements, then, does he provide for the guarding of the guardians? How is responsibility to be assured on the part of functional actors?

We may note as a brief prelude to Mitrany's answer those safeguards which have appeared in the workings of modern democratic governmental systems, in order to be the more ready to recognize the functionalist suggestions.

[28] John Dewey's suggestive comment makes the last question both relevant and significant: "The characteristic of the public as a state springs from the fact that all modes of associated behavior may have extensive and enduring consequences which involve others beyond those directly engaged in them. When these consequences are in turn realized in thought and sentiment, recognition of them reacts to remake the conditions out of which they arose. Consequences have to be taken care of, looked out for. This supervision and regulation cannot be effected by the primary groupings themselves. For the essence of the consequences which call a public into being is the fact that they expand beyond those directly engaged in producing them. Consequently special agencies and measures must be formed if they are to be attended to; or else some existing group must take on new functions." Dewey, *The Public and its Problems* (Denver: Alan Swallow, n.d.; first published 1927), p. 27.

Basically there are but two. One is an institutional arrangement which assures oversight by a public-at-large, perhaps, in practice, simply through a selection process allowing one of two or more alternative elites to exercise legitimate general political leadership only after an option by a relatively large number of voters. The operative ideal of this system is the responsiveness of political leadership to the general electorate. The other safeguard is the constitutional engineering of some controlling device, whether passive or active, such as the separation of powers, checks and balances, federalism, judicial review, bills of rights, and written constitutions themselves. Here the operative ideal is a limitation and diffusion of governmental power.

For Mitrany, there is no suggestion of alternative elites or an option by a general public: expertise is the standard, and the best qualified must rule. Presumably the experts would be selected by those "who really know something about the task in hand," along with "the relevant non-governmental organisations." Mitrany's functional representation scheme, taken as the sole foundation for that end of his bridge resting upon the bank of democratic control of functional action, would in any case prove cause for circumspection. This uneasiness is increased by the treatment of representation elsewhere in his work. As he writes in *A Working Peace System*, "one might hope that gradually the functional agencies would acquire a purely technical form of management, based no more even on contributions but on the capacity of the managers for their jobs—it would be, one might say, equality in non-representation."[29]

Nor do we find a constitutional device. There is at most an emphasis on autonomy of functional units which might be taken as roughly comparable with the ideal (if not the assurance) of diffusion of power.

[29] 1943 edition, pp. 40-41.

The functionalist emphasis lies elsewhere. The function itself selects and by implication limits its own jurisdiction, its organs and powers. "Technical self-determination" guides these exercises. Ultimately there is a human element in the formula. The responsibility is that of the governor to his station and duty, the *functionnaire* to his function. Mitrany's formulation reminds us that no mechanism can of itself assure the appropriate conduct of authority, that all systems demand an undergirding notion of individual responsibility in official action. But it also raises certain other questions: What are the roots of this undergirding notion in the functionalist scheme? To what extent must the notion be elaborated and assimilated as a common framework of expectations by functional actors, their clienteles, and publics-at-large?

The functional approach would solve problems in the social and economic sectors, its proponents argue. Yet there can be neither social nor economic problems without the people whose problems these are, just as there can be neither society nor economy without human beings. The "objective" side of these problems involves people as well as things: their solution necessarily involves the ordering or re-ordering of human behavior. Yet the generation of new behavioral norms in problem-solving suggests questions which the functionalists have largely avoided. Most important is the question of why these norms should and will come to be. Here lies the greatest deficiency in the functionalist argument—its inadequate consideration of the nature and operation of politics.

The functionalist antipathy toward politics is evidenced not only by disparaging comments and the lack of any sustained discussion of the political but also by a certain amount of ambiguity when the term is employed. In the functionalist literature "political" is generally used to denote that portion of the universe of human relations which lies beyond the functional pale. As such the functional is by definition the non-political, and thus is synonymous

with "non-controversial" or "technical" in terms of procedure, and "economic" or "social" in its substantive aspect.
Politics is a residue. Indeed, the strategy of the functional
approach is "to shift the emphasis from political issues
which divide to those social issues in which the interest of
the peoples is plainly akin and collective. . . ."[30] And the
functional way of dealing with these issues is the non-
political way, the way of technical self-determination.

Mitrany shifts his own emphasis momentarily during
his allusions to the *initiation* of functional projects. In
so doing he compromises his denigration of politics and
the political. Here the functional is temporarily subsumed
within the political. Mitrany cautions, for instance, that
"in this awkward field [of international relations] we
cannot make progress by propounding schemes which
have a pleasant symmetry without regard to the rough
and shifty terrain on which they have to be grounded,"
and concludes that "we are bound to look for a new political device," and to find, in that quest, the functional
approach.[31]

Sometimes Mitrany comes perilously close to inconsistency, even within the compass of a single page. "Functional co-operation is a political device . . . like other
forms of union . . . ," he writes. But "functional unions
. . . are a service, not an alliance; and therefore they are

[30] Mitrany, "The Functional Approach to World Organization,"
p. 359. Cf. Zimmern's assessment of an earlier but comparable
spirit: "[T]here emerged, in League circles, what may be described
as a new form of the old Fabian or gradualist doctrine, based upon
the assimilative power of the Geneva spirit and of the institutions
which it was creating. Little by little, so it began to be believed, the
morass of 'high politics' would dry up along its edges, as one issue
after another was drained off to Geneva. Thus eventually there
would be a world-wide cooperative system held together by a network of contacts between government departments (other than
Foreign Offices), professional organisations and individual experts.
It was, indeed, a curious combination of Fabianism and Cobden-
ism." *Op.cit.*, p. 322.

[31] Mitrany, "The Functional Approach to World Organization,"
p. 354.

not exclusive, as political unions are bound to be."[32] Apparently he intends to distinguish between the genus "political device" and two of its species, functional unions and political unions.

More crucial to the present argument is the fundamental weakness which these vagaries of usage appear to symptomize. As intimated already, the functionalist argument appears to rely on an inadequate appreciation of *obligation*—a crucial element in the practice and study of politics.

In order to lay a foundation for the criticism of this functionalist shortcoming it will be necessary to elaborate on the centrality of obligation to a political philosophy. Our contention is that the functionalist argument, through its failure to come to grips with "the political," falls short of providing an adequate basis for interpreting the origin and status of present international institutions. The demonstration of this argument must rest ultimately upon subsequent empirical findings. Here we seek to economize and focus that quest.

Let us define politics, arbitrarily though tentatively, as the rationalization of the exercise of power by and upon society. Such an open-ended definition makes it possible to draw together several elements relevant to this study. It implies a key role for society, without specifying the essence and bounds of that society or the nature and writ of the instrumentality with which society undertakes its "authoritative allocation of values."[33] It leaves unsounded and uncompartmentalized "power," that vast conceptual space so often assigned to data processing or storage, willfully leaves it to assume its appropriate position in the interstices of the subsequent discourse. Most important, it captures in a single word, "rationalization," two

[32] Mitrany, "International Cooperation in Action," p. 646.
[33] David Easton, *The Political System* (New York: Alfred A. Knopf, 1953), pp. 129ff.

ideas previously encountered, which will now be clothed in a different garb.

When one encounters the word "rationalize" or "rationalization" he is well advised to ponder the context before concluding its meaning. If he is reading Max Weber's work, he will understand rationalization to be the fitting of appropriate means to the achievement of a given end. As such, rationalization implies an economizing of effort. Its slogan is "efficiency," without raising the question "efficiency for what?"—if for no other reason than that the "what" is assumed. Although the end may be unspecified, in practice it is apt to be material in nature; the progress of rationalization may be read by the economic indices and perhaps in some columns of the census reports.

To rationalize power in this sense is to guide it, to attune it to the task-at-hand, to husband and allocate it where a scarcity exists, and restrict it when too much would undo the effort's design. Power in this formulation bears a resemblance to raw energy, and the parallel extends to the patterns of outcome and output—maximum production of "goods" with minimum effort. In the vernacular of the political dialogue, this type of power-rationalization closely approximates that styled "administration" since some of the writings of Woodrow Wilson and Frank J. Goodnow.[34] And it is hardly a monopoly of the state and its apparatus.

[34] E.g., Wilson's "The Study of Administration," *Political Science Quarterly*, II (June 1887), 197-222, reprinted in abridged form in Dwight Waldo (ed.), *Ideas and Issues in Public Administration* (New York: McGraw-Hill Book Company, Inc., 1953), pp. 65-75; Goodnow's *Politics and Administration* (New York: The Macmillan Company, 1900), especially pp. 9ff., 18ff. See also Albert Lepawsky, *Administration* (New York: Alfred A. Knopf, 1949), pp. 40ff.; Waldo, *The Administrative State* (New York: The Ronald Press Company, 1948), pp. 53ff.; Samuel Haber, "Scientific Management and the Progressive Movement, 1910-1929," unpublished Ph.D. dissertation, Department of History, University of California (Berkeley), 1961.

When the functionalists address the objective aspect of problem-solving, when they employ such terms as "technical self-determination"—and this is most of the time—they seem to have in mind essentially this style of power-rationalization. But rationalization has another side. Rationalization in the second sense is ordinarily applied to the self-justification of his actions by an individual. It is broadened here to include the justification of power's use upon human beings; specifically, the justification of its employment by society upon itself. Rationalization of power in this sense means its legitimization. Another way of expressing this is through the notion of obligation, insofar as those upon whom power impinges are in a position of choice in determining the legitimacy of its exercise.

To speak of society imposing strictures upon itself is to invoke an image much too anthropomorphic. More accurately stated, a segment of society makes this imposition, and society (perhaps in fact the rest of society) *for some reason* accepts the stricture. Theories of the polity answer the question of why individuals and groups accept the imposition in quite divergent manners. On one extreme are those explanations which see man obedient solely because he fears the consequence of disobedience. The state's essence is its monopoly of violence, and might has bred right, over the long if not the short pull. At the other end of the spectrum rest those interpretations which hold man's obedience to be purely the product of his internalization of society's norms. By this light, law is but a species of custom, and man's obligation rests lightly indeed on his consciousness—he knows no alternative to obedience.

In between these polar interpretations lie the provinces of most political philosophizing. Here we find the contract as an instrument of agreement, here the various elaborations of rights, duties, freedom. In the central regions of the spectrum, man's range of choice as a political animal grows, both in terms of knowing and doing. Here man is neither simply the product of his fears nor his habituation, and the underpinnings of his acknowledgment of authority become more rational and yet more complex—now symbolized, perhaps, by the change in terminology from oblige and obedience to obligation. In this middle sector man's choice as a political philosopher likewise expands. For here he enjoys the freedom and the responsibility for dealing not only with questions which begin "What is" but also with those which start "What *should* be." Politics itself, as defined above, may be understood along one of its dimensions as the range of publicly relevant activities between what one is obliged by necessity to do or not do, on the one hand, and what he feels *obligated* to do or not do, on the other. Yet high politics would include even the transformation of obligation's bases. So understood, politics is an exercise in choices, although some choices are more important than others.

At what position along the spectrum does the functionalist argument rest? Does it recognize these questions, and if so how does it answer them?

First of all, the functionalists reject out of hand the thesis that man can be made to obey only through fear of the consequences of disobedience. Yet they do not readily embrace the opposing extreme, which takes man to be a creature of custom. The image behind the latter view is "traditional" society. Man's obedience in such a setting is undiluted by the differentiation of structural and normative patterns induced by social change. The functionalist view is hardly that of pre-industrialism, either in its understanding or its prescription. Still, it does bear a certain similarity to customary behavior, if the latter is construed so broadly as to take man's obedience to rest upon a foundation of habit. More precisely, the functionalist argument, in its manipulative moments, seems to see the transplantation of man's obedience as a matter of planned re-habituation. Leonard Woolf gives the thought pithy expression:

"Man in national or international masses is not yet an orderly or a reasonable animal. He is an animal of passion and prejudice. Any system or organisation or machinery for governing his affairs must, if it is to be accepted by him, allow play to those passions and prejudices. It is no good building him a brand new beautiful international institution. The human institutions really used by him are secreted by him much in the same way as some small repulsive insects secrete a kind of building around themselves. And the only way of influencing him is by tickling him to induce a more copious secretion on one side than on another, just as ants for this purpose tickle their cowlike aphides with their antennae."[35]

The points of similarity between the functionalists and the position originally sketched must not be overemphasized, however. To say that man's behavior is best understood as the overt manifestation of a configuration of internalized norms is to take his range of choice as being very limited. The functionalist contention, per contra, implies an extension of this range of human choice beyond what it is at present. Mitrany's expectation is far from that associated with traditional society, with its solidary constitution and ascriptive ties. The functionalist model is *Gesellschaft*, not *Gemeinschaft*. Mitrany's image is much nearer that of the pluralists, with its implications of individuation and discretion. As he writes, "the functional way . . . leaves the individual free to enter into a variety of relationships—religious, political and professional, social and cultural, and so on —each of which may take him into different directions and dimensions. . . ."[36] Man's choice is assured by multiple access to the associations of the modern world.

[35] Woolf, *op.cit.*, pp. 124-25.
[36] Mitrany, "International Cooperation in Action," p. 647.

The functionalist argument thus lies somewhere in the middle range of our spectrum. If man has before him the choice of associating as well as a variety of possible associations, the question of obligation is fairly raised. Why should man obey the directives of a functional system? Why should groups of men adhere? The functionalist answer may be indicated in summary form:

1. Man's obligation to certain types of norms stems from the technical ability which was exercised in their formulation. Legitimate action in functional areas is the action of experts, closely backed by those "who really know what the scope of legislation in [a] particular field should be, and . . . also have the knowledge and the direct interest to watch on behalf of the political community at large how policy is carried out in that field."[37]

2. Beyond the proposition that the experts' guidance should be heeded, there is a utilitarian strand woven into the functionalist conception of obligation. "The functional body wins its way by the offer of service." Man should follow because of the benefits which accrue thereby to him and his fellow beings. Similarly, groups of people—as for instance nation-states—should feel obligated to join their efforts for similar reasons, "one purpose at a time," by way of "limited liability association[s] between units."[38]

We may tentatively express disappointment at the functionalist conception of obligation; it seems to offer naught but a foundation of sand. Subsequent chapters will provide perspective for an evaluation of this feeling. A rhetorical question ends the present discussion. If it were possible to see one, what would a community erected upon these principles of obligation look like?

[37] Mitrany, "An Advance in Democratic Representation," p. 137.
[38] Warren Roberts, "Community as Matrix," in Carl J. Friedrich (ed.), *Community* (New York: Liberal Arts Press, 1959), pp. 197-98; Mitrany, "International Cooperation in Action," p. 646.

The functionalist argument may seem weak in logic at some points, indefensible as to its ultimate vision in other respects. Yet these observations, even if apt, must not lead arbitrarily to a categorical rejection of the argument. Theories with more grievous failings than those heretofore examined have lived long and productive lives. We have thus far dealt only with the words in the functionalist argument; though the nature of the game prevents a complete break with the verbal medium, it is now appropriate to reorder the investigation through an application of symbols more closely attuned to the universe of the senses. How well does the functionalist argument explain actual developments in international organization?

An explanatory theory must meet the facts; that is, it must, given the conditions it exacts, find its own projected consequences realized in the course of actual events. This much is obvious: certainly the chief test of any purported explanatory theory is that it facilitate prediction, or at least the projection of trends.

Another purpose behind theoretical undertakings is too often overlooked. A theory may do no more than explain or illuminate *how* and *why* a phenomenon or a class of phenomena take place, yet if it opens the way to the observer's enlightenment it proves itself "useful," to employ that adjective so favored by social scientists. The obvious standard for a theory's usefulness in this respect is simply the question "Does it illuminate?" But the application of this standard involves certain difficulties to be assayed later in the present chapter.

How may the empirical confrontation of the functionalist theory of international organization be undertaken? Perhaps the best preparation will be to select elements from the functionalist argument which may be utilized in constructing operational propositions for imposition upon a universe of empirical data. Criteria of relevance in the form of suitable operational statements should provide not only an economizing principle for the quest but also a certain assurance of propriety: if the cases chosen are appropriate, they must follow closely the *conditions* set forth in the functionalist writings.

Another objective is a balance in which prophecy may be compared with the actual course of events. What *consequences* are foreseen for functional programs? Can these consequences be stated in a manner specific enough to apply to real happenings? To state consequences is to set forth the nature of functional progress and its opposite; to draw up indices or indicators is to rule off bench marks by which that progress or regress may be measured in the specific cases selected for study. In order to weigh the functionalist prophecy, consequences and indices must be brought together.

Finally, it is desirable to educe and systematize the functionalists' *explanation*. How do they account for the development of functional consequences from antecedent functional conditions? Let us assume that the functionalists did accurately foresee certain developments subsequent to implementation of those conditions initially demanded. Must we not also inquire whether these developments were actually the result of factors suggested by the functionalists? It may not always be easy or even possible to make this sort of assessment, but certainly it is desirable that it be tried, in order to avoid the *post hoc, ergo propter hoc* fallacy.

Our operational propositions rest to a considerable extent on what has been said already. There is no effort at this point to join specific conditions, consequences, and reasons. For purposes of clarity it will be well to remember a formula which represents the components of an interlinked operational proposition—"If . . . , then . . . , because. . . ." But here the statements are simply grouped under their three labels.

CONDITIONS: Which international activities are functional?

    I. Functional international activities are specific in their focus.

    II. These specific activities are in non-controversial areas (i.e., "social" or "economic," by definition distinguished from "political").

    III. These activities are at the outset organized separately—separately from each other, and from international political organs.

Mitrany has indicated which activities fall within his definition: "During the past century or so, quite a number of functional unions have come into being. . . . All specialised agencies of the United Nations are of this nature; but so far the most developed is the [European Coal and Steel Community]."[39]

CONSEQUENCES AND INDICATORS:[40] What developments do the functionalists foresee, and how may these developments be observed?

[39] Mitrany, "International Cooperation in Action," p. 646.

[40] The chief functionalist claim is world peace, as emphasized in Mitrany's title, *A Working Peace System*. It will be possible to assess this claim to some extent later in the inquiry, but one major qualification will have to be kept in mind: the forecast of peace as a consequence of the functional approach exacts as its proviso the continuation of many functional programs over an extended period— a condition manifestly not satisfied at present. The consequences selected from the functionalist argument for application in the present investigation are much more specific, but they are ultimately related to the functionalist conception of peace. For the functionalists, community is a necessary and sufficient condition for peaceful as for bountiful life. It will be recalled from the previous discussion that "peaceful change" with a functional content is regarded as a crucial process; it is one test of community's existence, and presumably one factor in that community's attainment in the first place. Cf. Richard W. Van Wagenen, *Research in the International Organization Field: Some Notes on a Possible Focus* (Princeton: Center for Research on World Political Institutions, 1952), pp. 10-11, as quoted by Karl W. Deutsch, *Political Community at the*

I. Structural change

   A. The development of the initial functional starts will be marked by

      1. An increase in structural support capacity for the performance of original tasks

      Structural indications of growth in capacity to perform original task:

         a) Financing operations

            (1) Quantitative secular increase in financing outputs

            (2) Changes in pattern of commitments and disbursals

            (3) Modifications of income pattern

               (a) Systematization of income from original source—member states

               (b) New sources of income

                   i) Revenues from agency transactions

                   ii) Borrowings

                   iii) Systematized contributions from sources other than member states

         b) Representation and participation patterns

            (1) Wider representation of nation-state actors (in cases where the functional need is itself more extensive than mirrored in the original pattern of representation)

International Level (Garden City: Doubleday & Co., Inc., 1954), p. 33; Deutsch *et al.*, *Political Community and the North Atlantic Area* (Princeton: Princeton University Press, 1957), p. 5. Consequences listed here draw their meaning from the functionalist notion of peaceful change. Indicators have been formulated with a look ahead at the programs from the UN system selected for study.

      (2) Increased participation of non-state actors

        (a) Individual experts

        (b) Non-governmental organizations

   c) Field capacity

      (1) Development of administrative expenditures for field activities

      (2) Relevant staff reorganizations

      (3) Field personnel and coordination

II. Problem-solving

  A. Problems will be solved in the social and economic areas where functional projects are initially undertaken

    Indications of the solution of problems:

      1. Actual implementation of a high percentage of decisions made by functional agencies

      2. Acknowledgment of the solution of problems by those previously labeling them problems, insofar as this is not counterbalanced by a causally linked outcry from another source

  B. Problems in sectors other than those where initial functional projects were undertaken will be approached (thereby expanding the original task) . . .

    Indications:

      1. Relevant changes in basic instruments

        a) By specific amendment

        b) By usage

      2. Official and quasi-official statements

        a) By Secretariat and executive members

        b) By significant segments of representation

3. Structural manifestations (see I, above)

C. . . . with comparable success in solving them
   Indications:
   1. (See II-A)

III. Attitude Change

A. A "new conscience"[41] will be bred by functional endeavor . . .
   Indications:
   1. Reduction of the percentage of votes required to arrive at decisions from unanimity to qualified or simple majority
   2. Modification of the principle of state equality in weight of vote allotted various nation-state actors
   3. Substance of decisions made

B. . . . and spread outward from its point of origin in "constantly widening circles."[42]
   Indications of widening circles of cooperation, listed in sequence:
   Cooperative behavioral manifestations in speeches and writings of
   1. Secretariat members
   2. Experts in specific fields involved
   3. International non-governmental representatives
   4. National non-governmental representatives
   5. Nation-state and bloc actors
      a) Recipients of functional benefits
      b) Combination recipient-benefactor participants in functional programs
      c) Benefactors of functional programs

REASONS OR EXPLANATIONS: *Why* did peaceful

[41] Mitrany, A *Working Peace System*, 1943 edition, p. 40.
[42] Reinsch, *Public International Unions*, p. 2.

change (as manifested in the consequences foreseen) actually take place? How does this aid in creating permanent conditions necessary for further peaceful change?

I. Functional activity as preventive: the elimination of sources of friction

"A preventive orientation does not stress the static aspects of peace—armistice, conference and treaty—but rather the task of post-war reconstruction and continued collaboration for the solution of economic and social problems."[43]

"[One] cause of the existing unrest and disharmony on the international scene can be found, in our view, in the disparity in the economic and social fields which characterizes our present time and divides the world into the very rich and the very poor. These unbalanced standards . . . sow the seeds of discontent and jealousy. . . ."[44]

"If we sit here just enjoying our material resources, if we are content to become fat and flabby at 50, and let the rest of the world go by, the time will not be far away when we will be hearing a knock on our door in the middle of the night. . . ."[45]

II. Functional activity as reorientation of endeavor: the division of problems and diversion of efforts

[43] George B. de Huszar, "The Need for a Preventive Policy," in Huszar (ed.), *Persistent International Issues* (New York: Harper & Brothers Publishers, 1947), p. 8.

[44] Ibrahim Abboud, President of the Republic of the Sudan (General Assembly, Sixteenth Session, A/PV.1036, 13 October 1961), as quoted in "Africa Speaks to the United Nations," Norman J. Padelford and Rupert Emerson (eds.), *International Organization*, XVI (Spring 1962), 311.

[45] President Lyndon B. Johnson, as quoted by Tom Wicker, "Johnson Bids U.S. Aid World's Poor," *New York Times*, 22 April 1964, p. 18.

"Principles are abstract; methods are concrete. The general term 'peace' must be broken down into its specific aspects. The French political maxim *il faut serier les problèmes* is applicable here."[46]

"I emphasise the importance of contact outside the Foreign Offices of State. I believe it is of real urgency . . . to multiply the sources of contact between States. The more we can localise action, the more it can be dealt with in terms, not of prestige, but of technique, the greater is the opportunity for the growth of technique. The normal channels of diplomacy centralise issues in a way of which the consequences may come to possess far more significance than is warranted. . . . Technique keeps the trivial in its right perspective. . . . And to keep discussion technical has the great additional advantage of keeping it undramatic. It cannot easily be made a journalistic sensation. It cannot be surrounded with that miasma of report and scandal which have poisoned so many international conferences. . . . It makes the notion of a triumph much less accessible when, *a priori*, the nature of the triumph is not intelligible enough to be news."[47]

"It merely adds to the strain upon the individual to appeal to his humanity while the state appeals to his selfishness. It is safer to regard emotions simply as a force which can be mobilised in the service of some specific purpose. As such and in itself it is neither good nor bad. As in the case of the internal combustion engine, where all depends on whether it is put into a fire engine or into a

[46] Huszar, *op.cit.*, p. 13.
[47] Harold J. Laski, A *Grammar of Politics* (rev. ed.; London: George Allen & Unwin Ltd., 1938), p. 619.

tank, so it all depends on whether the emotional drive is harnessed to a good or a bad social end."[48]

"[B]y concentrating all attention on a practical public service, [the functional method] is likely more than anything else to breed a new conscience in all those concerned with such international activities."[49]

"[The functional approach] should help to shift the emphasis from political issues which divide, to those social issues in which the interest of the peoples is plainly akin and collective; to shift the emphasis from power to problem and purpose. In all societies there are both harmonies and disharmonies. It is largely within our choice which we pick out and further."[50]

"[Some of the functionalists] have intimated, rather vaguely, that the accumulated agenda of constructive work under functional organizations will produce such a preoccupation that men will abandon war in a fit of absent-mindedness; they will forget to fight because they will be 'too busy with things that matter.' "[51]

"Let both sides explore what problems unite us instead of belaboring those problems which divide us. . . . And if a beachhead of co-operation may push back the jungle of suspicion, let both sides join in creating a new endeavor. . . ."[52]

[48] Mitrany in *Proceedings*, p. 82.
[49] Mitrany, *A Working Peace System*, 1943 edition, p. 40.
[50] Mitrany, "The Functional Approach to World Organization," p. 359.
[51] Claude, *op.cit.*, p. 381, quoting from John Maclaurin, *The United Nations and Power Politics* (London: George Allen & Unwin Ltd., 1951), p. 306.
[52] President John F. Kennedy, Inaugural Address.

III. Functional activity as habituator: the training-
ground of cooperation

"Perhaps the most important result of the
League [of Nations] system of non-political cooperation was that it, along with the Secretariat, produced a kind of international civil service [made up
of] internationally-minded persons. . . ."[53]

"[I]s the real task [perhaps] that of . . . *preparing*
people, changing them, making them fit for world
government? . . . What is required is the profound
alteration of attitudes, loyalties, attachments, and
values, which in turn involves an attack upon the
basic conditions of human society that provide the
context within which men are shaped. This is
clearly not an overnight process, and it is clearly
not to be conducted like a propaganda campaign.
In fact, it is precisely the kind of work which the
United Nations system, particularly in its functional agencies, is carrying on."[54]

"Each of us . . . is in effect a collectivity of functional loyalties; so that to build up a world community . . . is merely to extend and consolidate it
also as between national sections and groups."[55]

"The void which the old cosmopolitan ideal left
between the individual and humanity is . . . being
filled by the creation of living institutions through
which the individual may gradually learn to co-
operate, in many groups, with all his fellow men."[56]

"Cooperation is the key to life and society.
Neither the individual nor the nation is self-suffic-
ing. There is a broader life; there are broader in-

[53] Martin, *op.cit.*, p. 277.
[54] Claude, *op.cit.*, p. 415. Emphasis in original.
[55] Mitrany, "International Cooperation in Action," p. 647.
[56] Reinsch, *Public International Unions*, p. 3.

terests and more far-reaching activities surrounding national life in which it must participate in order to develop to the full its own nature and satisfy completely its many needs. Even as the individual receives from society both protection and stimulus, so the nation would suffer intolerable disadvantages were it to exclude itself from world intercourse. . . . It is not outside of, but within, the great international society of the world that states will advance and develop what is best in their individuality. . . . [By] recognizing interdependence with the other civilized nations of the world, a state strengthens itself as does the individual who plunges with full energy into the life of his community, being stimulated thereby and having all his faculties developed."[57]

"The truth is, of course, that the more nations work together, and grow to depend on each other in certain matters, the more likely they are to come to agreement on other questions, and so the less likely to strain their relations to the danger point. Joint action between nations in questions of public health, control of the opium traffic, etc., is not only worth while because it lessens the sum-total of human suffering, but is indirectly valuable in that it strengthens the machinery and habits of co-operation and induces mutual confidence and good feeling."[58]

"[A]nyone who once sees that the problems of his own country—and its achievements—are not so dissimilar from the problems and achievements of other countries, is not so likely to divide the world into 'good' people, i.e. his countrymen; and

[57] *Ibid.*, pp. 4, 6, 8.
[58] Howard-Ellis, *op.cit.*, p. 477; quoted by Martin, *op.cit.*, p. 171.

scoundrels and knaves, i.e. everyone else, especially his neighbors."[59]

"In the camaraderie of technical experts, the distinction between east and west has lost its meaning in many instances."[60]

IV. Functional activity as invisible hand: the motive forces implied by the "widening circles" simile

A. The *technai* as media of functional ramification

"The technical and industrial advance which characterizes our era has already brought about an internationalism, which is slowly and carefully being embodied in the forms of political organization. . . . Science knows no natural boundaries. . . . [U]niversal factors have in our era become of prime importance. They . . . are filling the entire world with that spirit of cooperation upon which real advance is dependent."[61]

B. "Function" as instrument of functional ramification

"The nature of each function tells precisely the range of jurisdiction and the powers needed for its effective performance. And for the same reason, unlike rigid political arrangements, functional arrangements can be adjusted, without political friction, when the conditions of the function are seen to have changed."[62]

[59] C. Hart Schaaf, "The United Nations Economic Commission for Asia and the Far East," *International Organization*, VII (1953), 476.

[60] David Wightman, "East-West Cooperation and the United Nations Economic Commission for Europe," *International Organization*, XI (Winter 1957), 7.

[61] Reinsch, *Public International Unions*, pp. v, 3, 186.

[62] Mitrany, "International Cooperation in Action," p. 647.

"The function of an organization is something so inherent that it constitutes the very law of existence of any institution. And if the function refers to a task which is shared with other organizations, this immanent law of existence transcends the particular organization and its incidental 'interests,' linking it with inescapable necessity to the operation of those other institutions."[63]

"Each act of successful co-operation . . . achieved will at the same time create the need and the preconditions for co-operation in other fields. . . ."[64]

"If we act where we may, in those areas where action is possible, the inner logic of the programmes which we adopt will work for us and inevitably impel us still farther in the direction of ultimate union."[65]

C. Personal influence as vehicle of functional ramification

"[Non-political cooperation in the League of Nations produced internationally-minded League civil servants whose influence] upon subsequent international thinking probably cannot be over-exaggerated. Their practical suggestions have been of great value. But even more important has been the influence they have had upon the minds of students of international affairs, an influence which continues to move ever-outward like ripples on the surface of a pond."[66]

[63] Gerhart Niemeyer, *Law Without Force* (Princeton: Princeton University Press, 1941), p. 234.

[64] UN Economic Commission for Africa Secretariat, "Approaches to African Economic Integration," 7 May 1963, p. 6.

[65] H.I.M. Haile Selassie I, opening address at the Conference of Heads of African States and Governments, Addis Ababa, Ethiopia, 22 May 1963.

[66] Martin, *op.cit.*, pp. 276-77.

V. Functional activity as creator of community: the organismic analogy and its implications

In exemplifying the previous categories of functionalist explanation it has seemed adequate to set down relevant quotations. For the final category, analogical explanation, more is necessary as caveat and as background.

Few would deny the heuristic efficacy of the analogy. And yet, quite apart from the failure to meet exacting logical standards which some would demand for enlightenment no less than proof, the analogy presents stubborn difficulties because of its highly personalized lessons. Its weaknesses are both logical and psychological, both personal and interpersonal. The analogy is apt to operate as a switch throwing the explicator (or his reader or listener) onto a spur track, causing an inadvertent departure from the route toward individual or shared understanding. Even if an analogy proves useful to one person's understanding, there is no assurance it will aid the next. One man's source of insight may prove another's source of confusion. Or, to put it in the contemporary language of social science, there is no assurance of replicability through the use of analogies. In principle this need bother only the most rigorous positivist—he who would accept as legitimate data only those phenomena which are knowable in a more substantial sense than analogies will allow. For our purposes, the more obvious dangers have been parried, hopefully, by utilizing analogies mainly to ask whether a consequence successfully foreseen by the functionalists has taken place *for the reasons offered* by the functionalists.

Another characteristic of analogies must be noted: their tendency to facilitate an easy and almost imperceptible transition from explanation to prescription. Here is a modern example of analogical norm-derivation: "Physiology is largely the science of how cells live together in an organism; and sociology, which is concerned with how men live together in a society, is related to physiology in that a society is a sort of epi-organism. So far cells seem to get on together better than do men; so physiology may have something of value to say."[67]

These are qualifications, but together they hardly disqualify the analogy. The point is its *indeterminacy*. There can be little assurance that the original analogy-maker's insights have been communicated, much less substantiated or undercut. Verification might be employed, it will be said by some, but verification of analogies directed to society is not easy, even if it could be assumed that it is possible to reduce all analogical insights to some scheme of verification, a difficult position to defend. What is model but analogy? Is such a common gambit to be proscribed because it is seldom consummated in verification? Surely this fashion in the social science fraternity attests a rather general willingness to reach beyond the firm grasp of one's perception—and to strive to convey fragile insights to others. By what standards, again, is the analogical prescription to be judged? Certainly neither standards of logic nor standards integral to the particular analogy in question will suffice. Still, remedy-by-analogy has hardly disappeared for want of a proper, handy evaluative instrument, nor should it.

Different ages and peoples have employed various analogies to express their understanding and wishes for society. Two analogies stand out for modern man. One takes society as akin to a machine, and draws forth deductions of a mechanistic dynamism and mechanical stability. The other holds society to be like an organism, more often than not the human organism, and provides by this image a view of unitary progression and organic harmony.[68]

[67] Ralph W. Gerard, "A Biologist's View of Society," *Common Cause*, III (July 1950), p. 630. Gerard has developed this analogy most persuasively. See, e.g., his "Higher Levels of Integration," in Robert Redfield (ed.), *Levels of Integration in Biological and Social Systems* (Lancaster, Pa.: The Jaques Cattell Press, 1942), pp. 67-87.

[68] Writes Barker: "[I]t may be contended, and it has often been

Sometimes the mechanistic and organismic analogies approach each other. Thomas Hobbes is properly regarded as being essentially mechanistic in his thought. Hobbes portrayed the human atom in much the same terms as did his physicist friends; for him, political artifice was an effort to restrict human "motion," not to re-educate or even rechannel it. Yet some of his language, read now with an intellectual backdrop of twentieth-century history, conjures up a very different picture. The elaborate metaphor by which Hobbes introduces his "artificial man" leaves the modern reader at least temporarily oblivious to the mechanistic character of Leviathan.

Ernest Barker finds common etymological roots for the analogies. He writes: "The biological analogy may be the best of the various analogies; and indeed we may frankly confess that it is. But we may also confess that 'organism' is itself an analogy drawn from mechanism; for 'organ' means a tool or an instrument, and when we speak of 'organs' of the body we are using an engineering analogy. The 'social organism' is an analogy which is based upon an analogy; and if biology can supply political science with a good metaphor for the understanding of the nature of Society and the State, it has itself been supplied already with a good metaphor in advance."[69]

Much of the functionalist explanation rests upon an organismic analogy or, more accurately, upon organismic metaphor.[70] It is necessary only to recall the strong plural-

---

contended, that Society and the State are themselves of the nature of biological structures, or organisms, in the sense that they are so analogous to such structures that they must be interpreted in the same terms and by the same language. . . . It is a point of view which would make both law and political science indebted to biology for the conceptions which they use to interpret their material, and the language which they employ to express their conceptions." Gierke, *op.cit.*, pp. xxviii, xxix.

[69] *Ibid.*, p. xxx.

[70] "Organismic" and "organic" are commonly employed interchangeably. In the present usage, "organismic" will refer to organisms and "organic" to organs.

ist bent in Mitrany's argument to sense that the device is engaged mainly for purposes of illustration. But its persistent appearance demands a closer look.

The functionalists take mankind as the relevant unit. Humanity is portrayed either as a potential organism or as an actual organism without self-consciousness. William Rappard, speaking of the League of Nations' evolution in an address delivered to the Geneva Institute of International Relations in 1927, depicted the political division of mankind as a vexatious though superficial and transitory attribute.

"Divided into separate units for purposes of political self-expression, humanity is, economically and socially, one great organism. As its component parts become more conscious of their interdependence, this organism tends to express its unity by means . . . other than political institutions. . . . The higher the political barriers, the more imperious the necessity of international cooperation. But the closer and more continuous international cooperation becomes, the more irksome and the less indispensable the high political barriers will doubtless in time become. Thus, checked in its frontal attack on the citadel of war by the as yet invincible forces of national sovereignty, the League is by means of its technical bodies executing a vast flanking movement around and against it."[71]

If humanity is already a social organism, it awaits but a clarion call to self-awareness of its accomplished unity; if only a *potential* organism, the demand must be for the building of the body of Man. The organism does not exist: it must be created. Mitrany's prescription is not surprising, from such a perspective; it is an excellent summary statement of the functionalist philosophy. Functional efforts would provide a connective tissue binding together the whole. "Every [functional] activity . . . would constitute a layer of peaceful life, and a sufficient

[71] Rappard, "The Evolution of the League of Nations," p. 818.

number of them would cover the world with a web of common endeavour and achievement, with common benefits to all peoples everywhere. Together they would create the living body of a true world community, and inevitably therefore a community within which the absence of war would be as natural as it now is within each of our own countries."[72]

To view the prospect solely in anatomical terms, however, provides only a gross structural picture of the projected outcome. The developmental process involves an interplay between organism and environment. This interplay is called "need" when viewed as the stimulus to action emanating from environment and "function" when taken as an appropriate response by the organism to a persistent need. A continuing interplay between organism and environment begets structural manifestations, for structural change is the means by which permanent support is given to a function and the continuing need which that function satisfies. The continuation of a minor need may be met by division of an existing structural unit, as (for the organismic analogue) by mitosis, the indirect division of a somatic cell. A number of more considerable needs might promote a kind of epigenetic development— the appearance of a series of new formations or successive differentiations in the structure. Major continuing needs may even necessitate the development of new organs to provide a functional response. And the further development of these new organs is proportional to their use, to move on to Lamarck's third law.[73] With these developments the organism itself undergoes a metamorphosis, whether the organism be the body physical or the body

[72] Mitrany, "International Cooperation in Action," p. 648.
[73] Ibid., p. 646: "When . . . Lamarck summarized his views on evolution in four laws, the second advanced the central theory that the development of a new organ in an animal body resulted from a new need which had made itself felt. That perfectly describes the growth of functional unions—they come into being because of a *felt common need*." Mitrany's emphasis.

politic. Mitrany's example is the New Deal; its "new functions and . . . new organs, taken together, have revolutionized the American political system. . . . A great constitutional transformation has . . . taken place without any changes in the Constitution."[74]

The organismic analogy or metaphor is indeed provocative. Its clues must be carried in the search for understanding. But before closing this section of the study we must make explicit several questions suggested by an elaboration of the analogy. These questions are asked in a spirit of skepticism, but it is neither a passive nor an unbounded skepticism. The failure to substantiate an analogical contention may nonetheless lead toward a consideration of problems in understanding which otherwise might not even have been recognized.

1. In the organismic analogue the layman speaks of certain elements or events as vital to the existence of living creatures. One such term is "conception," the creation of a new life. The life of the more complex animals begins as two germ cells unite, bearing and then combining the potential characteristics and limiting framework of the offspring's makeup. The process of conception likewise implies physical union of sexual opposites, at least outside laboratory conditions. The sexual partners are ordinarily of the same species. And modern man, at least, is conscious of the cause-effect relationship by which human offspring are created.

Does this suggest the desirability of exploring carefully those circumstances surrounding the origin of functional agencies? Certainly an understanding of the beginnings of life is imperative for the biologist. Or does the functionalist argument part ways with modern biological theory here? Some of the functionalist writings approach an abiogenetic explanation of the origins of functional life; the functional bodies are said by one writer to "have

[74] Mitrany, A Working Peace System, 1943 edition, p. 22.

come into being spontaneously, independently, and according to no concerted plan."[75] Or does the functionalist explanation hold that the organismic analogy is appropriate for an understanding of origins, but at the same time imply that we should think of the functional units as analogous to elementary one-cell animals—devoid of self-consciousness, capable of simple reproduction by producing offshoots which are also amoebic in their adaptability to external circumstance, and yet destined to evolve in some future age into the highest forms of life? If so, the Great Community will presumably be a long time emerging.

2. Another layman's word is "growth." One aspect of growth is nourishment, and we are likely, upon reflection, to think of nourishment in terms broader than physical sustenance. But growth involves more than nourishment even taken in this broad sense. We sometimes regard both existence and growth as implying an inner impulse, and perhaps call this the "survival instinct" or "life-force." Such phrases man has used to convey his belief in a biological energy which is expended by the organism and directed toward its well-being. What is the "nourishment" of functional growth? What is the nature of its growth-impulse—its energy and its energy-allocation?

3. Organisms mean life. What is life's analogue in the functionalist explanation? If we are to utilize organismic and organic analogies a solid bridge is needed, yet we find that while most of the functionalists analogically assume the preexistence of "life," the basic argument is that an organism is *being* built, and a life *created*. Can social organisms be built? Or, to phrase the question in different terms, can a world community be raised upon a foundation of overlapping *Gesellschaft* memberships? Is it possible to move by organization to organs, and from organs to organism?

[75] Pitman B. Potter, *An Introduction to the Study of International Organization*, p. 275; quoted by Martin, *op.cit.*, p. 52.

With these questions we are brought once again to an ambiguous legacy within the more general functionalist heritage—the irreconcilability of the notions "function" and "purpose." Joseph Tussman has both illuminated the difficulty and made it relevant to the present focus:

"[A]ny art or artifact supports a teleological question and . . . it is appropriate to ask about the purpose of a tribunal or a system of tribunals. We are, perhaps, more comfortable with 'function' than with 'purpose,' but function, while it has a broader range, is, when applied to artifacts, at least crypto-purposive. Thus, 'how does the heart function?' may be answerable without purposive overtones, but if we ask 'what is the function of a carburetor?' no theological issue is raised if the answer is 'the purpose of the carburetor is to . . .' So, questions about the function of the Cabinet or the Joint-Chiefs or the Rules Committee are, in part, answerable by 'it is supposed to . . .' or 'its job or purpose is . . .' We judge tribunals as ill-designed or well-designed and this assumes a task to be performed. A public tribunal, in short, has a purpose or purposes; it is the guardian of some end or good or value, however well- or ill-defined or even half-forgotten."[76]

The exponents of a functional explanation of certain types of international organization portray these developments as "natural," and the organismic analogy, "functions," and "organs" are the proper coin for this transaction. Yet "natural development" satisfies fully neither the functionalist objective of analysis nor that of prescription. The functionalists may describe functional development, like Topsy, as if it just growed. But when emphasizing another element in this development—the element of human choice—it seems necessary to invoke a concept

[76] Joseph Tussman, *Obligation and the Body Politic* (New York: Oxford University Press, 1960), pp. 67-68.

such as technical self-determination in order to impart to function a purposiveness it did not have before.

The difficulty seems intrinsic to the change of focus from natural organism to man-made artifice—or is it a difficulty intrinsic to the change of position from observer to builder? Regardless, the dichotomized perspective is implicit in the distinction between the phrases "functional development" and "functional approach," which the functionalists employ interchangeably. An organism would function regardless of its detached observer's existence. But even functional architecture requires architect and blueprint, purposer and plan.

PART II. FINANCING ECONOMIC
DEVELOPMENT THROUGH
THE UNITED NATIONS SYSTEM

III

The Financing of Economic Development:
A Narrative Introduction

WE TURN now from a consideration of issues raised by the functionalist argument and move toward the central task in this inquiry. Previous chapters introduced the functionalist argument, drew forth and examined its premises, and challenged it on some counts. The next objective is to achieve a better tactical position from which to pursue these questions: Are the functionalists good prophets? Does their interpretation of the process of international organization lead toward insights otherwise unattainable?

Meaningful answers to the questions "whether" and "why" presuppose a confrontation between the functionalist argument and the actuality which it purports to foretell and explain. For this purpose one complex of international programs has been selected from many possibilities. Its relevance and its boundaries, for purposes of the present study, will be further outlined below.

The present chapter is groundwork for this confrontation. Subsequent chapters will apply the functionalist guidelines; this one strives to project a series of gross images upon which both relevant detail and appropriate observation may be superimposed later.

In *A Working Peace System*, David Mitrany uses as illustrations of the functional approach to international organization two hypothetical organs which he calls an "International Investment Board" and an "International Development Commission." The narrative in this chapter will refer to agencies in the UN system exercising the function which Mitrany apparently had in mind. Various actual agencies carry a putative assignment approximating that which Mitrany suggested for his own International

Investment Board and International Development Commission—"executive" and "advisory," respectively.[1]

For this narrative presentation it has seemed desirable to begin with the notion of "economic development" as the function rather than with specific agencies. This approach is commended by several considerations. First of all, it seems more appropriate to an application of *functional* analysis and interpretation than would a discussion oriented about international organizations as such.

Second, the more general opening topic helps compensate for the eventual narrowness which will be assumed in our interpretation. Ultimately the discussion will center on the operations of four agencies—the International Bank for Reconstruction and Development (IBRD), the International Finance Corporation (IFC), the Special Fund (SF), and the International Development Association (IDA). This categorization is arbitrary: its bounds are due to the necessity for limiting the scope of the inquiry, not to the nature of the materials themselves. "Financing economic development" might well include a double handful of UN bodies not encompassed within the present study, especially if the protean phrase "technical assistance" were equivalent to a ticket of admission. Our designation might, contrariwise, exclude the Special Fund as irrelevant to this inquiry by virtue of the nature of its operations. It is hoped that these choices will be justified by the subsequent investigation. But in the meantime, the

[1] See *A Working Peace System*, 1943 edition, pp. 36, 40f. It will be noted in the course of the subsequent account that one of the agencies proposed by Britain prior to the first edition of *A Working Peace System* bore a title similar to one of Mitrany's. Elsewhere it has been suggested that the paper which became *A Working Peace System* was "circulated privately for official use previously"; see the biographical note on Mitrany in "International Cooperation in Action," p. 644. It would be interesting to follow the question which this suggests; unfortunately, we are not at present in a position to do so. This study does not, of course, depend on any inference of Mitranian natural intellectual parenthood for the specific agencies with which we shall be concerned.

broader initial approach to exposition has seemed a desirable aid to perspective.

Third, a commitment at the outset to the broader narrative framework seems better to fit this story than could an alternative approach. As will be seen, more international attention is given to related matters than to the *financing* of economic development during the earlier portion of the period covered by this account. For that matter, *development* emerges as a serious focus only in the course of time. We have sought to let the narrative follow the sequence of events by which, in more recent years, international financing has itself tended toward the status of a function in the UN system.

Finally, making "economic development" the initial aperture allows and encourages us to encompass one aspect of the financing programs which we have previously taken the functionalists to task for underemphasizing in their conceptual apparatus. This chapter is above all an account of origins, of the beginnings of international agencies; indeed, it is meant to provide little more than this and a satisfactory answer to the considerations already mentioned.

I

The notion of a multilateral arrangement to assist in the economic development of less-developed areas antedates the international conclaves which planned the United Nations itself.[2] In March 1942, under the auspices

[2] The idea of a substantial peace-creating role for an international banking institution goes back at least as far as the Saint-Simonian journal of 1825-1826, *Le Producteur*. In its pages the followers of Henri de Saint-Simon, after the death of the master, called for the formation of a "General Loan and Borrowing Bank" to receive funds from the "leaders of the idle," those who possessed and "reposed," and lend by contract to those capable of industrial undertakings. Georg G. Iggers, a student of the Saint-Simonians, writes further that *Le Producteur* contributors conceived of banking as "an instrument for the pacification and unification of the world. . . . [A joint stock company, *société commanditaire de l'industrie*,] would tend to 'moralize' the economy. . . . With the formation

of the United States Treasury Department, a memorandum was prepared entitled "Preliminary Draft Proposal for United Nations Stabilization Fund and a Bank for Reconstruction and Development of the United and Associated Nations."[3] In August of the same year the British Embassy in Washington transmitted to the State and Treasury Departments for informal consideration copies of a draft entitled "Proposals for an International Clearing Union," later known as the "Keynes Plan." This statement included a reference to the need for a Board for International Investment.[4]

During the same general period preparatory work was undertaken in the U.S. State Department; in this general effort, Leo Pasvolsky directed the Division of Special Research and Leroy D. Stinebower was chief of the Division of Economic Studies. The latter prepared a plan for an International Investment Agency which would make loans and facilitate the flow of private capital.[5]

---

of [a] committee of experts, science and industry would be integrated and scientific and industrial capacities brought together. . . . [T]he society because of its international character would offer a check to international enmity. The industry of one country would no longer be the enemy of that of another country, and thus the economic basis of popular nationalism would be taken away." *Le Producteur*, I, 44ff. It was suggested, too, that racial strife in Haiti might be ended by industrial loans. Iggers, *The Cult of Authority* (The Hague: Martinus Nijhoff, 1958), pp. 24-26, 119, 144-46.

[3] John Parke Young, "Developing Plans for an International Monetary Fund and a World Bank," *United States Department of State Bulletin*, XXIII (13 November 1950), 779. Cf. the following accounts: Ruth B. Russell, assisted by Jeannette E. Muther, *A History of the United Nations Charter* (Washington: The Brookings Institution, 1958), p. 62; William Adams Brown, Jr., "The Inheritance of the United Nations," in Robert E. Asher *et al.*, *The United Nations and Promotion of the General Welfare* (Washington: The Brookings Institution, 1957), pp. 182-87, especially pp. 185-86. Eugene R. Black, in "Ventures in World Order," *Princeton Alumni Weekly*, 1 June 1962, emphasizes the role of Vice President Henry A. Wallace.

[4] Young, *op.cit.*, pp. 780, 785.

[5] *Ibid.*, p. 780.

At this time the United States had not officially announced its policy toward an international development agency.[6] In June 1943, at an informal conference of representatives from nineteen countries meeting in Washington, Treasury Secretary Henry Morgenthau, Jr. mentioned that consideration of an International Bank for Reconstruction and Development might well follow that of an international stabilization fund.[7]

The plan for an International Investment Agency prepared in the State Department was sent to Harry D. White of the Treasury Department on September 4, 1943, by Assistant Secretary of State Adolph A. Berle, Jr.[8] Both the State and Treasury Department plans envisaged an institution to encourage and complement private international capital movements by guaranteeing private loans and by careful lending based on sound financial principles with regard to repayment prospects. The Treasury proposal exacted two lending conditions not demanded by that of the State Department: the former plan provided that the proceeds of loans must be "tied" to expenditure in the country of the currency loaned, and it required a guarantee for each loan by the member government involved. The U.S. Export-Import Bank backed a tied-loans requirement during debate in the American Technical Committee; the Bretton Woods proposal by the U.S. was a compromise between the positions of State and Treasury in this regard.[9] As we shall see, IBRD's Articles of Agree-

---

[6] Richard N. Gardner has suggested that the 1942 U.S. elections —in which the Democratic Party lost Congressional ground—acted as a restraining factor on postwar economic planning. See Gardner, *Sterling-Dollar Diplomacy* (Oxford: The Clarendon Press, 1956), p. 77.

[7] Young, *op.cit.*, p. 784. The U.S. Treasury's plan for a Stabilization Fund had been released the previous April.

[8] *Ibid.*, p. 784. White headed an interdepartmental group known as the American Technical Committee during these years. See Young, *ibid.*, p. 779, for a list of other principal participants, and the relationship of this group to the U.S. "Cabinet Committee."

[9] *Ibid.*, p. 785.

ment require a guarantee on loans by the member government involved, whether in the capacity of recipient or
guarantor.

Meetings took place between British and U.S. representatives during the fall of 1943, where this plan was presented and discussed. "A Preliminary Draft Outline of a
Proposal for a Bank for Reconstruction and Development
of the United and Associated Nations" was published by
the U.S. Treasury Department on November 24, 1943.
Bilateral conversations were conducted between the United States and representatives of various countries during
late 1943 and early 1944, and, though the proposal for a
stabilization fund received most of the attention, a great
deal of interest was shown by the war-devastated in reconstruction aid, and by others in assistance toward economic development.[10]

[10] *Ibid.*, p. 785. The discussions of this period eventuated in the
"Joint Statement by Experts on the Establishment of an International Monetary Fund," made public in April 1944. Its chief provisions were subsequently embodied in the Articles of Agreement of
the International Monetary Fund (IMF). For an account of the
negotiations between White and Keynes, and the subsequent "compromise," see Gardner, *op.cit.*, pp. 110-21, 261ff. Gardner writes
(pp. 111, 112) of the White-Keynes confrontations: "In the conduct of negotiations they were not unlike two vain and rather
jealous economics professors striving to impress a university seminar.
. . . 'Well, Harry,' Keynes would say, 'what shall it be to-day—
passivity, exchange stability, or the role of gold?' With this informal
beginning the two . . . would exchange observations on some theoretical issue. Occasionally bitterness would creep in. Keynes would
take White out of his depth; White would feel, but not admit, his
intellectual inferiority; he would say something to remind Keynes
that he, not Keynes, represented the stronger party in the negotiations. There would be angry words; papers would be thrown on the
floor; one of them would stalk out of the room. The other negotia-
tors would stay to patch up the quarrel. The next day the same
procedure would be repeated."

The "third leg" of postwar economic collaboration was to be an
institutional arrangement for assuring cooperation in the area of
commercial policy. The U.S. State Department's Division of Commercial Policy set about the framing of principles during 1943, and,
in the U.K., James Meade led the drafting of a plan which came to
be known as the "Commercial Union." These early efforts paved

A preliminary consultation session was held at Atlantic City during late June 1944, in order to facilitate the work of the forthcoming United Nations Monetary and Financial Conference, scheduled for Bretton Woods, New Hampshire, the next month. Financial experts from seventeen countries were present at this preliminary meeting.[11] Here Lord Keynes, heading the British delegation, unveiled a proposal for a bank which diverged considerably from the U.S. State-Treasury plan previously discussed with the British. According to one account, Keynes' proposal "met with almost immediate approval by the experts of the other nations including the United States," all the same.[12] The United States proposal had outlined an institution with gold and national currency resources capable of allowing substantial lending operations. Keynes' suggestion was to provide for only a small portion of the Bank's capital (20 percent) to be paid in and available for loans; the remaining 80 percent of the joint national obligation would constitute a backlog to strengthen the Bank's position in guaranty operations and enable it to meet other obligations. Furthermore, of the paid-in portion of subscriptions, only a fraction—2 percent of the

---

the way for the subsequent International Trade Organization (ITO) proposal. For accounts of this period, later attempts at U.S.-U.K. compromise, and the political forces contributing to the eventual demise of ITO, see Gardner, *op.cit.*, pp. 101ff., 145ff., 269ff., 348ff.; Percy W. Bidwell and William Diebold, Jr., "The United States and the International Trade Organization," *International Conciliation*, No. 449 (March 1949); Diebold, *The End of the I.T.O.* (Princeton: Department of Economics and Social Institutions, 1952).

[11] Australia, Belgium, Brazil, Canada, Chile, China, Cuba, Czechoslovakia, France, Greece, India, Mexico, the Netherlands, Norway, the U.K., the U.S.S.R., and the U.S.

[12] Young, *op.cit.*, p. 786. Young reports that this Keynes proposal had been prepared "in collaboration with the delegates of several European governments in exile." Gardner relates the Keynes amendment to Britain's financial position; see *op.cit.*, p. 118, and primary sources cited.

total obligation—was to be made in gold or dollars. The remaining 18 percent was to be in local currency.[13]

The Atlantic City meeting adjourned just before the conclave at Bretton Woods, which convened July 1, 1944. Forty-four governments were represented at the latter, and the Danish Minister in Washington attended in an unofficial capacity. The Conference operated for much of its duration through three "technical commissions," which were in turn broken down into committees and subcommittees.[14]

The Articles of Agreement of the International Bank for Reconstruction and Development, which were subsequently to be acceded to by almost all the Bretton Woods participants, bear the imprint of several demands pressed at the Conference. In response to a request by the Soviet Union, the Bank was directed to "pay special regard to lightening the financial burden" of members suffering "great devastation from enemy occupation or hostilities." Pressure by the Latin American representatives to earmark half the Bank funds for development purposes, in turn, led to the compromise injunction that resources should be allocated "with equitable consideration to projects for development and projects for reconstruction alike." And the latitude for loan-making policy was broadened somewhat. The U.S. Treasury plan had restricted loans to specific projects. After considerable discussion,

[13] Brown, op.cit., p. 185; Young, op.cit., p. 786.
[14] The forty-four participants were Australia, Belgium, Bolivia, Brazil, Canada, Chile, China, Colombia, Costa Rica, Cuba, Czechoslovakia, the Dominican Republic, Ecuador, Egypt, El Salvador, Ethiopia, France (French Committee of National Liberation), Greece, Guatemala, Haiti, Honduras, Iceland, India, Iran, Iraq, Liberia, Luxembourg, Mexico, the Netherlands, New Zealand, Nicaragua, Norway, Panama, Paraguay, Peru, the Philippine Commonwealth, Poland, Union of South Africa, U.S.S.R., U.K., U.S., Uruguay, Venezuela, and Yugoslavia. For the records of the Conference, see U.S. Department of State, Proceedings and Documents of the United Nations Monetary and Financial Conference (Washington: U.S. Government Printing Office, 1948), I and II.

this was qualified by the words "except in special circumstances."[15]

Congressional authorization for U.S. participation in both the Bank and the International Monetary Fund was given in the Bretton Woods Agreement Act of July 1945, which also set up the National Advisory Council on International Monetary and Financial Problems to advise U.S. delegations. Representatives of thirty countries signed the Articles of Agreement and deposited their appropriate instruments for both institutions in Washington on December 27, 1945, thereby bringing the Bank and the International Monetary Fund into existence. The first meeting of the Bank's Board of Governors was held in Savannah, Georgia, March 8-18, 1946.[16]

Long before British and American preparations and consultations leading up to the Bretton Woods organizations, Anglo-American pronouncements had suggested support for certain principles related to the objective of economic development. The Atlantic Charter, a joint declaration of the leaders of the two governments signed August 12, 1941, proclaimed that their "hopes for a better future for the world" were predicated in part on principles of "economic advancement" and "freedom from . . . want."[17] In February 1942, Article VII of the Mutual

[15] IBRD, Articles of Agreement, Article III, Sections 1 (a) and (b), 4(vii); Brown, op.cit., pp. 185-86; Young, op.cit., p. 787; Antonín Basch, "International Bank for Reconstruction and Development, 1944-1949," International Conciliation, No. 455 (November 1949), p. 795.

[16] Young, op.cit., pp. 789-90. For an account of the debate prior to Congressional authorization, see Gardner, op.cit., pp. 129-43; Jack N. Behrman, "Political Factors in U.S. International Financial Cooperation, 1945-1950," American Political Science Review, XLVII (June 1953), especially pp. 434ff.

[17] For a discussion of the give-and-take preceding the declaration, see Gardner, op.cit., pp. 42-47; Russell, op.cit., pp. 34ff. The phrase "economic advancement" apparently was a British initiative; cf. Winston S. Churchill, The Grand Alliance (Boston: The Houghton Mifflin Company, 1950), p. 435. It would seem that the "free-

Aid Agreement between the two had emphasized better standards of living, among other objectives. But aside from the references to "development" already noted in connection with the plans for IBRD, that word did not find its way toward the endorsement implicit in its inclusion within an international legal instrument until a Canadian amendment proposed in the drafting subcommittee at the San Francisco Conference in 1945 offered the following change to paragraph IX-A-1 of the Dumbarton Oaks draft:

> With a view to the creation of conditions of stability and well-being . . . *members agree to cooperate fully with each other and with the United Nations with the object of:*
>
> (a) *attaining higher standards of living and economic and social progress and development.* . . .

General acquiescence in the substance of this modification was over-shadowed by fierce contemporaneous disagreement over the inclusion of the words "full employment." Article 55 of the United Nations Charter, which precedes a general agreement or pledge by members "to take joint and separate action in cooperation with the Organization for the achievement of the purposes set forth" therein, retains the "economic . . . development," now modified somewhat by the prefatory "conditions of."[18]

Thus was laid the foundation for United Nations programs concerned with economic development. Virtually all deliberations following this period have made reference either to some portion of Article 55; to the Charter's Preamble, which proclaims the willingness of the peoples of

---

dom from want" has a Rooseveltian ring. The Atlantic Charter appears as Appendix B to Russell's study; see p. 975.

[18] Brown, *op.cit.*, p. 179; Russell, *op.cit.*, p. 783, and UNCIO documents cited. The Canadian-proposed amendment is set off by italics, above.

the United Nations to "employ international machinery for the promotion of the economic and social advancement of all peoples"; or to the International Bank's Articles of Agreement. Yet of course the framing of the Charter and Articles of Agreement of the Bank was only the beginning.

I I

IBRD's status as a specialized agency was broadly defined by Article 57 of the Charter, and the Bank subsequently entered into a formal relationship with the United Nations under the terms of Article 63.[19] The Charter also directed the Economic and Social Council (ECOSOC) to "set up commissions in economic and social fields."[20] The question of which commissions to establish provoked considerable discussion by the United Nations Preparatory Commission, which convened in London in the fall of 1945. An economic commission was one of the first proposed. This proposal was shortly acted on by the Economic and Social Council, which created the Economic and Employment Commission and three subcommissions —a Temporary Subcommission on the Economic Reconstruction of Devastated Areas, a Subcommission on Employment and Economic Stability, and a Subcommission on Economic Development.[21]

To the Economic and Employment Commission,

[19] So permissive are the terms of this agreement that IBRD, along with its younger affiliates and IMF, is often said to lie completely beyond the UN pale, never truly having been "brought into relationship" with the principal organs and their subsidiaries in the sense of Articles 57 and 63. Writes Andrew Shonfield: "Admittedly, the president of the World Bank does have to make a formal report to the meetings of the United Nations Economic and Social Council. But his manner on these occasions is rather that of a visiting potentate about to receive an honorary degree. . . ." *The Attack on World Poverty* (New York: Vintage Books, 1962), p. 121.

[20] Article 68.

[21] Walter M. Kotschnig, "Structure of the System," in Asher, *op.cit.*, p. 49.

ECOSOC, in 1946, assigned responsibility for "the promotion of economic development and progress with special regard to the problems of the less developed areas";
the Subcommission on Economic Development was directed to "study and advise the Commission on the principles and problems of long-term economic development,
with particular reference to the inadequately developed
parts of the world." The General Assembly, in the continuation of its initial session during the last months of
1946, in turn called on ECOSOC to study means by
which economic advice might be provided to those de-
siring it, after a pointed observation that not all UN
members were equally developed. Technical assistance
was already in the wind.[22]

"Pure" and "applied" aspects of the problem of economic development were joined in the reports which
followed shortly. When ECOSOC convened in 1947 it
had before it comments from three commissions, including Economic and Employment, and a note from the Secretary-General. Referring to the Council's resolution 51
(IV) of March 28, 1947, Robert Asher writes that the
upshot of these reports was an ECOSOC request that
the Secretary-General "establish machinery within the
Secretariat for helping Member governments through
experts, research facilities, and other resources that the
United Nations and the specialized agencies might make
available, including the dispatch of teams of experts to
study the problems of underdeveloped countries. This
action provided the necessary legal authority for the mission to Haiti that the Secretary-General organized in 1948,
and it served to put the United Nations actively into the
business of providing technical assistance in the whole

[22] Economic and Social Council, *Official Records, First Year:
Second Session*, p. 392; ECOSOC resolution 1 (III) of 1 October
1946; General Assembly resolution 52 (I) of 14 December 1946.
Citations from Asher, *op.cit.*, p. 584.

field of economic development rather than solely in respect of social welfare services."[23]

The first report of the Subcommission on Economic Development was more audacious than those of the three commissions previously submitted. This later report emphasized "industrialization" as a *sine qua non* of economic development.[24] The Subcommission followed this up at its next session with a detailed examination of the types of technical assistance already in use through the United Nations system, and stressed the need for special budgetary appropriations to provide more of the same. The General Assembly adopted a resolution on December 4, 1948 which appropriated $288,000 for technical assistance in economic development, and made the Economic and Social Council responsible for reviewing the program at regular intervals. Asher sums it up well: "The four types of assistance in which considerable experience had already been accumulated were, so to speak, legitimized."[25]

The debate on the Economic and Social Council's report at this same session of the General Assembly was the occasion for charges that ECOSOC was dominated by

[23] *Ibid.*, pp. 584-85.

[24] *Ibid.*, pp. 585-86, citing Economic and Employment Commission, Subcommission on Economic Development, *Report—First Session*, E/CN. 1/47 of 18 December 1947. In particular, see p. 11 of the report for the emphasis on the role of "industrialization," which the Soviet expert, A. P. Morozov, pressed home, and p. 18 for indications of the perceived need for increased financing: "a considerable measure of foreign financing will be required for promoting . . . economic development [of the underdeveloped countries, and] . . . examination of the main sources of international loans for development indicates that the total volume of available funds is entirely inadequate to the needs of development." The Subcommission also heard reports on this problem by representatives of IBRD and IMF, and offered its own comments; see pp. 19ff.

[25] Asher, *op.cit.*, pp. 586-87; Economic and Employment Commission, Subcommission on Economic Development, *Report—Second Session*, E/CN. 1/61 of 1 July 1948, p. 17; General Assembly res. 200 (III) of 4 December 1948. Sponsors of the resolution included Burma, Chile, Egypt, and Peru.

the developed countries. The onslaught, led by Hernan Santa Cruz of Chile, sought a UN program which would include the financing of all costs involved in technical assistance, not simply the salaries of those sent into the field.[26]

Furthermore, IBRD was held up to reprobation. Major criticisms were the Bank's slowness and its niggardliness; one delegate, at least, went further. Iraq's K. Khalf described the International Bank as the "spoiled child of the United Nations."[27] What had been the Bank's experience since its origin?

At its Savannah inaugural the Bank's Board of Governors first listened to greetings by President Truman and Fred M. Vinson, U.S. Secretary of the Treasury and Governor to the Bank, then turned to the business at hand: formulation, debate and acceptance of committee reports, resolutions, and bylaws. Among the decisions made were the site for the Bank (Washington, D.C.), the procedure for election of Executive Directors, and adoption of a request, pursuant to Article IX(a) of the Articles of Agreement, asking the Executive Directors "to interpret the Articles of Agreement . . . as to the authority of the Bank to make or guarantee loans for programs of economic reconstruction and the reconstruction of monetary systems, including long-term stabilization loans."[28]

[26] According to Daniel S. Cheever and H. Field Haviland, Jr., upon whom this portion of the account relies, Chile's erstwhile parliamentary diplomatist was once called "Santa Claus" by Andrei Vishinsky of the Soviet Union. *Organizing for Peace, op.cit.*, p. 548.
[27] "Iraq Urges Bank's Aid," *New York Times*, 14 November 1948, p. 22; Cheever and Haviland, *op.cit.*, p. 548.
[28] Inaugural Meeting of the Board of Governors of the IBRD, Savannah, Georgia, 8-18 March 1946, *Selected Documents* (Washington: IBRD, 1946), pp. 46-47, 57, 61-62, 71-73. Article IX(a) provides that "Any question of interpretation of the provisions of this Agreement arising between any member and the Bank or between any members of the Bank shall be submitted to the Executive Directors for their decisions." The particular request submitted at the inaugural Board of Governors meeting was initiated by the United States. The Executive Directors subsequently agreed that

The Savannah meeting bred ill feelings between U.S. and U.K. delegates. Fragile compromises underpinning the IMF and IBRD Articles of Agreement involved certain contingencies which the British delegation felt were threatened at the initial meeting of the Boards of Governors. U.S. procedures seemed high-handed to them in pressing toward decisions on site and on the functions and remuneration of Executive Directors. *The Manchester Guardian* phrased this criticism in more general terms: "It had been hoped that the 'Bretton Woods' scheme would be managed by truly independent experts, judging economic needs on their merits and giving impartial advice to all. It would be difficult enough to make such a spirit grow in the political setting of Washington, but the arrangements now made seem to have made this even less likely."[29]

---

such loans as were mentioned in the resolution were within the Bank's authority: see IBRD, First Annual Meeting of the Board of Governors, Washington, D.C., 27 September-3 October 1946, *Proceedings and Selected Documents*, p. 30, and Appendix E, pp. 40-45.

One part of Vinson's Savannah address bears quotation, as much for what it adumbrated as what it exhorted: "I repeat . . . that written words [i.e., those which express the Articles of Agreement] do not convey this full [Bretton Woods] meaning in themselves. I read them and I know what they mean to me. I do not know, I could not know that they mean precisely the same to you. In fact, if we were so disposed, probably we could sit here in this very room and wage intellectual and academic warfare about nuances in their meaning until the end of time. From the escapist point of view this form of intellectual acrobatics would be easy. . . . [But] ours cannot be the escapist course of the intellectual cloister. Ours must be the practical, concrete course. Ours is a race against time for sanity."

[29] *The Manchester Guardian*, 20 April 1946; quoted by Gardner, *op.cit.*, p. 260. Keynes had seen much the same trend in the Bretton Woods Agreement Act by which Congress authorized U.S. participation: "The proposal to make the American Director subject to an advisory council is . . . a purely domestic matter, to which we cannot object. Some of us, however, had been hoping that the officials of the two bodies would, in the course of time, come to regard themselves as primarily international officials, taking a world, objective outlook, and only where clearly necessary grinding their own axes. So one would have wished to minimise, rather than maximise,

By the First Annual Meeting of the Board of Governors of the Bank in Washington, beginning September 27, 1946, the new U.S. Secretary of the Treasury and Chairman of the Board of Governors, John W. Snyder, could report in his welcoming address: "We are now beyond the blueprint stage of Bretton Woods. Last March at the Savannah Conference we established the basic operating structure under which these institutions of international cooperation would function. The period since the Savannah Conference has been one of building the organizations. Basic procedures and policy have been explored by the Executive Directors . . . and the important task of choosing key personnel has been practically completed."[30]

The Bank's Executive Directors had chosen Eugene Meyer as the Bank's first President. In his address presenting the First Annual Report, Meyer reiterated the decision previously made to call in the first portions of members' capital subscriptions. He also reported on his study of the prospects for Bank borrowing: "I have spent a good deal of time in discussions of the problem of marketing the Bank's securities. Commercial bankers, investment bankers, representatives of insurance companies and savings banks, dealers in securities and officers of the Federal Reserve Banking system have been consulted. I have also requested the Executive Director of the Bank representing Canada to take up with his Government the possibilities of marketing the Bank's securities in Canada. As circumstances justify, we will study the marketing possibilities in other countries."

With regard to lending operations, the Bank's President answered those who thought it "curious that the Bank has not already negotiated a number of loans" by stressing that

their national representative character and their position as delegates from outside authorities." Letter to E. M. Bernstein, quoted by Gardner, p. 266.

[30] IBRD, First Annual Meeting of the Board of Governors, *Proceedings and Related Documents*, p. 5.

the Bank had not as yet "received such properly documented applications as would make it possible for us to act."[31]

The next Board of Governors meeting was held in London, September 11-17, 1947. Here the tone of opening addresses was more sombre than that of the previous year. Hugh Dalton, Chairman of the Board of Governors, noted that in the last year and "particularly in the last few months" there had occurred a "marked and rapid worsening in the economic position and prospects of almost all the countries represented," and he quoted with obvious agreement the assessment in the IMF and IBRD annual reports which admitted, respectively, that the "magnitude of the reconstruction task" had not been "foreseen in 1945 and 1946," and that "the requirements of recovery today are not limited to the rehabilitation and reconstruction of individual productive facilities," but "include rehabilitation and reconstruction of entire national economies. . . ."[32]

Though the diagnosis was sombre, the prognosis was somewhat less dire. The Bank's *Annual Report* pointed back to the 1930's as the origin of the confidence crisis in international investment, then expressed its hope that "by its activities in the fields of reconstruction and development" the Bank could "help to restore that confidence." The Bank's new President, John J. McCloy, who reported in his address presenting the Second Annual Report in September 1947 that during the last year he had "had very close and continuous contact with the American investment community," emphasized what he saw as the route to this renewal of confidence: "the Bank must attach importance to the views of the American investor and must conduct its activities in such fashion that its

[31] IBRD, First Annual Meeting, *Proceedings and Related Documents*, pp. 10, 11, 20-21, 22-23.
[32] IBRD, Second Annual Meeting, *Proceedings and Related Documents*, p. 4.

bonds will be considered a sound business risk by the United States financial community." World recovery plans and the investor's interest were compatible, as McCloy noted; indeed, as he put it, "it is only as capital is stimulated to move into reconstruction and development that the world can prosper." Furthermore, sound loans would aid "healthy international relations," while more generous but less productive loans would be apt to lead to "the impairment . . . of relations within the international community."[33]

The Bank had undertaken its first operations as borrower and lender during the months prior to the Second Annual Meeting. The first loan was made in May 1947—$250 million to the French Credit National. By the end of 1947, $497 million had been loaned to European countries including, besides France, the Netherlands, Denmark, and Luxembourg. (Lending, however, was to decline to $28 million in calendar year 1948.) In July 1947, the first public offering of its own bonds was successfully undertaken by the Bank in the New York market.[34]

The reconstruction of war-torn areas was clearly in the forefront of Bank attention at this time. McCloy's address at the Second Annual Meeting contained but a single reference to development—its next-to-last paragraph—and one of his sayings might, along with his justification for a sound lending policy, be taken as the signpost of this period: "the world cannot endure half skyscraper and half rubble."[35]

[33] *Ibid.*, pp. 4-5, 7.

[34] IBRD, *Second Annual Report*, 1946-1947, pp. 18-20; IBRD, Press Release No. 109 of 4 August 1948; Asher, *op.cit.*, pp. 309-10, 317; Cheever and Haviland, *op.cit.*, pp. 540-41; Charles P. Kindleberger, "Bretton Woods Reappraised," *International Organization*, v (February 1951), 45.

[35] IBRD, Second Annual Meeting, *Proceedings*, p. 5. McCloy's public addresses during this period were often directed to the debate in the U.S. which preceded legislative endorsement of the Marshall Plan. After ERP's beginning, the Bank's President continued to emphasize the need for European recovery.

It was perhaps this emphasis on reconstruction over development that had raised the ire of representatives from certain of the underdeveloped members in the General Assembly. At a different level, the Subcommission on Economic Development continued to stress the need for more development financing in the report on its third session, which appeared April 12, 1949. The Subcommission again emphasized its belief that "industrialization" formed the "decisive phase in economic development," and stated the reasons for its finding that "substantially more foreign financing than has heretofore been available for economic development can, under appropriate conditions, be effectively utilized by under-developed countries." Although the Bank had more recently expressed its intention to "expand its activities in financing economic development projects in under-developed countries," the report continued, as a "realistic assessment," it must be concluded that the Bank had neither the magnitude of resources nor the latitude of lending policy "to make a significant contribution to the massive investments required for economic development."[36]

This time, however, the statement of the experts was not unanimous. E. G. Collado, who had replaced Beardsley Ruml as the United States expert, took exception to much of the report in a dissenting footnote.[37]

[36] Subcommission on Economic Development, *Report, Third Session*, E/CN. 1/65, pp. 2, 20ff. As noted earlier, the Subcommission on Economic Development was established by ECOSOC along with two other subcommissions and the parent Economic and Employment Commission. Its seven members at the Third Session were M. Bravo Jimenez, J. Nuñez Guimaraes, D. K. Lieu, A. P. Morozov, V. K. R. V. Rao, E. G. Collado (for B. Ruml), and J. Patek (for E. Slechta).

[37] *Ibid.*, p. 16, n.1: "I am unable to concur. . . . I believe sincerely that the most effective and desirable pattern of organization of the domestic economy from the economic and social points of view is that which gives greatest emphasis to free private enterprise and institutions guided and even regulated and supplemented by government where necessary in the broadest interests of the people and the nation. This is the pattern which has brought great bene-

The report included as an appendix a proposal which was to become the focal point of debate for years to come. The Subcommission's Chairman, V. K. R. V. Rao, an Indian economist, submitted his idea for a new international financing agency, a "United Nations Economic Development Agency," as he called it. Without recommending its creation, the Subcommission reported that in view of the International Bank's limitations, it had "discussed the possibilities of opening new sources of international finance under United Nations auspices," and it commended Rao's proposal for further study.[38]

Rao's proposal did not find immediate endorsement. The Economic and Employment Commission, parent body of the Subcommission, agreed at its May 1949 meeting that a new international financing agency was not necessary.[39] But this finding was in turn brought into some question when the General Assembly's fifth session, seized of Rao's UNEDA proposal the next fall, adopted

---

fits to my own country. . . . It is of course the right of any people to determine the form of organization of the domestic economy in which they choose to live and the manner in which they will receive foreign capital and technology. It is likewise, I believe, the right of a great capital-exporting nation, always adhering to the principles of the United Nations Charter, to parallel in its external activities the pattern of its internal economy. I therefore believe strongly that the United States should co-operate fully in sound economic development of under-developed countries, that it should look primarily to American private enterprise to provide abroad investment of capital and technique, and that it should rely fundamentally on the International Bank for Reconstruction and Development for financing or collaborating in financing closely circumscribed types of projects basic to development not readily susceptible of implementation by purely private financing."

[38] *Ibid.*, pp. 20-21. Rao's proposal comprises pp. 26-28. For a later proposal by Rao, see his "International Aid for Economic Development—Possibilities and Limitations," an address delivered at the University of Leeds on 15 November 1960. The latter occasion was the Eighteenth Montague Burton Lecture on International Relations, and Rao's status that of Director of the Institute for Economic Growth, Delhi.

[39] ECOSOC, *Official Records, Ninth Session, Supplement 11,* para. 32.

a resolution by which it asked the Commission's own parent organ, the Economic and Social Council, to "consider practical methods, conditions and policies for achieving the adequate expansion and steadier flow of foreign capital" to underdeveloped countries and "to pay special attention to the financing of non-self-liquidating projects" —the very kind of loan which the Bank had eschewed.[40]

In May 1951 a group of experts made explicit the organizational implications of the General Assembly resolution by recommending, *inter alia*, the establishment of an "International Development Authority" which would have among its purposes the distribution of grants to underdeveloped countries, with the proviso that these grants be for specific purposes well-chosen to enhance development.[41]

The experts' recommendation was considered at both the May 1951 session of the Commission (now called the Economic, Employment and Development Commission) and the thirteenth session of ECOSOC, meeting in August and September of the same year. The latter adopted a resolution which, "without either accepting or rejecting the principle of the establishment of an international fund to assist in the financing of economic development of under-developed countries or of an international development authority" such as the experts had specified, nonetheless requested that the Secretary-General "formulate a series of methods which he deems practicable for dealing with the problem of grant assistance...."[42]

Before the Secretary-General's report was completed the General Assembly acted once again. By way of a resolution in January 1952, the Assembly requested ECOSOC submission of "a detailed plan for establishing, as soon as circumstances permit, a special fund for grants-

40 General Assembly res. 400 (V).
41 *Measures for the Economic Development of Underdeveloped Countries*, E/1986. See recommendation 14 of the experts.
42 ECOSOC res. 368 (XIII).

in-aid, and for low-interest, long-term loans to under-developed countries for the purpose of helping them, at their request, to accelerate their economic development and to finance non-self-liquidating projects which are basic to their economic development."[43]

Three months later the Secretary-General's report was made available to Council members. As directed by the ECOSOC request, this report was a survey of "a series of alternative approaches" rather than a specific recommendation, and it was presented as a working paper.[44]

This fourteenth session of the Economic and Social Council suggested by way of a resolution that the substance of the General Assembly's request of the previous January required more time, so that "thorough study of the many and complex aspects" of the problem could be fully reviewed. Such a study could not be culminated in time for the seventh (1952) session of the General Assembly to consider a proposal, the Council felt, but it did provide for a committee of not more than nine persons to be appointed by the Secretary-General for this purpose. Terms of reference for the "Committee of Nine" were the views of the Council, the Assembly, and the Secretary-General's working paper.[45]

During its 1952 session the General Assembly took note of this ECOSOC decision as an accomplished fact, but requested that the Council keep in mind the necessity of financing economic development "through international co-operation within the framework of the United Nations." The same Assembly resolution called for a detailed plan to be ready for its next session and stated that this plan should include "recommendations for a special

[43] General Assembly res. 520 A (VI).

[44] ECOSOC, *Economic Development of Under-Developed Countries*, Working Paper by the Secretary-General, E/2234.

[45] ECOSOC res. 416 A (XIV); see also *Historical Résumé of the Proposal for a United Nations Capital Development Fund*, A/AC.102/3, para. 7, p. 3.

fund for grants-in-aid and for low-interest, long-term loans."[46]

The Committee of Nine met between January and March 1953. Its work is indicated in the *Report on a Special United Nations Fund for Economic Development*.[47] Like the Secretary-General's previous working paper, the report is somewhat hypothetical in tone, though not without recommendations. The Committee sketched the outline of a fund (SUNFED) made up of voluntary annual contributions by non-governmental organizations and individuals as well as by member states, rather than capital subscriptions such as for the International Bank.[48] The experts advised against establishment before adequate resources could be made available—$250 million contributed by at least thirty governments was the minimum suggested.[49] One guideline for disbursement policy should be the widest possible impact on the entire economy of the receiving country—"economic development which raises the welfare of the population as a

[46] General Assembly res. 622 A (VII).

[47] E/2381; UN Sales No. 1953. II. B 1. The Committee was composed of S. Amjad Ali of Pakistan, Ambassador and President of the Economic and Social Council of the UN during 1952; Fernand Baudhuin, Professor of Economics at the Catholic University of Louvain, Belgium; C. V. Bramsnaes, member of the Board of Directors and former Governor of the National Bank of Denmark; Miguel Cuaderno, Governor of the Central Bank of the Philippines; Cyril Jones, Director of the Mercantile Bank of India, Ltd., London, England, and the former Finance Secretary to the Government of India; Leo Mates, Ambassador Extraordinary and Plenipotentiary, Permanent Representative of the Federal People's Republic of Yugoslavia to the UN; Hernan Santa Cruz, President of the Economic and Social Council of the UN during 1950 and 1951 and former Permanent Representative of Chile to the UN; Eduardo Suarez, member of the Board of Directors of the Nacional Financiera S.A. and the Bank of Mexico and former Secretary of Finance of Mexico; and Wayne C. Taylor, former President of the Export-Import Bank and former Under-Secretary of Commerce of the United States.

[48] *Ibid.*, pp. 9-10.

[49] *Ibid.*, pp. 9-10.

whole."[50] As for allocation among underdeveloped countries, the experts recommended a combination of criteria: the probability of quick results for the project in question, reasonable geographic distribution, and "the merits of individual applications."[51]

The Committee set forth a new principle in discussing the relative merits of loans and grants. In neither type of transaction should the interests of borrower and lender be regarded as evenly balanced: for grants and loans alike the recipient's interests should be understood as "the paramount consideration." Perhaps the major advantage of loans was the added possibility which they gave for revolving resources and thereby spreading benefits. The fund, if established, should be allowed considerable latitude as to the form of each transaction, and as to the terms of loans.[52]

In terms of structure, the Committee suggested a General Council composed of representatives of all members, an Executive Board of eight to twelve members, and a Director-General. The Executive Board would be equally balanced in its membership between representatives of the major contributors and the other members. The fund should be a "separate administration but within the framework of, and in close proximity to, the United Nations." It should make use of existing information and research facilities and work closely with the agencies already involved in development objectives.[53]

The report had been unanimously adopted by the nine experts. In the sixteenth session of the Economic and Social Council, however, it met considerable opposition from major potential contributors and others.[54] The Council's resolution called for Assembly consideration

[50] *Ibid.*, p. 15.   [51] *Ibid.*, p. 19.
[52] *Ibid.*, p. 26.   [53] *Ibid.*, pp. 34ff.
[54] See ECOSOC, *Official Records, Sixteenth Session,* especially the statements by the U.S. delegate (E/SR.726, pp. 146-47); also A/AC.102/3, *op.cit.*, p. 13.

(using the ECOSOC discussion as well as the experts' report as terms of reference) of "other preparatory steps [which] might usefully be taken towards the establishment, when circumstances permit, of an international fund designed to assist development and reconstruction of the under-developed countries."[55]

This resolution and related matters occupied the General Assembly during its eighth session, which convened in September 1953, shortly after ECOSOC adjournment. By way of resolution 724 B (VIII), the Assembly called on member governments to submit detailed comments on the Committee of Nine report and on "the degree of moral and material support which may be expected from them for such a fund." Raymond Scheyven, then President of the Council, was chosen to examine and collate replies, to clarify them, if necessary, by consultation, and to report to the Council and the Assembly at their respective 1954 meetings. This report was to be supplemented by a working paper from the Secretary-General on the degree and methods of coordination that a fund should maintain with existing organs. The Secretary-General was asked to aid Scheyven in fulfilling the latter's assignment.

An interim report was ready for the Council's eighteenth session in the summer of 1954,[56] but not until August—shortly before the Assembly convened—was the final report completed.[57] Much of the report was devoted to a description of the plight of the underdeveloped countries, analysis of the types of aid already being given, and specification of the reasons that international action —and in particular, the financing of non-self-liquidating projects—was necessary.[58]

Scheyven concluded on the basis of responses from gov-

[55] ECOSOC res. 482 A/I (XVI).

[56] ECOSOC, *Official Records, Eighteenth Session, Annexes,* Agenda Item 3 (a), E/2599.

[57] General Assembly, *Official Records, Ninth Session, Supplement* 19, A/2728.

[58] *Ibid., passim.*

ernments that although there were certain encouraging aspects to the situation, "the essential conditions for the establishment of a UN fund for economic development in the near future do not at present exist."[59]

Scheyven had divided the responses into three categories. One group of respondents indicated strong support for the fund and optimism as to the feasibility of its prompt establishment. These replies Scheyven referred to as being "from under-developed countries"; Yugoslavia was included in this category, along with non-European members. A second group of responses conveyed a strong sense of the inappropriateness of the present time or circumstances for establishing a fund. Scheyven noted that these replies were "all . . . from industrialized countries." On the basis of their answers, he included in this category the Federal Republic of Germany, Canada, the United States, New Zealand, the United Kingdom, Sweden, and Switzerland.

The other replies appeared to indicate some shift of position since Rao's UNEDA proposal. Scheyven reported that these respondents "express the view that it would be regrettable to make the creation of a special fund dependent upon a general reduction in armaments expenditure. . . . [and] declare themselves ready to give their material support," although, as he added, some of these countries made the question and extent of their participation dependent upon "the fulfillment of a number of conditions." Respondents in the third group included several industrialized nations. Scheyven cited Denmark, Italy, Norway, and the Netherlands as having made explicit declarations of material support, and Belgium, France, Japan, and Luxembourg as extending conditional pledges.[60]

Having reviewed Scheyven's interim report, the Economic and Social Council took note of what some members proclaimed as growing support for a fund. The Coun-

[59] *Ibid.*, p. 21.   [60] *Ibid.*, pp. 15-16.

cil recommended that the General Assembly urge governments to continue to review their positions toward material support of a fund "in accordance with changes in
the international situation and other relevant factors."
In the same resolution, the Council suggested that Scheyven's appointment be extended so as to permit him to
continue his consultations with governmental representatives.[61]

At its ninth session, in 1954, the General Assembly
fulfilled these requests, and did more. On December 11
it extended Scheyven's appointment. To this it added a
hope that the fund would be "established as soon as
practicable." Scheyven was asked to prepare a further
report, this one to give "a full and precise picture of the
form or forms, functions and responsibilities which such
a . . . fund might have," and to indicate its relationship
to other agencies. In preparing this report Scheyven was
to be aided by the Secretary-General and an ad hoc group
of experts appointed by the Secretary-General in consultation with Scheyven. Specialized agencies concerned and
the Technical Assistance Board (TAB) were also to be
brought into consultation in preparing the report.[62]

This Committee, headed by Scheyven and composed of
eight experts, met during March 1955. Besides its own
deliberations, it consulted with representatives of IBRD
and TAB. The Scheyven Committee report was jointly
submitted to the Economic and Social Council and the
General Assembly. In general, this report reviewed and
amended the recommendations in the previous findings
of the Committee of Nine so as to bring its own conclusions more in line with the interim response from governments received by Scheyven.[63] In his letter of transmittal,

[61] ECOSOC res. 532 A (XVIII).

[62] General Assembly res. 882 (IX).

[63] General Assembly, *Official Records, Tenth Session, Supplement
No. 17*, A/2906; A/AC.102/3, *op.cit.*, p. 18. Experts: John Abbink
(U.S.), A. Nazmy Abdel Hamid (U.A.R.), B. K. Madau (India),
Francis Mudie (U.K.), Jacques Oudiette (France), Nenad Popovic

Scheyven commended his cohorts, and stated that, since "we found ourselves in agreement on most of the questions we examined together, I have invited the experts to join me in submitting the report. . . . The unanimity among us and the standing of the experts I consulted give the recommendations we are submitting to the General Assembly infinitely more weight than if they were mine alone." Those recommendations included a special fund to "provide underdeveloped countries with grants or loans repayable in local currency. . . . [but with] no authority to grant low-interest loans on the indeterminate and extremely liberal terms envisaged by our predecessors and against which the International Bank puts forward many objections."[64]

The Economic and Social Council, at its twentieth session in July-August 1955, reviewed not only the report but the current willingness of principal prospective contributors to participate. In the course of the review of this report and the ensuing debate on related issues, the United States delegate reported that his government's position in regard to SUNFED "had often been clearly stated and remained unchanged": the U.S. "would not join or contribute to such a fund in present circumstances." Speaking for the United Kingdom, Sir Alec Randall observed pointedly that his government "could take on fresh commitments towards SUNFED only by cutting down existing ones," a decision "that could not be contemplated," as he "was sure other members of the Colombo Plan would agree." The delegate from the Soviet Union, on the other hand, stressed that his government's support in principle had already been established, and stated that the Soviet Union "was ready to consider participating in SUNFED." The Czechoslovakian delegate added his gov-

(Yugoslavia), Jorge Schneider (Chile), Jan Tinbergen (Netherlands).

[64] A/2906, *op.cit.*, pp. iii, 18.

ernment's "support [for] the creation of SUNFED" the same day.[65] The Council adopted a resolution recommending that the General Assembly request comments by governments on the report and establish an ad hoc committee to analyze these replies, submitting an interim report to Council and Assembly alike in 1956, and a final report to the Council at its session in the spring of 1957.

The Council's recommendations were adopted by the General Assembly at its tenth session, in 1955. Governments were invited to transmit no later than March 31, 1956 their views on "the establishment, role, structure and operations" of a fund.[66] A list of eight specific questions was appended to the resolution to guide this response. The President of the Assembly was to appoint an intergovernmental review committee; its task: summarizing and classifying views submitted, and setting forth any conclusions which might be drawn from them. This committee was to be made up of representatives of sixteen governments.[67]

It will be recalled that on April 12, 1949, there had appeared a report by the Subcommission on Economic Development which reemphasized the need for "substantially more foreign financing," doubted the Bank's capac-

[65] ECOSOC, *Official Records, Twentieth Session,* E/SR. 886, pp. 165, 167; *idem,* E/SR. 887, pp. 172, 174. For analysis and interpretation of the abrupt Soviet shift in strategy toward UN economic programs revealed in mid-1953, see Alvin Z. Rubinstein, *The Soviets in International Organizations* (Princeton: Princeton University Press, 1964), pp. xiii, 32ff., 94-95; Harold Karan Jacobson, *The USSR and the UN's Economic and Social Activities* (Notre Dame: University of Notre Dame Press, 1963), pp. 237ff.

[66] General Assembly res. 923 (X).

[67] The General Assembly's President named Canada, Chile, Colombia, Cuba, Egypt, France, India, Indonesia, the Netherlands, Norway, Pakistan, Poland, the U.S.S.R., the U.K., the U.S. and Yugoslavia. Later, the Assembly increased the Committee's membership (by General Assembly res. 1031 [XI] of 26 February 1957) to nineteen countries; Italy, Japan, and Tunisia were designated the new members.

ity for meeting the need, and carried as an appendix the UNEDA proposal by its chairman, V. K. R. V. Rao of India. About a week later a report by the Subcommission on Employment and Economic Stability was made public. It too was sharply critical of the Bank. This investigation had been undertaken by a group of experts who had sounded national sentiment by means of special questionnaires. They found a fear of over-cautious lending by IBRD and the U.S. Export-Import Bank, especially if the current "incipient downturn" were to become a full-fledged depression. Emanuel A. Goldenweiser, an expert from the United States, strongly urged expansion of the potential range of action which both agencies might undertake. The Subcommission endorsed Goldenweiser's plea for an international conference on the lines of Bretton Woods to recast the Bank's basic instrument.[68]

The Bank was not long in responding to these reports. Robert L. Garner, Vice President, told a press conference on April 25 that the Bank intended to continue to make loans on economic rather than "social or relief grounds."[69] On May 11 the Bank transmitted to the Economic and Employment Commission a memorandum discussing both the report of the Subcommission on Economic Development and that of the Subcommission on Employment and Economic Stability. The major point emphasized in the Bank's press release, prepared from the memorandum, was the inconsistency, as seen by IBRD, between investment for economic development and counter-cyclical activity, the major functions proposed by the respective subcommissions.[70]

The Bank gave more extended attention to the report on economic development. "The Bank will not be de-

[68] "World Bank, Fund Hit in U.N. Report," *New York Times*, 20 April 1949, p. 41.
[69] "World Bank to Keep Present Loan Basis," *New York Times*, 26 April 1949, p. 41.
[70] IBRD, Press Release No. 134 of 11 May 1949, para. 13, p. 6.

flected from its determination to make loans only for sound and productive projects," the pronouncement stated. The "Proposal for [a] so-called UNEDA" was discussed in terms of the particular purposes envisaged for such an agency, considered *seriatim* in the Bank's memorandum. The first such purpose in Rao's plan was the financing of projects "which are not financially productive in a banking sense." To it the Bank responded that this assignment was its own by common agreement at the time of its establishment, and that inasmuch as the "obstacles which have thus far prevented a greater volume of investment by the Bank have been imposed by external circumstances and not by charter limitations," the "mere creation of a new lending agency [would] do nothing to remove" these obstacles. Furthermore, since the Bank was already lending on marginal terms, it seemed "clear that any greater liberality in the terms of UNEDA loans would amount simply to [making them in effect] disguised inter-governmental grants."

Another aspect of Rao's proposal was held to be more than merely the Bank's assignment by prior agreement. "The second purported function of UNEDA, aid to 'underdeveloped countries in the preparation and/or execution of their programs of economic development,' is one which the Bank has been performing for some time."[71]

Yet another purpose, that of coordinating the several technical assistance programs and integrating technical assistance with financial assistance, was, said the Bank, "stated in terms which are too broad to give a useful idea of its intended scope." The Bank reminded its memorandum's reader that it was already in close consultation with other agencies on coordination of technical assist-

[71] Early in 1949 the Bank had announced that it was sending missions to India, Turkey, Colombia, and Peru. It added that this practice had already "become a very important element in [the Bank's] operations." IBRD Press Release No. 123 of 10 January 1949.

ance, and stated that plans were "well advanced."

Finally, the proposed purpose of executing "projects of economic development extending over more than one national frontier and not likely to be taken up by any one of the countries concerned . . . on its own initiative" drew the Bank's comment that once again "an aspect of development which falls squarely within the Bank's sphere of responsibility" was involved. The Bank went on to note that it had been "considering several such schemes," and that the lack of any agreement as yet was "an index of the practical difficulties involved rather than inactivity."[72]

The Bank's next press release came one week later. It announced: "The Executive Directors of the International Bank for Reconstruction and Development today accepted the resignation of John J. McCloy as President of the International Bank and Chairman of the Executive Directors, and elected Eugene R. Black President of the Bank and Chairman of the Executive Directors."[73] Another press release the same day carried a statement by McCloy. His message included his view of the Bank's future role. "The reconstruction phase of the Bank's activities is largely over," McCloy said. "The development phase . . . is under way. By its charter, the Bank can assist in financing only sound and productive projects."[74]

The change in management did not signify an apparent shift in Bank policy. Eugene Black, the Bank's new

[72] IBRD, Press Release No. 134 of 11 May 1949, para. 15, pp. 7-8. It was at approximately this time that the Economic and Employment Commission itself became seized of the two subcommission reports, along with Rao's UNEDA proposal. Isador Lubin and Richard Hall, U.S. and British delegates to the Commission, were critical of the suggestions as to financing methods. Lubin suggested that confidence, not new machinery, was the missing factor in the current situation. See "U.S. Seeks Safety for Funds Abroad," *New York Times*, 12 May 1949, p. 14.

[73] IBRD, Press Release No. 135 of 18 May 1949. McCloy's resignation had been hinted for several weeks prior to the official announcement.

[74] IBRD, Press Release No. 136 of 18 May 1949.

President, hastened to reiterate the desirability of continued operation on strict business principles.[75] Furthermore, the criticism of Bank policy by some of the less-developed countries continued. In February 1950, for instance, Black listened to a series of critical retorts to his report at the Economic and Social Council.[76]

In December 1951, the Bank responded to a critical report by a group of experts.[77] In particular IBRD sought to answer the report's suggestion that the International Bank could lend $1 billion a year to developing countries. Speaking before the Economic and Financial Committee of the General Assembly, Black described the proposal as "unrealistic" and called attention both to the strictures on Bank policy and to the necessary factor of time inherent in the process of economic development.[78]

Nor did criticism of the Bank's policy by underdeveloped members of the UN and of the Bank itself cease during the middle fifties.[79] Much of this energy, however,

[75] But cf. this observation by Kindleberger, *op.cit.*, p. 45: "In a long and detailed statement of its lending policies in its Fifth Annual Report for 1949-50, the Bank, under the guise of defending these policies, fundamentally modified them in the directions indicated by the criticism. None of these changes, it should be noted, ran contrary to the letter of Bretton Woods, but many represented wide departures from the spirit in which the articles were drafted, substituting, for example, the exception as the basis of practice in place of the rule."

[76] A. M. Rosenthal, "World Bank Asked to Ease Standards," *New York Times*, 17 February 1950, p. 13.

[77] Department of Economic Affairs, *Measures for the Economic Development of Underdeveloped Countries*, Report by a Group of Experts Appointed by the Secretary-General of the United Nations, E/1986. Cf. Asher, *op.cit.*, pp. 344-46.

[78] "World Bank Head Rejects UN Plan," *New York Times*, 11 December 1951, p. 21. The Economic, Employment, and Development Commission and ECOSOC largely ignored the experts' report; the latter simply recommended (by res. 368C [XIII]) that existing facilities continue to increase their lending operations. See Asher, *op.cit.*, pp. 345-46.

[79] See, e.g., Charles E. Egan's report on the eleventh annual meeting of the Board of Governors: "Black Tells Critics World

began to be directed toward achievement of new means to the same objective.

I I I

To this point the narrative recounts activity in and about the central UN organs on the one hand and IBRD on the other. In the mid-fifties other agencies enter the narrative.

The first of these newer agencies was the International Finance Corporation (IFC).[80] Its institutional origin was antedated by several years as a name and an idea. An international finance corporation which could make loans to private enterprise without the government guarantee exacted by the International Bank and nonvoting equity investments in participation with private investors was suggested in a report to the President of the United States in March 1951.[81] It has been argued that the proposal originated with the IBRD Staff.[82] Within two months the proposed agency was commended to UN study by the experts' report entitled *Measures for the Development of Underdeveloped Countries.* The Economic, Employment and Development Commission considered such an agency at its sixth session. There the United States first questioned the desirability and possibility of "establishing new credit institutions," then admitted that an international finance corporation "might prove a useful instrument," eventually joining in the recommendation that

---

Bank Will Maintain Loan Standards," *New York Times*, 28 September 1956, p. 38.

[80] Our discussion of the International Finance Corporation, in these paragraphs and later in the present study, relies upon the diligent research of B. E. Matecki and the coverage of Robert Asher, as will be readily seen by succeeding references to both.

[81] U.S. International Development Advisory Board, *Partners in Progress: A Report to the President*, generally called the "Rockefeller Report" after its chairman, Nelson A. Rockefeller.

[82] See B. E. Matecki, *Establishment of the International Finance Corporation and United States Policy* (New York: Frederick A. Praeger, 1957), pp. 64-67; Asher, *op.cit.*, n. 81, p. 361.

the United Nations explore the possibility of the agency.[83]

At the first portion of its thirteenth session during the summer of 1951, the Economic and Social Council included in its omnibus resolution on the financing of economic development a request that the Bank investigate and report on the possibility of such an agency.[84] The Bank's first report on an international finance corporation, released the next spring, suggested that this agency could "fill an important gap in the existing machinery for financing economic development."[85] At the 1952 ECOSOC meeting some industrially advanced member states regarded the proposal with favor.[86] The United States, however, was once again "cool to the proposal and reluctant to discuss it in detail."[87] A number of the less-developed member states showed considerably more interest in a public international grant agency along the lines of Rao's UNEDA than an agency such as the proposed IFC.[88] The Council's resolution simply observed that the Bank was continuing its study and asked that it be kept informed. The General Assembly added its endorsement at its seventh session, on December 21, 1952.[89]

In 1953 and 1954, IBRD submitted its second and third reports—on the "question of creating" an international finance corporation and the "status of the proposal," respectively. The first pointed to the "significant

[83] Matecki, op.cit., p. 97, quoting Leroy D. Stinebower of the United States, from ECOSOC, Summary Records, UN Doc. E/CN.1/SR. 120.

[84] Asher, op.cit., citing ECOSOC res. 368 (XIII).

[85] Quoted in "Bank's Report on Project for a Finance Corporation," United Nations Bulletin, XII (1 June 1952), 456.

[86] "U.N. Council Hears Black's Plan for New World Finance Company," New York Times, 17 June 1952, p. 37.

[87] Asher, op.cit., p. 362.

[88] Matecki, op.cit., pp. 107-08, citing ECOSOC, Official Records, Fourteenth Session. ECOSOC, it may be recalled, also authorized at this session the appointment of a committee of nine experts to study and report on a special development fund.

[89] Asher, op.cit., p. 362, citing ECOSOC res. 416 (XIV) and General Assembly res. 622 (VII).

fact" that even "while maintaining their interest in the proposal, countries on whom the corporation would necessarily have to depend for the greater part of its funds [had] not as yet indicated that they are ready to commit themselves to subscribe to its capital." From this the Bank concluded that no benefit would accrue to any attempted "formalization of the project at the present time." The second report indicated that the situation was unchanged in this crucial respect.[90]

Bank President Eugene Black advanced a modified proposal to the U.S. Treasury in the late months of 1954. The "Black Plan" dropped the proposed IFC authority to make equity investments and substituted for it authority to buy convertible income debentures, holding them only until they could be sold to purchasers in the private sector who might convert them into capital stock. Black also suggested that the initial capital outlay of $400 million proposed by the Rockefeller Report be reduced to $100 million "in order to get the institution going."[91]

In November 1954, the U.S. Secretary of the Treasury, George Humphrey, announced his government's willingness to solicit Congressional approval for U.S. participation. The next month the General Assembly, at its ninth session, adopted a resolution initiated by the United States which asked the Bank to prepare draft statutes for the new agency. The IFC Articles of Agreement proposed by the Bank were not long in preparation or in acceptance: they were submitted on April 15, 1955, approved as the IFC statute by the General Assembly on November 3, 1955, and accepted by the necessary combination of governments and subscriptions within a few months. IFC began its operations on July 24, 1956, and on Febru-

[90] "Outlook for Finance Corporation: Bank Thinks Time Unripe for Concrete Plan," *United Nations Bulletin*, XIV (15 June 1953), p. 433; "The International Bank," *The Times* (London), 27 September 1954, p. 11.

[91] As quoted by Matecki, *op.cit.*, p. 137.

ary 20, 1957, the Assembly gave its approval to an agreement making the Corporation a part of the UN system as an affiliate of IBRD.[92]

The second new agency geared into the UN's economic development program was the Special Fund (SF). Like IFC, the Special Fund's existence was preceded by its status as an idea, although there is an important difference in the two cases—unlike IFC, the Special Fund as finally realized bore little resemblance to the initial proposal. "Special Fund" is a rather sharply abbreviated version of the original "Special United Nations Fund for Economic Development" in a manner symbolic of more substantial differences between the two.

The Special Fund story commences in 1955.[93] The General Assembly, as noted earlier, had authorized an intergovernmental committee to "analyse" member governments' responses to eight specific questions concerning the establishment and the nature of a Special United Nations Fund for Economic Development. This Intergovernmental Committee, whose membership had been extended to include nineteen members, first met in the spring of 1956. Apparently some members construed its task as negotiation as well as analysis. Its initial report came before the Economic and Social Council's twenty-second session in the summer of the same year. Pressure to proceed with the actual drafting of statutes developed, but a compromise was the outcome: those governments not having submitted their written response to the questions were urged to do so as soon as possible, and the General Assembly was requested to consider additional measures which might promote an early establishment of SUNFED. It was at this session that an abbreviated

[92] Asher, *op.cit.*, pp. 362-63.
[93] This account relies heavily upon the admirable little volume by John G. Hadwen and Johan Kaufmann, *How United Nations Decisions Are Made* (Leyden: A. W. Sythoff, 1960). See especially chapters V and VI.

version of the proposal was presented. Argentina brought up a modified plan which would have financed regional training centers and systematic surveys of natural resources with voluntary contributions—a "special fund for regional co-operation." This less ambitious suggestion was not offered as a formal proposal, however. Apparently the Argentine delegation found little promise in its soundings.[94]

The pressures for action at ECOSOC's twenty-second session were not dissipated, only forestalled. At its eleventh session, beginning in November 1956, the General Assembly found as part of its agenda not only the request carried by the ECOSOC compromise resolution but also a draft resolution presented by forty-one countries which would have asked the Committee of Nineteen to go on to prepare a draft statute for the fund. The discussion was marked by a number of "clarifications" and the presentation of new proposals, some of which would have had the effect of replacing the SUNFED scheme with quite different arrangements. Again Argentina presented its intermediate proposal. And once again a compromise was reached in the form of resolution 1030 (XI), which asked the Intergovernmental Committee to take on the assignment of indicating "the different forms of legal framework on which a Special United Nations Fund for Economic Development may be established and statutes drafted" and suggesting the types of projects which the fund might finance. This supplementary report was to be conveyed, along with the final analysis of governments' replies, to ECOSOC at its next meeting, and the Council was requested to forward both reports and its own recommendations to the General Assembly in time for consideration at the latter's twelfth session.[95]

[94] ECOSOC res. 619 A (XXII); UN Doc. A/AC.102/3, *op.cit.*, pp. 36-37; Hadwen and Kaufmann, *op.cit.*, pp. 92-93.

[95] UN Doc. A/AC.102/3, *op.cit.*, pp. 37-38; Hadwen and Kaufmann, *op.cit.*, p. 93.

It was during this eleventh session of the General Assembly that an article by Paul Hoffman appeared in the *New York Times Magazine* suggesting a "United Nations experimental fund of $100,000,000 (to which the United States would contribute in the usual proportion) to be used for surveys of mineral, water and soil resources, and for a limited number of pilot projects."[96] Since Hoffman was at the time the U.S. representative on the Economic and Financial Committee of the Assembly, the article "naturally provoked among delegates informal discussion of his proposal."[97]

At its third meeting in the spring of 1957, the Intergovernmental Committee of Nineteen arrived at the principal alternatives for a legal framework, as well as some points on which a measure of agreement had been reached. The deliberation process evidently was not an easy one.[98]

The Council was first to consider this report, and at its twenty-fourth session in mid-1957 three views emerged. Some of the principal prospective contributors to a fund (Canada, the United Kingdom, and the United States) continued to oppose establishment prior to a disarmament agreement. Another group of members, including Egypt, Greece, Indonesia, Mexico, the Netherlands, Poland, the U.S.S.R., and Yugoslavia, favored immediate establishment of the fund. A third group of countries expressed discouragement over the immediate prospects, and supported the initiation of less ambitious alternatives. Be-

[96] Paul G. Hoffman, "Blueprint for Foreign Aid," *New York Times Magazine*, 17 February 1958; quoted by Hadwen and Kaufmann, *op.cit.*, pp. 93-94.

[97] According to two who were there, Hadwen and Kaufmann, who make us privy to these exchanges on p. 94.

[98] *Ibid.*, p. 94. These observers write that the "condensation" by which the second section of the report was readied "disguises a certain degree of selection," since "a number of presumably less essential views were eliminated in the process. . . ." The report itself is UN Doc. A/3580; see also A/AC.102/3, annex.

sides Argentina, this final group included Brazil and Pakistan.[99]

This time the final resolution manifested the pressures of the SUNFED supporters. It urged the General Assembly both to take steps leading to the "immediate" establishment of the fund by setting up a preparatory commission for that purpose, and to select a number of projects to be financed through voluntary contributions on an experimental basis pending SUNFED's full operation. The resolution was adopted by 15 votes to 3, with Canada, the U.K., and the U.S. the dissenters.[100]

Hadwen and Kaufmann report that a short time before the convening of the General Assembly at its twelfth session (1957), "it became known that the United States Government . . . favoured the establishment of a small U.N. fund ["Special Projects Fund"] to undertake certain special projects which could not be financed from the existing Expanded Programme of Technical Assistance (EPTA)."[101] In the General Assembly the U.S. proposal was introduced in draft resolution A/C.2/L.354 of November 18, 1957.

Another draft resolution (A/C.2/L.331 of October 16, 1957) submitted by SUNFED supporters had already proposed changes which moved somewhat away from the SUNFED organizational ideas toward a "multilateral fund of the U.N.," to be christened the "Economic Development Fund." This proposal was reportedly advanced to meet the criticisms of those who opposed "a new international bureaucracy."[102]

Resolution 1219 (XII), adopted by the General Assembly on December 14, 1957, embodied the decision to establish "as an expansion of the existing technical assist-

[99] A/AC.102/3, op.cit., pp. 94-95.
[100] ECOSOC, *Summary Records, Twenty-Fourth Session*, 994th meeting, para. 48; A/AC.102/3, op.cit., pp. 38-40.
[101] Hadwen and Kaufmann, op.cit., p. 95.
[102] *Ibid.*, pp. 95-96.

ance and development activities of the United Nations and the specialized agencies a separate Special Fund which would provide systematic and sustained assistance in fields essential to the integrated technical, economic and social development of the less developed countries. . . ." In view of the limited prospective resources available, of which the resolution took note, it was resolved that "the operations of the Special Fund shall be directed towards enlarging the scope of the United Nations programmes of technical assistance so as to include special projects in certain basic fields to be defined by the Preparatory Committee," which was provided for by another paragraph of the same resolution. The resolution looked forward to the establishment of the Special Fund as of January 1, 1959—an expectation subsequently realized, following the work of the Preparatory Committee and General Assembly resolution 1240 (XIII) of October 14, 1958. The latter's final paragraph foreshadowed a review process which was to include and continue beyond the deliberations issuing in establishment of the next addition to the UN economic development agency complex:

"[A]s and when the resources prospectively available are considered by the General Assembly to be sufficient to enter into the field of capital development, principally the development of the economic and social infrastructure of the less developed countries, the Assembly shall review the scope and future activities of the Special Fund and take such action as it may deem appropriate."[103]

The words "International Development Authority" had appeared in printed form at least as early as 1951. But

103 General Assembly res. 1219 (XII) of 14 December 1957; A/AC.102/3, op.cit., p. 42; Hadwen and Kaufmann, p. 97, and Appendix II, pp. 124ff. For further information on the organizational features of SF, see General Assembly res. 1240 (XIII), which is included in Hadwen and Kaufmann's Appendix II, pp. 128-37, and *The Priorities of Progress: The United Nations Special Fund, 1961* (New York: United Nations, 1962), UN Pub. Sales No. 62.I.2.

not until 1958 was an IDA (now International Development Association) proposal carried beyond the stage of study and report by a group of experts.[104] On February 23 of that year the *New York Times* announced a plan by A. S. (Mike) Monroney, U.S. Senator from Oklahoma, to gain the Senate's support for a resolution favoring study of an international agency, to be associated with IBRD, which would make long-term, mixed-currency, low-interest loans to underdeveloped countries. The next day the *New York Times* carried a report that Eugene Black had stated that the International Bank "would be willing to explore" the general idea.[105]

On March 18, 1958, three days of hearings began on the proposal before Monroney's International Finance Subcommittee of the Senate Banking and Currency Committee. The first witness, Secretary of the Treasury Robert B. Anderson, admitted the plan was "a valuable . . . suggestion," which should be studied "with all reasonable diligence." But he found several arguments against the scheme, and no substantial reasons for implementing it.[106]

Another witness, Paul Hoffman, gave Monroney's idea enthusiastic backing. Although somewhat less critical of existing bilateral arrangements than Monroney, and perhaps a bit less optimistic as to the speed with which an IDA could be made workable, Hoffman stated that it

[104] For background coverage leading up to the latter date, see James A. Robinson, *The Monroney Resolution: Congressional Initiative in Foreign Policy Making*, Eagleton Foundation Case Studies in Practical Politics (New York: Henry Holt and Co., 1959), pp. 1-3; David Charles Botting, "New Concepts in Economic Assistance for Underdeveloped Countries," *Western Political Quarterly*, XIV (June 1961), 507-08.

[105] E. W. Kenworthy, "Monroney Urges a 2d World Bank," *New York Times*, 23 February 1958, pp. 1f.; "Black Asks Study on 2d World Bank," *New York Times*, 24 February 1958, pp. 1f.

[106] E. W. Kenworthy, "Anderson is Cool to 2d World Bank," *New York Times*, 19 March 1958, pp. 1f.

would be "tragic" if Congress were to fail to act promptly on the "exciting proposal."[107]

C. Douglas Dillon, then Deputy Under Secretary of State for Economic Affairs, told the Subcommittee that since repayments on most IDA loans would be in local currencies, these funds "could not be used for relending"; consequently, replenishment of the original hard currency capitalization would be necessary. Dillon did give the proposal his approval "in principle," but he conveyed the Administration's skepticism as to participation by other hard currency nations. Dillon suggested an agency on a "modest scale" as an adjunct to the U.S. Development Loan Fund.

Governor Averell Harriman of New York gave the plan his full support by telegram, and Senator Prescott Bush of Connecticut expressed his sympathy for the idea, "assuming it's practical," on the same day. The latter suggested that the Administration (acting through the Departments of State and Treasury) sound out other hard-currency nations.[108]

About two months later, with the Development Loan Fund appropriation by Congress apparently assured, the Administration began to look somewhat more favorably upon the "Monroney Plan." The Senator from Oklahoma received letters in May from Dillon and from Julius B. Baird, Acting Secretary of the Treasury, proposing a "few changes" in the resolution's language, and offering their departments' approval for this call to study the IDA proposal, with their revisions.[109]

[107] *Ibid.*, p. 3.
[108] E. W. Kenworthy, "750 Million Urged for Needy Lands," *New York Times*, 20 March 1958, p. 14; "U.S. For Principle of Aid Bank Plan," *New York Times*, 21 March 1958, p. 5.
[109] The principal change was that the study requested by Senator Monroney be conducted by the National Advisory Council on International Monetary and Financial Problems, which included the Secretaries of State, Treasury, and Commerce, the Chairman of the Export-Import Bank, and the Chairman of the Board of Governors

The Senate Banking and Currency Committee filed its report on the proposal July 12, 1958. As formulated and backed by the Committee, the resolution would express as the "sense of the Senate" a request for study of the proposal. Dissenting were the Committee's two senior Republicans, Senators Homer A. Capehart of Indiana and John W. Bricker of Ohio. They charged that the proposed new agency would duplicate the activities of existing organizations, and Capehart, listing the agencies which already drew U.S. financial support, later warned that the United States would "run out of money" if it continued to participate in such loan programs. Capehart sought to append an amendment to the resolution on the Senate floor which would have required a preliminary study of all existing international loan programs, but the change was rejected (47 to 40) by a lineup basically along party lines. The Senate then adopted the resolution by a 62-25 roll-call vote.[110]

In late August 1958, President Eisenhower gave his official endorsement to an international development association while urging, at the same time, an expansion in the capital resources of both IBRD and IMF. Commented the *London Times'* City Editor: "President Eisenhower has now amply set the stage for the World Bank and International Monetary Fund meetings early in October."[111] So it was to prove, for at the annual meet-

---

of the Federal Reserve System. See E. W. Kenworthy, "U.S. Favors Study on 2d World Bank," *New York Times*, 26 May 1958, p. 10. For a behind-the-scenes account of the two month interval between Administration coolness and Administration endorsement as viewed from a Congressional vantage-point, see Robinson, *op.cit.* Both Robinson and Kenworthy report informal discussions between U.S. government officials and Eugene Black.

[110] "New Loan Agency for World Gains," *New York Times*, 13 July 1958, p. 55; "Senate for Study of Foreign Loans," *ibid.*, 24 July 1958, p. 14; Robinson, *op.cit.*, pp. 15-16.

[111] "U.S. Plan to Increase I.M.F. and World Bank Funds," *The Times* (London), 27 August 1958, p. 12; see also "Aid for Less Advanced Nations," *The Times* (London), 27 August 1958, p. 8.

ing of the Boards of Governors of Bank and Fund in New Delhi, U.S. Secretary of the Treasury Anderson called for the executive boards of both institutions to complete their study of the expansion proposals by the end of December 1958, and he indicated that the U.S. wished the IDA proposal to be the subject of informal discussion.[112]

In August 1959 a "guidelines paper" setting forth U.S. views on the IDA proposal was sent to the Bank's sixty-seven other member governments by Secretary Anderson. This confirmed an earlier report that a resolution calling for the Bank's Executive Directors to "study the question" would be introduced at the annual meeting the next month.[113]

At the annual meeting in Washington in late September both President Eisenhower and Secretary Anderson called for increased participation in financing economic development. Eugene Black again offered his public endorsement. The sixty-eight member governments on October 1 unanimously approved the study by the Bank's Executive Directors, but only after a few reservations had been entered on the record. Several governors emphasized that they would not agree to join IDA until they had seen the final draft of its provisions.[114]

The Bank forwarded the IDA articles to prospective

[112] "World Bank Told of Asia's Dire Need for Aid," *The Times* (London), 7 October 1958, p. 8.

[113] E. W. Kenworthy, "U.S. Will Propose New World Bank for Poor Nations," *New York Times*, 16 August 1959, pp. 1f.

[114] Edwin L. Dale, Jr., "Europe Exhorted to Help Others," *New York Times*, 29 September 1959, pp. 1f.; "U.S. May Tighten World Financial Policies if Aid Burden Isn't Shared," *Wall Street Journal* (Western Edition), 30 September 1959, p. 3; Dale, "Anderson Warns Europe on Trade; Cites U.S. Deficit," *New York Times*, 30 September 1959, pp. 1f.; Dale, "World Loan Plan Gaining Support," *New York Times*, 1 October 1959, pp. 1f.; "68 Nations in World Bank Approve New Loan Agency," *New York Times*, 2 October 1959, pp. 1f.; "World Bank to Study U.S. Plan for Loan Agency to Aid Nations," *Wall Street Journal* (Western Edition), 2 October 1959, p. 12.

members early in 1960. On February 18, President Eisenhower asked Congressional authorization for participation by the U.S., and a participation bill was introduced in the British House of Commons in March by the Chancellor of the Exchequer. Subsequent approval by these governments provided IDA with its two largest subscribers, and before the annual meeting of the Board of Governors in September 1960 the $650 million minimum commitment of funds had been assured, thereby clearing the way for the agency's formal establishment. The International Development Association officially began its operations in November 1960.[115] Certainly the plot which was its prehistory had featured very different actors and arenas than that of its immediate predecessor.

I V

The resolution which had pronounced the General Assembly's decision to establish the Special Fund temporarily covered over a divergence of views among member states. That resolution, it will be recalled, contained in its final paragraph a reference to a future hypothetical Assembly decision to "review the scope and future activities of the Special Fund and take such action as it may deem appropriate." In the course of the debate preceding adoption of a subsequent resolution accepting the Preparatory Committee's report and establishing the Special Fund itself, the issue came into the open once again. At that time a proposal to include a reference to the possible evo-

[115] "World Bank Acts to Set Up $1 Billion Loan Fund for Poorer Nations on Easy Terms," *Wall Street Journal* (Western Edition), 1 February 1960, p. 5; Dale, "World Bank Sets Global-Aid Rules," *New York Times*, 1 February 1960, p. 41; "I.D.A. Articles Ready," *The Times* (London), 1 February 1960, p. 18; Dale, "President Urges U.S. Participation in New Aid Group," *New York Times*, 19 February 1960, pp. 1f.; "Aiding Under-Developed Countries," *The Times* (London), 11 March 1960, p. 20; Richard E. Mooney, "West Germany Is Urged to Give Aid to Under-Developed Nations," *New York Times*, 27 September 1960, p. 5; "I.D.A. Begins Operations," *The Times* (London), 10 November 1960, p. 22.

lution of the Special Fund into a capital development fund was debated and rejected.

Later in the same Assembly session, however, the supporters of a UN capital development fund were able to gain support for a separate resolution which recalled "previous resolutions of the General Assembly and of the Economic and Social Council on the establishment of a United Nations fund for financing the economic development of the less developed countries" and urged members "to continue working for the establishment of a United Nations capital development fund." Supporters of this resolution thus served notice that they would refuse to allow the history of UNEDA and SUNFED to be buried in the Special Fund's present and future. Furthermore, the resolution endorsed the continuation, as a standard Assembly agenda item, of a review of "progress in . . . financing the economic development of the less developed countries" in general, and "progress towards the establishment of a United Nations capital development fund" in particular. This resolution gained 67 affirmative votes, no dissents, and 14 abstentions.[116]

The months prior to adoption of this General Assembly resolution were those of the debate on the "Monroney Plan" in the United States. Monroney's IDA proposal—and the slightly modified version emanating from his consultation with the executive branch—envisaged an agency closely tied to IBRD and following the Bank's system of executive representation (Executive Directors) and voting (weighted according to member states' respective subscriptions). The sponsors of resolution 1317 (XIII), however, sought as an organizational principle for their projected agency a relationship which would place a future capital development fund closer to the UN's central po-

[116] General Assembly res. 1317 (XIII); Hadwen and Kaufmann, op.cit., pp. 99f., 137-38; Yearbook of the United Nations, 1958 (UN: Office of Public Information, 1959), pp. 141-42. See latter for the voting lineup.

litical apparatus—in particular, the General Assembly—
and thus make it more readily answerable to the Assembly's representation and voting patterns. A United Kingdom amendment which would have designated the hypothetical agency "a capital development fund within the
framework of the United Nations" was not accepted, and
the subsequently adopted designation, a "United Nations
capital development fund," symbolized an organizational
principle which, without retrenchment by either position,
barred the combination of Monroney's plan with that of
the proponents of the capital development fund in a
single agency—at any rate, for the time being.[117]

At its mid-1959 session, the Economic and Social Council was presented with a report by the Secretary-General
which referred to the suggested capital development fund
as one possible means of financing economic development.[118] At this session of the Council considerable sup-

[117] Hadwen and Kaufmann, op.cit., p. 100. Speaking for the
Netherlands, a co-sponsor of the resolution, Johan Kaufmann
"pointed out that the words 'a United Nations capital development
fund' had been used deliberately. . . . There would appear to be
no reason why an international development association and a
United Nations capital development fund should not exist side by
side." General Assembly, Second Committee, Official Records,
Thirteenth Session, A/C.2/SR.564, p. 242.

V. K. R. V. Rao, in his Montague Burton Lecture for 1960,
"International Aid for Economic Development—Possibilities and
Limitations," op.cit., indicated his favor for a "reformed and re-
juvenated" IDA to become "the main instrument for the promotion
of economic development. . . ." The United States, per contra,
held that IDA had fulfilled "the promise held forth" by earlier Assembly resolution 724 A (VIII)—which had looked toward increased financing of development—without even waiting for the
progress toward disarmament which was, by that resolution, enun-
ciated as the condition for such further financing. The United
States representative went on to point out that IDA would start
with a capital base four times that recommended for SUNFED,
and would support projects recommended by the Intergovernmental
Committee of Nineteen; he also warned of what he saw as a danger
in dissipating resources available for financing by multiplying the
distributory machinery.

[118] Analytical Summary of Various Suggested Means of Acceler-

port for further action toward a capital development fund appeared among less-developed members, and some industrialized countries as well. The Council unanimously adopted a resolution calling upon members of the UN and the specialized agencies to "give further consideration" to the Assembly resolution which had endorsed work toward a capital development fund, and to "continue to examine the possibility of contributing financial resources that may serve to accelerate economic development, giving consideration to the means envisaged in that resolution [*viz.*, a capital development fund] as well as to other means . . . proposed or referred to in the discussions or documents of the Council or the General Assembly."[119]

The question of means for building economic and social infrastructure in the developing countries again drew the attention of the General Assembly at its fourteenth session. The use of United Nations machinery in financing this process was a focal point of the discussion, and the representatives of Bolivia, Chile, the Philippines, and Greece all supported the establishment of a UN capital development fund as a major component. Other members —for instance, the U.S., the U.K., Japan, Italy, and the Netherlands—expressed a desire to wait for some time before supporting a new multilateral financing agency beyond IDA.[120] On December 5, 1959, the Assembly adopted, by a 67-0-15 roll-call vote, a resolution calling once again on members to "give further consideration" to previous resolutions and to "reappraise their positions as regards extending material support for the early establishment of a United Nations capital development fund,"

---

ating Economic Growth in Less Developed Countries Through International Action. Report by the Secretary-General, E/3259.

[119] ECOSOC res. 740 D (XXVIII), 31 July 1959; *Yearbook of the United Nations,* 1959 (UN: Office of Public Information, 1960), pp. 139-41.

[120] Robert Asher's comment on a similar series of earlier events has a certain relevance here, also. He states that the earlier question gradually shifted from "whether" to "when." *Op.cit.,* p. 630.

asked the Secretary-General to "examine, in consultation with" member governments, "ways and means of making further progress towards the early establishment" of such a fund, and invited him to report to both the Council and the Assembly in 1960.[121]

The next year the push toward a capital development fund resumed. At the thirtieth session of ECOSOC, the Council considered the replies of fifteen member governments to the Secretary-General's request for their views. The replies showed no significant changes of position.[122]

The General Assembly's fifteenth session was the occasion for a more determined drive. In the Second Committee, forty-four underdeveloped countries, many of them new UN members, joined in sponsoring a draft resolution whereby the Assembly would express its decision to establish a United Nations capital development fund and its resolve that a draft statute for this fund should be prepared by a committee of twenty-five representatives of member states designated by the President of the Assembly on the basis of equitable geographic distribution. This committee's report was to be submitted to ECOSOC's mid-1961 session, and the Council, in turn, was to transmit the document, along with its own comments, to the As-

[121] General Assembly res. 1424 (XIV). Those abstaining were Australia, Belgium, Canada, Denmark, Finland, France, Italy, Luxembourg, New Zealand, Portugal, Spain, Sweden, the Union of South Africa, the United Kingdom, and the United States. Japan and the Netherlands voted in favor of the final resolution, even though they had earlier expressed some reservations. *Yearbook of the United Nations, 1959, op.cit.*, pp. 139-41.

[122] *United Nations Review*, VII (October 1960), 74. Eighteen member governments had responded by the time the Assembly reviewed the replies. Eleven favored the early establishment of a capital development fund: Byelorussian Soviet Socialist Republic, Ceylon, Czechoslovakia, Ecuador, Guatemala, Iraq, the Sudan, Turkey, Ukrainian Soviet Socialist Republic, the U.S.S.R., and Yugoslavia. Six opposed early establishment: Australia, Canada, France, New Zealand, the U.K., and the U.S. Norway also gave a somewhat qualified "no." A/AC.102/3, *op.cit.*, p. 51 and nn. 159, 160, and 161.

sembly's sixteenth session. The draft resolution, with an "in principle" added to the proposed Assembly decision, cleared the Second Committee by a vote of 68-4-8 and gained the approval of the Assembly in plenary session as resolution 1521 (XV) of December 15, 1960. The seventy-one affirmative votes included those of representatives from several developed countries. There were ten abstentions, but only Australia, South Africa, the United Kingdom, and the United States voted against the resolution in the plenary session.[123]

On March 27, 1961, the President of the General Assembly asked twenty-five states to provide representation on the Committee on a United Nations Capital Development Fund provided by the Assembly resolution.[124] The Committee organized at its first meeting on April 17, electing U Thant of Burma as its chairman. On May 15 it turned to the assignment of "consider[ing] all concrete preparatory measures, including draft legislation," necessary for the establishment of the fund. The Committee was handicapped by a want of time and consensus. The representatives of Canada, France, Italy, Japan, the United Kingdom, and the United States declared that their participation in the Committee's work and their commitment to its purpose and recommendations would be sharply limited. The Committee's draft product upon

[123] Chad became the forty-fifth sponsor of the draft resolution. Mario Rossi, "Fund Slated in UN to Develop Small Nations," *Christian Science Monitor*, 2 November 1960, p. 1; "Capital Development Fund," *United Nations Review*, VIII (January 1961), 24, 66; *United Nations Review*, VIII (March 1961), 30; A/AC.-102/3, *op.cit.*, pp. 51ff.; Hadwen and Kaufmann, *op.cit.*, second edition, 1962, pp. 101ff.; *Yearbook of the United Nations*, 1960 (UN: Office of Public Information, 1961), pp. 285ff. See p. 285 of the latter for a list of the original forty-four sponsors.

[124] *Yearbook of the United Nations*, 1961 (New York: Columbia University Press, 1962), p. 237. The states designated were Argentina, Brazil, Burma, Canada, Chile, Czechoslovakia, Denmark, France, Ghana, India, Indonesia, Iraq, Italy, Ivory Coast, Japan, Netherlands, Nigeria, Pakistan, Peru, Sudan, U.S.S.R., U.A.R., U.K., U.S., and Yugoslavia.

its adjournment June 5 proved somewhat less definitive than the Assembly resolution had indicated. Besides *requesting* draft legislation for a capital development fund through an invitation to ECOSOC and the General Assembly to renew its own mandate, the Committee recommended that the Secretary-General be asked to prepare a report assessing the capital needs of developing countries, evaluating the impact of existing institutions financing economic development, and defining fields in which additional international efforts were necessary. In lieu of a draft statute, the Committee (voting 17-4-1) adopted twelve principles to govern the establishment and operations of a fund.[125]

No significant position changes by member states were evident at ECOSOC's session in mid-1961. On August 3 the Council voted unanimously to take note of the Committee report and transmit it to the General Assembly.

On November 3 the Assembly's Second Committee, with a vote of 70-4-7, approved a draft resolution extending the mandate of the Committee of Twenty-Five and instructing it to proceed to draft a fund statute for submission to ECOSOC in 1962. The proposal was adopted as General Assembly resolution 1706 (XVI) on December 19, 1961.[126]

When the Committee on a United Nations Capital Development Fund reconvened on February 14, 1962, it asked the Secretariat to undertake another probe into this sensitive area. Mindful of the Committee's difficulties as a decision-making body, and stung, perhaps, by several ECOSOC speakers' expression of disappointment that the

[125] *Ibid.*, pp. 237-38; "Issues Before the Sixteenth General Assembly," *International Conciliation*, 534 (September 1961), pp. 144-45; *United Nations Review*, VIII (May 1961), 2-3; *ibid.*, VIII (July 1961), 5, 45; "Twelve Principles Proposed for Capital Development Fund," *ibid.*, VIII (August 1961), 26ff.

[126] *Yearbook of the United Nations, 1961, op.cit.*, pp. 238-39; *United Nations Review*, VIII (December 1961), 30; *ibid.*, IX (February 1962), 33.

twelve capital development fund principles were even less precise than those formulated years earlier in conjunction with SUNFED proposals, a majority of the intergovernmental committee decided to request the Secretariat to prepare for it a working paper "setting forth, in legal form, the technical, organizational and administrative provisions of a draft statute for a United Nations Capital Development Fund, based on [the] framework prepared by [the Intergovernmental] Committee of Nineteen in 1956-1957. . . ." This working paper was to be forwarded to the respective committee members for consideration by their governments.[127]

As the Committee's second regular session began May 25, 1962, the United States, Britain, and France stated their determination to avoid active participation in the work of the Committee. Canada followed suit the next day, along with Japan, whose representative, joined subsequently by the Danish representative, thought it futile to draft a statute in the face of the negativism demonstrated by major potential contributors. The Dutch representative also qualified his participation in the deliberations, indicating a preference, in these circumstances, for a modification of the Special Fund mandate and machinery that would allow SF to undertake capital investment as well as pre-investment. The proposal to transform the Special Fund into a capital fund had been cast in the SF terms of reference, as already noted, and revivified as an option from time to time with allusions by various delegates in ECOSOC and the General Assembly. Delegates from the Soviet Union participated in the Committee deliberations but announced, at the final meeting, that they would be unable to support either the statute or the proposed fund because certain principles which they deemed vital had not been included. A Committee majority nonetheless approved a twelve-article draft "statute"

[127] *Ibid.*, IX (March 1962), 70-71.

for submission to ECOSOC and the General Assembly.[128]

At ECOSOC's thirty-fourth session in mid-1962, the Council considered the second report of the Committee on a United Nations Capital Development Fund and transmitted the report to the General Assembly by resolution 921 (XXXIV) of August 3, which also urged "economically advanced countries to reconsider [their stands], in consultation with the Secretary-General. . . ." The General Assembly, in turn, added its endorsement to this appeal, requested the Secretary-General to transmit the draft to governments for comment, extended the Committee's mandate, asked it to "propose practical measures designed to ensure the beginning of the operation" of the fund, and instructed it to report in 1963.[129]

The transformation of SF into a capital development fund received further impetus though not exclusive attention during the third session of the Committee, which met September 5-13, 1963. A continuing study of needs for capital and the status of its flow expressed as to appropriate machinery was requested of the imminent General Assembly session, along with a further extension of the Committee's mandate.[130]

On November 12 the Second Assembly Committee voted, 85-0-10, to recommend Assembly approval of a request to the Secretary-General to prepare a study on practical steps to transform the Special Fund into a Capital

[128] "Issues Before the Seventeenth General Assembly," *International Conciliation*, 539 (September 1962), pp. 118-19; *United Nations Review*, IX (July 1962), 3, 48-49; "New U.N. Lending Agency is Opposed by 3 Powers," *New York Times*, 26 May 1962, p. 3; "Boycott Fails to Halt Plans for a New U.N. Aid Agency," *New York Times*, 30 May 1962, p. 27; "U.N. Aid Group to Accept Appeals From All States," *New York Times*, 5 June 1962, p. 24.

[129] "Issues Before the Eighteenth General Assembly," *International Conciliation*, 544 (September 1963), p. 158; *United Nations Review*, IX (September 1962), 63-64; *ibid.*, X (January 1963), 10, 69, 95-96; *ibid.*, X (February 1963), 39. The General Assembly endorsement was expressed through resolution 1826 (XVII) of 18 December 1962.

[130] *United Nations Review*, X (November 1963), 46.

Development Fund. This gained approval as General Assembly resolution 1936 (XVIII) of December 11, 1963.[181]

The Secretariat study on practical steps involved in transforming the Special Fund appeared March 9, 1964.[132] As its point of departure in estimating financial requirements for a capital development fund, the report adopted the minimum figure of $200 million to $250 million for the initiation of a fund recommended in 1957, when SUN-FED was under discussion.[133] The Secretariat's report suggested, at the same time, that a smaller amount might nonetheless make it feasible "to consider the possibility of a *gradual* transformation of the Special Fund into a Capital Development Fund which would mature at such speed and in such direction as the successive allocation of additional funds and functions would allow."[134] Changes in both the SF terms of reference and its organization would be necessary, the study indicated. Investment activities by the new fund would necessitate strengthened SF arrangements for the evaluation, execution, and follow-up of projects. Separate accounts for pre-investment and investment would be necessary. Procedures for the allocation of resources between the two accounts would need to be established; allocation might be accomplished through "the decisions of an authorized organ" or by the designation of individual contributors at pledging conferences.[135]

---

[131] *Ibid.*, X (December 1963), 43, 48; *ibid.*, XI (January 1964), 52-56; "West Voted Down on U.N. Investments," *New York Times*, 13 November 1963, p. 13.

[132] "Transformation of the Special Fund into a United Nations Capital Development Fund," E/CONF.46/66.

[133] "Final Report of the Ad Hoc Committee on the Question of the Establishment of a Special United Nations Fund for Economic Development," A/3579, Part III, para. 4. See also "Report on a Special United Nations Fund for Economic Development," UN Sales No. 1953.II.B.1, para. 55; "Special United Nations Fund for Economic Development, Final Report by Raymond Scheyven," A/2728, Ch. IV, Section 1.

[134] E/CONF.46/66, para. 6. Emphasis in original.

[135] *Ibid.*, pp. 4-6.

The Secretariat study was circulated at the United Nations Conference on Trade and Development (UNCTAD), which convened in Geneva March 23, 1964. UNCTAD's Third Committee, assigned the consideration of financing measures to expand international trade, heard various proposals relating to targets for the United Nations Development Decade, the establishment of compensatory financing to offset short-term (or secular) "shortfalls" for commodity exports, the modification of existing terms for UN system development financing, and the genesis of a capital development fund. On May 12, for instance, this UNCTAD committee of the whole voted to recommend both an enlargement of SF activities "so as to include increased financing of demonstration projects and to undertake investment proper as additional resources become available," on the one hand, and "the early establishment" of a United Nations Capital Development Fund, on the other.[136] Both approaches to an investment fund were thus held open, although the SF-transformation plan may have received the requisite consensual mix to place it in the ascendancy.

As Hadwen and Kaufmann have said, "United Nations consideration of a problem such as the promotion of the economic development of the less developed countries has a beginning but not an ending."[137] At this point our account of some of the developments in these years must close, however. The challenge of providing for these selected events some semblance of order through analysis and interpretation has now been cast forth. Fortunately, we may begin by applying the guidelines in the functionalist argument. To that endeavor we now turn.

[136] UN Monthly Chronicle, I (May 1964), 55ff.; ibid., I (June 1964), 60-62.
[137] Hadwen and Kaufmann, op.cit., p. 100.

IV

Functional Consequences: Structural Support Capacity

THIS CHAPTER and Chapter V will be devoted to a more thorough examination of those programs within the United Nations system which participate in the financing of economic development. The investigation will proceed essentially along the lines suggested by the functionalist argument, following in particular the projections which represent the functionalist short-run prophecy. Here these questions provide the focus: Have the functionalist predictions been borne out? Which ones, if so, and to what extent?

These questions, with the propositions and indicators set forth above[1] to guide a selection of the relevant, provide a different organizing principle than that employed in the previous chapter. Once again the aim is to portray developments over time, but here the findings will be grouped into categories suggested by the functionalist writers.

There is a further difference. Events selected for inclusion in the previous chapter were, in general, those which accompanied the *establishment* of several agencies, and attempts to set up others—IBRD, UNEDA, SUNFED, IFC, the Special Fund, IDA, and a United Nations Capital Development Fund. Little was reported beyond the origin of agencies. That task has been reserved for the following pages.

Central to the functionalist argument is the claim that cooperation in solving common problems comes to provide its own dynamic. This dynamic bears with it several types of metamorphosis, the most apparent being structural

[1] See pp. 53ff.

change—that development of new organizational and procedural patterns which consolidates the gains made by functional activity. Structural change is regarded essentially as a clue to accomplished facts, facts of greater significance than the structure itself. But there is a suggestion in the functionalist thesis that even as "form follows function," that form, in turn, lends strength and permanence to the specific need and activity which brought it into being.

Despite its secondary status in the functionalist scheme, structural change provides the obvious starting point for an assessment of functionalist predictions. The phrase "structural support capacity" covers the inquiries followed in the present chapter. These inquiries will center upon financing operations, representation and participation patterns, and field capacity.

Financing Operations

Perhaps the appropriate opening question in a consideration of programs which finance economic development is "how much," and how has this quantity varied during the course of the respective programs. At the outset we are concerned with the large picture: magnitude and change on a comparative and secular basis. Figure 1 depicts IBRD and IDA loan commitments, IFC investments, and Special Fund allocations. The IBRD component includes loan commitments to member states and to borrowers for whom member states act as guarantors. IFC figures are based on the Corporation's original investment commitments, not including standby and underwriting commitments. For the Special Fund the compilation includes the amount allocated for contracts with the Fund's executing agents but not the contribution by the member government directly concerned. SF allocations are not loans, but commitments toward payments to the executing agent. IDA figures are for credits.

IBRD, IFC, SF, and IDA[1]

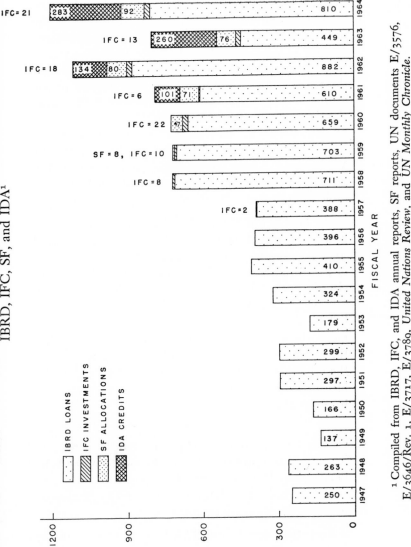

[1] Compiled from IBRD, IFC, and IDA annual reports, SF reports, UN documents E/3576, E/3646/Rev. 1, E/3717, E/3789, *United Nations Review*, and *UN Monthly Chronicle*.

This picture indicates an increase in the magnitude of financial commitments over the years, although the increase is not uniform on a year-to-year basis. Further questions must be asked about this pattern when the foundation for an inquiry has been laid.

Another fundamental aspect of financing operations is the terms under which they take place. Length of commitment, grace period, interest rate, other explicit conditions—here, too, the over-all pattern suggests further inquiries. Economic criteria are preeminent in IBRD's stated policy on loans; the same can be said for IFC. With regard to both length of loan and grace period, for instance, IBRD policy implies substantial reliance upon project-oriented considerations:

"In establishing the length of its loans, the Bank has generally followed the principle that the term should bear some relationship to the estimated life of the equipment or plan being financed. For example, the cost of a hydro-electric power plant consists partly of installations such as a dam, embankments, a powerhouse and so on, which last for a very long time, and partly of generating equipment which has a shorter economic life. For such projects the Bank has usually made loans for 20 to 25 years. On the other hand, loans made for the purchase of less durable goods, such as trucks or farm machinery, have often been for about seven years.

.   .   .   .

"The borrower is normally given a period of grace ranging from two to five years before the first principal installment comes due; the length of the period of grace is generally determined by the time estimated to be necessary to bring the project into operation."[2]

Recently, however, the Bank has apparently broadened

[2] IBRD Staff, *The World Bank* (Washington: IBRD, 1957), pp. 72, 73.

its application of standards to fit the borrower's situation, thereby easing (or at least attenuating) debt-servicing burdens of some member states. In early 1964, the Bank extended its first thirty-five year loan, for hydroelectric power development in Colombia. And eight years of grace accompanied a highway loan to Liberia at about the same time.[3] Furthermore, President George D. Woods announced on March 25, 1964, that IBRD would consider refinancing loans of " 'a few countries now caught in an acute cash squeeze' " if the member government in question would agree to undertake " 'appropriate disciplines.' "[4]

Members of the IFC Staff stress that the pattern of conditions for its investments is difficult to fit into a general survey of trends. As the April 1962 edition of *The World Bank, IFC and IDA* noted, IFC's "usual term . . . is from about seven to fifteen years with serial maturities, after an appropriate grace period" which allows time "for the project financed to come into profitable operation." Since underwriting its first issue of capital shares in June 1962, however, the Corporation has been active in various equity transactions. It would be fair to construe the trend toward equity investments as a constructive lengthening of term. The relationship of equity financing to effective grace period is less clear.[5]

Credits extended by IDA through fiscal year 1963 are

[3] Edwin L. Dale, Jr., "World Bank Starts New Policy With 35-Year Colombian Loan," *New York Times*, 8 February 1964, p. 28. These steps were adumbrated in the annual address by George D. Woods, President of IBRD, IFC and IDA, on 30 September 1963. See IBRD, *Summary Proceedings, 1963 Annual Meetings of the Boards of Governors*, p. 12.

[4] Quoted by Philip Shabecoff, "World Bank Head Urges Debt Shift," *New York Times*, 26 March 1964, p. 49. The announcement came in the course of the Bank President's address to the first United Nations Conference on Trade and Development in Geneva.

[5] IBRD Staff, *The World Bank, IFC and IDA* (Washington: IBRD, April 1962), p. 100; IFC, *Sixth Annual Report, 1961-62*, p. 10; *Seventh Annual Report, 1962-1963, passim*.

for identical terms and grace periods: fifty years, with amortization to begin after the first ten.[6]

Raymond F. Mikesell noted in early 1963 that the International Bank had made almost no loans "for so-called social impact projects such as housing, hospitals, rural improvement and educational facilities"—that it preferred to "confine its financing to projects making a more or less direct contribution to the physical output and productivity of the borrowing country," avoiding others which "do not fit the concept of 'bankability' and 'soundness' "—possibilities that would "present difficult problems in the application of the economic and engineering standards which the Bank has evolved in judging projects."[7] But more recently the Bank leadership has expressed its intention of transcending these criteria in some instances with a policy statement on education loans. Further shifts from the dominant project orientation of IBRD-IFC-IDA undertakings are also likely. A path-breaking IDA loan to cover straight import financing of "supplies, components and equipment needed by [Indian] private enterprise to keep operating" was announced on June 9, 1964.[8]

[6] IDA, *Third Annual Report, 1962-63*, p. 5.

[7] Raymond F. Mikesell, "The World Bank in a Changing World," *Challenge*, XI (February 1963), 15.

[8] Dale, "World Bank Starts New Policy . . . ," p. 31; Dale, "Two 'Firsts' Set for World Bank," *New York Times*, 10 June 1964, p. 61. IDA already has extended several loans for education. Negotiations for an IBRD loan to the University of the Philippines have been reported; this would be the Bank's first to an educational institution. "World Bank Pleases Romulo," *New York Times*, 28 June 1964, p. 8.

Dale reports that with these new directions "the bank will have to drop its customary practice of financing only the foreign exchange costs of a project." Local costs would also figure heavily in another venture contemplated by the Bank's Executive Directors—the financing of farm credit institutions. However, Bank officials observe that there were many prior exceptions to the "customary practice." One reckoning counts local expenditures as constituting most of the figure represented in Bank tabulations as "other disbursements." This category, in turn, mounts to almost one quarter of total disbursements.

Interest rates on IBRD loans have ranged from 3 to 6¼ percent.[9] Bank officials have often emphasized what they regard as the undesirability of severing IBRD interest rates from existing capital market conditions. IFC Staff members aver that the Corporation has never made a simple, fixed-interest loan: even prior to the equity era, IFC investments included profit-sharing devices, stock options, and other special features, sometimes in lieu of any fixed interest rate whatsoever. However, the justifiable claim that an exclusive focus on Corporation interest rates misrepresents the terms of these investments by neglecting their other features has not diminished the attention given fixed rates when they are part of the bargain. IFC rates varied between 5 and 10 percent through mid-1962; thereafter they are not compiled for presentation in the annual reports. The recent shift toward equity financing renders virtually impossible a satisfactory quantitative comparison of IFC trends in costs with IBRD and IDA rates. But the available evidence does not suggest that Corporation investments have been unprofitable.[10] IDA credits thus far

[9] IBRD, *Eighteenth Annual Report*, 1962-1963, Appendix K. Bank charges have three components, a fixed commission of 1% which goes to a special reserve against losses, a fraction of 1% for administrative costs, and the estimated cost to the Bank, at the time of the loan, of borrowing the same amount for a comparable term in the capital market. See note 13, below, for a recent development. Interest is charged only on the part of the loan actually disbursed; however, a smaller commitment charge is made on the undisbursed portion. See *The World Bank, op.cit.*, pp. 73-74.

[10] IFC, *Fifth Annual Report*, 1960-1961, pp. 12-13; *Sixth Annual Report*, 1961-1962, pp. 29-30; *Seventh Annual Report*, 1962-1963, pp. 5ff. It should be noted that a number of recent IFC investments carry no fixed interest. This is one attribute of IFC credits emphasized by its management in meeting criticism of the predominant high interest rates during the Corporation's earlier days. The IFC Staff also underlines the complexity of decisions on its terms compared to those accompanying IBRD and IDA commitments by pointing to the additional variables surrounding evaluation of the individual *enterprise* involved: IBRD and IDA look to governments as borrowers or guarantors, IFC eyes the country and its government as context for its potential investment, but also must

bear no interest charges.[11]

An interesting pattern emerges. Bank loans—the only ones in the picture prior to fiscal year 1957—were initially extended at 4¼ percent in 1947, dropped to their low for two short-term loans in 1949, rose to 6¼ percent for three long-term loans in February and March 1960, and have remained at about 5½ percent since September 1962. IFC credits, of course, were extended during the latter years of this period. Thus, recent interest rates on "bankable loans"—credits from the Bank and IFC—are comparatively high *relative to interest charges in earlier years*.[12] On the other hand, the newest lending agency, IDA—a "bank for the unbankable," as *Fortune* once dubbed it— is extending loans at the lowest rates yet offered by a multilateral agency in the UN system. When to this pattern is added the Special Fund's allocations during the last few years, which carry recipient contribution requirements but no interest costs (or repayment of "principal"), we find a divergence in credit charges which seems to be growing—a gap between "hard" and "soft" credit handled

---

calculate the risks attendant upon the specific venture, the local company and its personnel. This latter argument goes far to explain and justify IFC terms. However, in the distinction it seeks to draw between IFC and IBRD investment criteria, the contention rests in part upon an assumption of cursory IBRD attention to the human dimensions of Bank projects which appears to be betrayed by the record.

[11] A "service charge" of ¾ of 1% per annum is levied on amounts withdrawn and outstanding to "help meet IDA's administrative costs. . . ." IDA, *Annual Report, 1962-63*, p. 5.

[12] Bank Staff members rightly observe that the major component in the cost of IBRD loans only reflects the rising cost of money generally during the period. On the other hand, the difference between the cost of money to the Bank and its interest rate when lent, initially 1¼%, has now been reduced to 1%. Geoffrey M. Wilson, Vice President of IBRD and IDA, recently noted of his elder institution that "we are slow to move our rate upward and quick to bring it down" in an address to the Institute of Banking and Financial Studies, Paris. Emphasis on cost-cutting by the Bank, however, tends to highlight the predominant, uncuttable portion of Bank-exacted costs.

by different agencies. What implications does this pattern suggest?

Trends have been noted and questions introduced with respect to financing operations. Financial outputs have been the focus thus far. What of the input phase implied by these disbursements? Have there been modifications over time, and if so would they appear to raise questions for subsequent consideration?

Earlier we presented a paradigm to aid in indicating the strengthening or weakening of structural support capacity.[13] Before its application, some attention must be devoted to a description of the means by which these agencies gain the financial substance for their disbursements.

The basic financial structure of IBRD was agreed on in 1944, as already noted. The Bank's authorized capital stock was set at $10 billion, divided into 100,000 shares. Capital subscriptions as assigned at Bretton Woods ranged from $200,000 for Panama to $3,175,000,000 for the United States.[14] The capital subscription for each member was divided into three parts:

1. 2 percent, payable in gold or U.S. dollars, which could be used freely by the Bank in any of its operations;

2. 18 percent, payable in the currency of the subscribing member, which might be lent only with the consent of the subscribing member;

3. 80 percent, not available to the Bank for lending, but subject to call if required to meet Bank obligations on its borrowings or on loans guaranteed by it. Payments on such a call, which has not taken place, could be made in gold, U.S. dollars, or the currency required to discharge such obligations as necessitated the call.[15]

As it happened, the Bank never deployed for lending

[13] See p. 54.
[14] Each Bank member has 250 votes plus an additional vote for each $100,000 share subscribed by it.
[15] *The World Bank, op.cit.*, p. 22.

those funds available from the 2 percent paid in by members. In April 1947, a month before the Bank's first loan agreement was signed with France, the United States released for lending the 18 percent of its subscription falling within the second category above.[16] Subsequent years witnessed releases by other members. The remaining 80 percent of the initial capitalization began to play a more active role about 1947. This portion was conceived as a guaranty fund. Although the Bank's management chose not to underpin loans advanced by private initiative, the fund has been utilized to provide backing for debenture obligations issued by the Bank itself.[17]

In 1959 the Bank's potential was strengthened by a substantial change in its financial structure. With the total of Bank borrowing nearing the amount of the original uncalled U.S. subscription, the authorized capital of IBRD was increased to $21 billion. This additional capital—like the original four-fifths of the collective subscriptions—was not paid in. The Bank's "back-up" fund was swelled to nearly $18 billion by this step.[18]

A final primary source of funds[19] for Bank lending is its net earnings. The commission which comprises a portion of the interest charge on Bank loans has gone into a special reserve against Bank obligations, as specified by Article IV, Section 6, of the IBRD charter. Beyond this special

[16] According to members of the IBRD Staff. See also IBRD Staff, "A Note on the World Bank," Appendix to Eugene R. Black, *The Diplomacy of Economic Development and Other Papers* (New York: Atheneum, 1963), p. 168. But cf. IBRD, *Eleventh Annual Report, 1955-1956*, p. 13; *Twelfth Annual Report, 1956-1957*, p. 13; *Thirteenth Annual Report, 1957-1958*, p. 11.

[17] The decision not to employ the IBRD guarantee authority is discussed briefly in Chapter V, below.

[18] Eugene Black, "Financing Economic Development," *United Nations Review*, VIII (February 1961), 21.

[19] "Primary" refers to those sources which do not depend upon a recovery of funds initially lent, and upon which such secondary or revolving sources as sales from the Bank's portfolio and repayments of loan principal ultimately depend. See *The World Bank, op.cit.*, pp. 24ff. Bank portfolio sales are considered below.

reserve, accumulated net earnings amounted to the equivalent of $558,115,003 in mid-1963. IBRD's *Eighteenth Annual Report* indicated that these funds had been allocated to "a Supplemental Reserve Against Losses on Loans and Guarantees Made by the Bank," a process to continue "until further action by the Executive Directors or the Board of Governors."[20] The present disposition of both reserves will be examined shortly.

Financing procedures by IFC, Special Fund, and IDA are much less complex. IFC's initial capital of approximately $100 million came from a subscription of public funds by its member states. The Corporation is authorized to borrow funds against its own securities, although it had not done so through fiscal year 1964. Like the Bank, IFC has accumulated "a reserve against losses" from its net earnings—$18.9 million as of June 30, 1964.

The Special Fund exists on annual contributions pledged by UN members, to a considerable extent in conjunction with their pledges to the UN Expanded Programme of Technical Assistance (EPTA). The United States limits its contributions to 40 percent of the total; several other governments, including India and Japan, make pledges which are contingent upon attainment of a minimum total by the Special Fund and EPTA combined.[21] SF does not have the capability of issuing its own

[20] IBRD, *Eighteenth Annual Report, 1962-1963*, p. 51. The segregation of Supplemental Reserve funds is less rigid than might be thought from this stricture. At the 1963 Annual Meeting, IBRD President Woods felt impelled "to point out, in reply to the comments of one Governor, that it is wrong to speak of the Bank's reserves of $813 million as sitting idle and unutilized. To the contrary, as our reports point out, only the $255 million in the Special Reserve is held in liquid form. The remaining $558 million which is in our Supplemental Reserve is mingled with the Bank's general funds and treated as a part of the investible resources available and availed of for lending purposes." IBRD, *Summary Proceedings, 1963 . . . ,* p. 15.
[21] John G. Stoessinger, "Financing the United Nations," *International Conciliation*, No. 535 (November 1961), pp. 47-48; Special

securities, and, since its paper provision for a reserve fund remains substantially inoperative, it is unable to realize earnings by holding its assets in government bonds.

Initial capitalization of IDA was by government sub-scriptions, which were proportionate to the respective members' subscriptions to capital stock in the Bank. Com-bined subscriptions would have amounted to $1 billion if all Bank members had joined and fully subscribed to IDA.[22] The Association's members are divided into two groups: under the Articles of Agreement, Part I countries make subscription installment payments in gold or freely convertible currencies; Part II countries' payments are but 10 percent in convertible funds.[23] Given its lack of loan income to pay interest on borrowings, IDA as a practical matter has no borrowing capacity, even though the Asso-ciation is authorized to "borrow funds with the approval of the member in whose currency the loan is denomi-nated" by Article V, Section 5 of its charter. IDA realizes a modest if necessarily diminishing return from invest-ment of its resources above loans outstanding, but will presumably not exact loan charges as a further source of earnings. The initial pattern of loans suggests that there will be a substantial time lapse before amortization begins to provide revolved funds, and the rate of this process, once begun, will be slow.

With this introduction to major aspects of financing by the agencies, we can move on to analyze the status of financing capacity during this period in line with the pre-vious indices. Has there been a systematization of the orig-

Fund, *Target: An Expanding Economy* (New York: United Nations, 1963), UN Sales No. 63.I.7, n. 1, p. 27.

[22] See IDA, *First Annual Report, 1960-1961*, Appendix D, p. 13, for a statement of actual amounts and voting power at IDA's beginning.

[23] The remaining 90% is paid in the member's own currency, and may not be used without its consent. See IDA, *First Annual Report, 1960-1961*, p. 4.

inal means of income? Have new means of financing appeared over the years? If so, what means? What are the
respective magnitudes involved?

The original financial resources of three of the four
agencies were provided as subscriptions by member states.
IBRD, IFC, and IDA were set in motion thus. There has
been almost no systematization—or development—of subscriptions as a means to further financing, although a few
marginal cases should be noted.

Insofar as the *establishment* of agencies since IBRD's
own beginning may be considered a development of the
subscription mode of financing, additional government
commitments have occurred in the magnitude of approximately $100 million in 1956 (with IFC), and $1 billion in
1960 (with IDA).[24] The tenuous nature of this mode
should be evident from the previous chapter; it hardly
qualifies as a systematization of the subscription method.

A new round of subscriptions substantially increased the
Bank's "guaranty" fund in 1959. While the magnitude of
this supplementary capitalization dwarfs the initial subscriptions to IFC and IDA alike, the decision by Bank
members should probably be regarded as an ad hoc measure rather than a step toward systematization of a source
of income. Furthermore, it should be emphasized that the
"guaranty" fund is not itself a source of loan money—it is
not even held by the Bank.

Nor can it be said that Article III, Section 1 (a), of the
IDA charter[25] represents a substantial step toward sys-

[24] IDA subscriptions were to be paid over five years. Actual subscriptions for both IFC and IDA were and remain somewhat smaller
than these figures. See the successive statements on subscriptions
which appear as appendices to respective annual reports.

[25] "The Association shall at such time as it deems appropriate in
the light of the schedule for completion of payments on initial
subscriptions of original members, and at intervals of approximately
five years thereafter, review the adequacy of its resources and, if it
deems desirable, shall authorize a general increase in subscriptions.
Notwithstanding the foregoing, general or individual increases in
subscriptions may be authorized at any time, provided that an in-

tematization of government subscriptions as a means of financing. That provision is by no means self-executing. Sweden has voluntarily added one and one-half times the amount of its initial subscription, and Part I members (including Belgium and Luxembourg), along with Kuwait, intend to make available new resources aggregating $753.36 million in freely useable currencies.[26]

In appraising Article III, Section 1 (a) as an indication of systematized resource-procurement, furthermore, the designation assigned both the Swedish gifts and the Part I/Kuwait replenishment is also pertinent. These supplements are labeled "contributions" rather than "subscriptions," the style of the instrument in question.[27]

Hypothetically, *subscriptions* by member states to an international financing agency are supported by a mild sanction. In principle, a potential member cannot join unless its initial fee is paid, and when a subsequent gen-

---

dividual increase shall be considered only at the request of the member involved."

[26] According to its Annual Report for 1963, the proposal by IDA Executive Directors stipulated that "the obligation to contribute new resources should not become binding on any member unless 12 of the prospective contributing members, whose contributions aggregate at least $600 million, give the Association formal notification on or before March 1, 1964, that they will contribute the amounts proposed for each of them." IDA, *Annual Report, 1962-63*, p. 7. On 26 February 1964, the House of Representatives voted to reject and return to committee an Administration bill providing for the United States contribution. C. P. Trussell, "House Rebuffs Johnson in Vote Against Aid Loans [sic]," *New York Times*, 27 February 1964, p. 1. The measure was later retrieved by the Johnson Administration and approved by Congress on 13 May. Meanwhile, the Executive Directors of IDA had set a new deadline—30 June 1964. Twelve governments had formally pledged $670 million by 29 June, and the remaining five contributors were expected to follow shortly. IDA Press Release No. 64/2 of 1 March 1964; "World Bank Unit Set For 2 Years," *New York Times*, 8 July 1964, p. 45.

[27] Cf. IDA, *Annual Report, 1962-63*, pp. 7, 9, with the terminology in note 25, above. It must be noted, confusing though it renders this usage, that Article 19 of the UN Charter employs the phrase "financial contributions" just before the loss-of-vote warning.

eral levy is exacted the member state may be confronted by the possibility of having the weight of its vote lessened if it is not able or willing to resubscribe at the rate assigned.[28] At most, however, such a sanction is a forfeiture of potential or actual benefits and perquisites of state membership in an international association—by no means comparable to the penalty imposed upon the individual by the national state for a willful, extended refusal to pay his taxes. And in practice, even the operation of this relatively mild sanction is subject to vagaries of application.[29]

The potential exercise of the sanction, however, is sufficient basis for an analytical distinction between subscrip-

[28] E.g., Article III, Section 1 (c), of the IDA basic instrument states that "When any additional *subscription* is authorized, each member shall be given an opportunity to *subscribe*, under such conditions as shall be reasonably determined by the Association, an amount which will enable it to maintain its relative voting power, but no member shall be obligated to *subscribe*." Emphasis added. The "contributions" by Part I members did not, of course, devaluate votes of Part II members.

Here the reader's mind may turn to the contemporary dispute over members' financial obligations vis-à-vis other organs and activities in the UN system—Article 19 (*inter alia*) of the Charter and questions concerning interpretation or application, the financial veto or limitation on policy, sanctions for arrearage and both the desirability and feasibility of their implementation. Leaving aside such differences as the purpose and destination of funds, the period of time between financial requests upon member states, and the different decision-making units involved, "assessments" levied by the General Assembly are comparable to "subscriptions" here.

[29] Cf. the comments on arrearage and the non-application of sanctions in the League of Nations in John G. Stoessinger and Associates, *Financing the United Nations System* (Washington: The Brookings Institution, 1964), pp. 38, 39. Chapter V, below, recounts cases of IBRD arrearage in Vignette #1.

UN Congo operation assessments were once classified thus by Prime Minister Macmillan: "There is the compulsory subscription and the voluntary subscription. The only difference between them is this. The compulsory is the one that you do not pay if you do not want to, and the voluntary is the one that you need not pay unless you wish to." Quoted by Inis L. Claude, Jr., "The Political Framework of the United Nations' Financial Problems," *International Organization*, XVII (Autumn 1963), 850.

tions and another type of financial allocation which may be called "government contributions," as suggested by the IDA usage just indicated. Government contributions are financial resources, made available for general agency financing operations by member states, which arise from governmental decisions due to influence short of the threat of expulsion or curtailment of vote in the relevant international institution.

Three actual types of governmental decisions may be included in this category:

1. Since establishment of IBRD, the United States, Canada, and several European members have released for lending portions of their subscriptions which were initially part of the 18 percent paid the Bank in members' currencies but loanable only with the consent of the respective subscriber. These funds had already been accessible to the Bank for certain administrative expenses, but the release of the convertible currencies enhanced the Bank's lending position. (See Figure 2.)

2. SF funds originate as government contributions. As of March 31, 1963, $245 million had been pledged by UN members and members of the UN specialized agencies.[30]

3. As noted above, IDA lending resources have been swelled by the Swedish contributions, and will probably be augmented by a round of contributions from Part I members and Kuwait.

Subscriptions by member governments were necessary to establish the Bank, IFC, and IDA. Either subscriptions or contributions were necessary for the initiation of operations by all the agencies under discussion. Earlier the question of *additional* financing modes was raised—new means or sources developed during the course of functional ac-

[30] Special Fund, *Target . . . , op.cit.*, pp. 26-27. The 1964 SF figure was estimated at $80.7 million; see "Nations Pledge Contributions to EPTA and Special Fund," *United Nations Review*, X (November 1963), p. 33.

FIGURE 2. Cumulative Releases from 18% Capital Subscriptions for Lending or Allocating—IBRD[1]

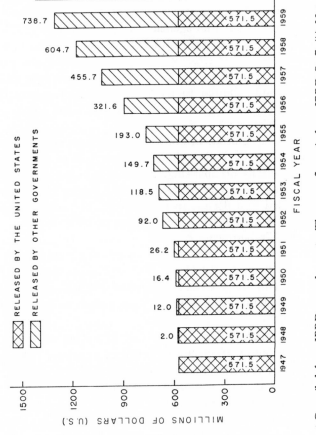

[1] Compiled from IBRD annual reports. The 1947 figure is from IBRD Staff, "A Note on the World Bank."

tivity. These have been described briefly; what remains is to categorize them in terms of the classification scheme set forth in Chapter II, and to indicate the magnitudes involved, where that information is available. Our three categories are (1) revenues from transactions by the agency; (2) borrowing capacity; and (3) regular, systematized contributions from sources other than states.

Three of the four agencies—the Bank, IFC, and IDA—have added their own earnings from transactions to total resources. Most striking among these is the Bank, which in fiscal year 1964 alone enjoyed a net income (not including funds allotted to its Special Reserve) greater than total SF contributions in the Special Fund's best year. (See Figure 3.)

The magnitude of borrowing operations may readily be discerned for IBRD, the only agency yet to make use of this means of financing. Figure 4 provides the picture. During the last two fiscal years, the Bank's fiscal position has led to a decline in its funded debt,[31] although gross borrowings exceeded $100 million in both years.

IFC's borrowing capacity appears to be on the verge of development under most congenial circumstances. An amendment to IBRD and IFC Articles of Agreement proposed by the Executive Directors will authorize International Bank loans of up to $400 million to the Corporation.[32]

If "contribution" is employed in a strict sense, private contributory agents are rudimentary at present. The Ford and Rockefeller Foundations met half the cost of the first three sessions of IBRD's Economic Development Institute; since 1958 the Bank has maintained this program at its own expense. More recently, the Rockefeller Foundation helped pay for library materials sent to member states

[31] This was due largely to the continuing high level of sales of IBRD loans to other investors.

[32] Edwin L. Dale, Jr., "Loan Surge Is Set for Poor Nations," *New York Times*, 2 September 1964, p. 49.

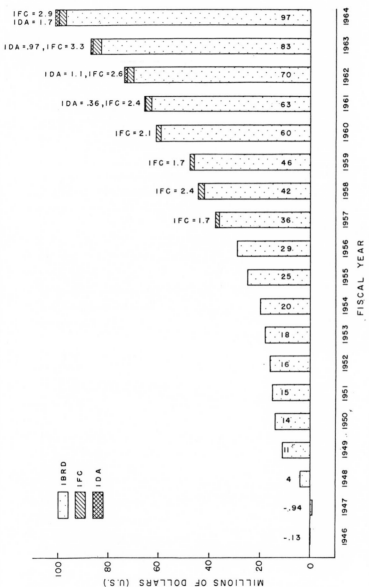

FISCAL YEAR

MILLIONS OF DOLLARS (U.S.)

IFC = 2.9
IDA = 1.7   97   1964

IDA = .97, IFC = 3.3   83   1963

IDA = 1.1, IFC = 2.6   70   1962

IDA = .36, IFC = 2.4   63   1961

IFC = 2.1   60   1960

IFC = 1.7   46   1959

IFC = 2.4   42   1958

IFC = 1.7   36   1957

29   1956

25   1955

20   1954

18   1953

16   1952

15   1951

14   1950

11   1949

4   1948

-.94   1947

-.13   1946

IBRD
IFC
IDA

[1] Compiled from IBRD, IFC, and IDA annual reports.

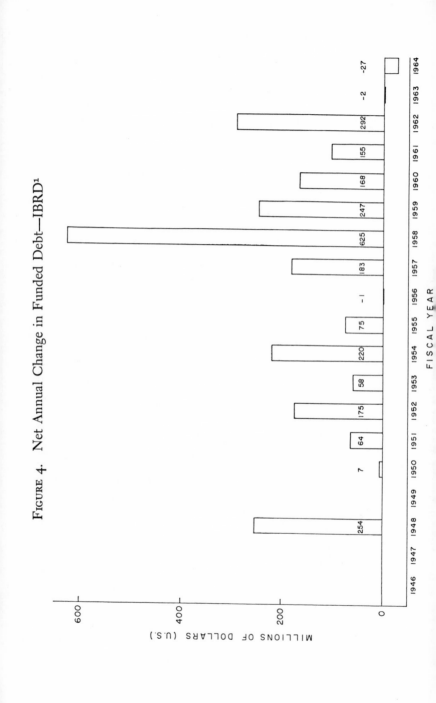

FIGURE 4. Net Annual Change in Funded Debt—IBRD[1]

by the International Bank. In both instances the contribution was tied to a specific project; in one case financing was terminated, and in the other it appears to be terminal. The Special Fund's terms of reference authorize it "to receive donations from non-governmental sources," but little development has taken place along these lines.[33]

A more striking development has occurred at a higher non-state level. In his address to the 1963 annual joint meeting, IBRD President Woods announced that the Executive Directors had agreed it was "no longer necessary automatically to allocate . . . net income . . . to the Bank's Supplemental Reserve." Six months later, at the United Nations Conference on Trade and Development in Geneva, Woods revealed that part of IBRD's future earnings would be transferred to IDA coffers. The Bank's Executive Directors subsequently recommended that $50 million be allocated the Association from IBRD net income for the year. These are not primary funds, as defined earlier, and the transfer between the accounts of international institutions is all in the family, so to speak. Still, the magnitude of the expected allocation and its concurrent transformation to "soft" resources is of some significance.

Another recent IBRD decision may portend further financing or servicing developments. IBRD loan commissions will no longer automatically be credited to the Special Reserve; after July 1, 1964, they are to be classed as "regular income" subject to allocation by the Executive Directors.[34]

[33] IBRD, *Thirteenth Annual Report, 1957-1958*, p. 21; *Sixteenth Annual Report, 1960-1961*, p. 15; General Assembly res. 1240 (XIII), para. 45; Norman J. Padelford, "Private Support of the United Nations," Brookings Institution United Nations Financing Project, Center for International Studies, M.I.T., C/62-11, p. 15.

[34] IBRD, *Summary Proceedings, 1963* . . . , p. 12; Richard E. Mooney, "Poorer Lands Get Warning from U.S. on Trade Accords," *New York Times*, 26 March 1964, p. 1; Shabecoff, "World Bank Head Urges Debt Shift," *op.cit.*, p. 49; IBRD Press Release No. 64/30 of 11 August 1964, p. 1.

If a less stringent definition of "contribution" is applied, several additional developments appear. First, there has been a long-term increase in the magnitude of sales from the IBRD portfolio. (Figure 5.) Total IFC sales now run to $22 million. The Corporation's management claims that in fiscal year 1964 IFC investments elicited seven times their own amount in commitments from participants. These are not contributions in the sense that they are without economic recompense, nor are they primary funds.

FIGURE 5.   Investments Sold or Agreed to be Sold—IBRD[1]

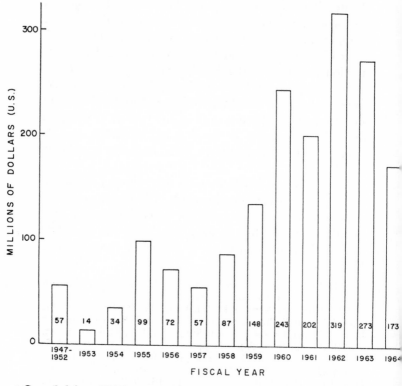

[1] Compiled from IBRD annual reports.

However, they do revolve the funds available for lending or investment, and thus "have the same effect as new capital in that they reduce the amount the Bank [and IFC] would otherwise have to obtain from other sources."[35]

Funds external to the agencies themselves also come from the country where the project is actually undertaken. Some of these funds come from local private investors. The Bank has long held as a guideline for its operating policy the mobilization of local private capital by way of its own loans, and this banner has been prominently displayed over the International Finance Corporation in more recent years.[36] IFC underwriting of share offerings in local capital markets probably contributes to the growth of local contributions, although it is not possible from the information at hand to quantify this development.[37]

In its effort to mobilize investment funds from local sources, the IBRD-IFC leadership has, in some situations, encouraged the adaptation of an existing structure to the dimensions of the need; in other situations it has fostered new growth of this type of organization. The genre is "development company"; beneath the name lurks a variety of actual institutions. They may and do emphasize industry or agriculture. They may utilize loan or equity capital—a distinction which is apt to be blurred in practice. They may be owned by the government, by private interests, or by a combination of public and private share-

[35] *The World Bank*, p. 24.

[36] *Ibid.*, p. 46. Cf. IFC, *Third Annual Report*, 1958-1959, pp. 7f.; *Sixth Annual Report*, 1961-1962, p. 11; *Seventh Annual Report*, 1962-1963, pp. 14ff. In his final address as IFC President in 1961, Robert L. Garner heralded a shift in Corporation policy which would encourage the spread of share ownership in the developing countries, and added: "The ability to draw capital from large numbers of people is a necessary element for sustained growth of modern business. It is the basis of people's capitalism."

[37] IFC, *Seventh Annual Report*, 1962-1963, pp. 3-4. On 4 May 1964 IFC reported that $410,000 in share capital for a tannery in Honduras was raised from private investors, mainly Honduran businessmen.

holders. They may, in their policy-making process, seem a cat's-paw of the governmental planning arm or anemometer of the market mechanism—though more likely, in practice, they may be responsive to both. They may be subnational, national, or regional.

The Bank and IFC have utilized development companies as local institutional adjuncts for their investment operations. The local institutions assess and extend credit to small and medium enterprises, and it has been thought they would promote the productive application of local funds which would otherwise be hoarded, speculated in "non-productive" ventures such as real estate, or invested abroad. It is impossible to analyze the quantitative results of this latter endeavor, though the sheer number of development companies benefiting from technical or material assistance from the IBRD complex would seem at least to indicate that a basis for growth of local contributory sources is rapidly being laid. As of June 1964, the three international agencies had extended a total of $293.3 million to eighteen development companies in sixteen countries.[38]

[38] IFC Staff, "Private Development Finance Companies," June 1964. For further information on development banks, development corporations, and the role of IBRD and IFC, see William Diamond, *Development Banks* (Baltimore: The Johns Hopkins Press, 1959); *The World Bank, IFC and IDA*, pp. 43, 102; "World Bank Holds to Strict Tenets," *New York Times*, 19 February 1950, p. F-1; Black, "The World Bank at Work," *Foreign Affairs*, XXX (April 1952), 407; Asher, *op.cit.*, pp. 349ff.; Black, address before 25th Session of ECOSOC, 17 April 1958; Robert L. Garner, address to the Fifth Annual Meeting of the IFC Board of Governors, 21 September 1961; *United Nations Review*, IX (April 1962), 48; IBRD, annual reports for: 1957-58, p. 21; 1958-59, p. 16; 1959-60, pp. 16-17; 1960-61, pp. 14-15; 1961-62, pp. 17, 20-21, 25-26; 1962-63, pp. 19, 22, 23, 25; IFC, annual report for 1962-63, pp. 4-5; Shabecoff, "Foreign Industry Gets More Funds," *New York Times*, 15 March 1964, pp. F-1, F-10; Shabecoff, "Brazil Is Wooing Foreign Capital," *New York Times*, 4 July 1964, p. 20. Mr. A. G. El Emary of the IFC Staff "assisted the UN Economic Commission for Africa in drawing up plans" for the African Development Bank; IFC,

Two modes of government financing rest comfortably in none of the categories prepared above. The local government payments which the Special Fund requires in conjunction with its own pre-investment allocations share some of the characteristics of the government contribution: they are public funds and come from a "member" government or governments. In other respects they more closely resemble the local private capital which ventures out to participate. They are project-oriented contributions, tied to objectives within the boundaries of the contributing state or region and perforce redounding to its direct economic benefit. Furthermore, aside from the earnest money SF exacts to prime its allocative mechanism, "matching" payments are concurrent rather than agency-collected. Pre-investment funds appear to be powerful money in drawing forth local public expenditures—$374 million earmarked by the SF Governing Council had educed $545 million in commitments by beneficiary governments, or about 60 percent of the total, as of June 1964.[39]

The second mode of financing difficult to classify is best represented by the international consortium. On September 19, 1960, when the Indus Waters Treaty was signed by representatives of the governments of India and Pakistan and the International Bank, representatives from Australia, Canada, West Germany, New Zealand, the United Kingdom, and the United States entered into another agreement with the Indus signatories for the creation of an Indus Basin Development Fund. It was agreed that this Fund would be jointly financed and administered by the Bank. Since then the consortia, strengthened by the participation of Austria (in the Indian consortium), Belgium, France, Italy, Japan and the Netherlands, have entered

---

Seventh Annual Report, 1962-1963, p. 9. Earlier, IBRD assisted the Inter-American Development Bank in its organizational phase. IBRD, *Eighteenth Annual Report, 1959-1960*, p. 7.

[29] *UN Monthly Chronicle*, I (July 1964), 52.

into further joint financial commitments to the Indian and Pakistani Five-Year Plans.[40] The magnitude and breakdown of these commitments is indicated in Figures 6 and 7. Again, financing is similar in several respects to

FIGURE 6

PROGRAM OF AID TO INDIA'S THIRD FIVE-YEAR PLAN
(in millions of U.S. dollars; Indian fiscal years)

	1961-62	1962-63	Two-Year Total	1963-64 1965-66	Total
Canada	28	28	56	—	56
France	15	15	30	—	30
Germany	225	139	364	61	425
Japan	50	30	80	—	80
United Kingdom	182	68	250	—	250
United States	545	500	1,045	—	1,045
World Bank & IDA	250	150	400	—	400
TOTAL	1,295	930	2,225	61	2,286

Reproduced from IBRD, *Sixteenth Annual Report*, p. 6.

the government contribution, as defined earlier. Public funds come from IBRD members. However, they are tied to a particular agreement and bound for a specific destination, rather than entering into the general lending resources of the IBRD complex. It may be noted that the operative financing criteria for the second round of commitments to India and Pakistan are less stringent than those applied in most IBRD-IFC-IDA financing: the consortium underwrote not a project but a plan.[41]

[40] IBRD, *Sixteenth Annual Report*, 1960-1961, pp. 6, 7; *Seventeenth Annual Report*, 1961-1962, p. 8; *Eighteenth Annual Report*, 1962-1963, p. 7; "World Bank Aids Pakistan Project," *New York Times*, 8 April 1964, p. 64; "Consortium Pledges $1 Billion to India," *New York Times*, 27 May 1964, p. 1.

[41] An IFC innovation in private investment participation was announced early in June 1964. ADELA, an Atlantic Community Development Group for Latin America comprising banks and industrial corporations in Western Europe and the United States, invested $500,000 in a Colombian steel forgings plant at the time of IFC's

Both the SF beneficiary contribution and the consortium arrangement stand part way between universal and bilateral financing patterns. An international agency plays

FIGURE 7

PROGRAM OF AID TO PAKISTAN'S SECOND FIVE-YEAR PLAN
(in U.S. dollars; Pakistan fiscal year 1961-62)

	Recommended Additional Commitments	Already Committed	Total
Canada	18.0	19.8	37.8
France	10.0	—	10.0
Germany	25.0	37.5	62.5
Japan	20.0	20.0	40.0
United Kingdom	19.6	22.4	42.0
United States	150.0	129.6	279.6
World Bank & IDA	77.4	—	77.4
TOTAL	320.0	229.3	549.3

Reproduced from IBRD, *Sixteenth Annual Report*, p. 7.

a leading role, supported on an ad hoc basis by individual state contributors. The procedure calls to mind contemporary financing experiences elsewhere in the United Nations system. Norman J. Padelford aptly describes this as financing by "parties at interest."[42] The parties may be disputants, or governments sufficiently concerned with a particular UN policy for other reasons. The most recent cases of support by parties at interest are the UN peace-seeking operations in Yemen and Cyprus.[43] The extent to

investment of $1 million and the Corporation's aid in underwriting an additional $1 million stock issue for the venture. This IFC-syndicate arrangement parallels the IBRD-public participant consortia.

[42] Norman J. Padelford, "Financial Crisis and the Future of the United Nations," *World Politics*, XV (July 1963), 563-64. Padelford mentions the Korean operation and the UN administration in Western Irian in 1962-63 (UNTEA) as examples. Cf. Stoessinger, *Financing the United Nations System*, p. 42.

[43] Richard N. Gardner, "Needed: A Stand-by U.N. Force," *New York Times Magazine*, 26 April 1964, p. 112.

which the UN operations in the Middle East (UNEF) and the Congo (ONUC) will prove in fact to have been financially underwritten by parties at interest remains to be seen. In any case, it may be predicted that hybrid support arrangements have a future in both UN security operations and programs financing economic development.

We close this inquiry with a qualification and a question. The appearance and expansion of financing modes which might have been especially significant in buttressing the functionalist contention is less conclusive than the latter part of the analysis might seem to indicate. For none of these means is "new" in the sense it was not foreshadowed by the relevant basic instrument; none is utterly detached from the circumstances accompanying the birth of the agency involved. The means of financing beyond government subscriptions and contributions might be described as *contingent* means. But to label them contingent raises further questions which must be followed in the chapter on interpretation: Contingent upon what? With what consequences?

Representation and Participation Patterns

A second indication of increased structural support for functional activity would be a development of representation and participation patterns beyond those existing at the initiation of any particular function. David Mitrany implies that increased participation is one means by which an expansion to fit common needs takes place. Paul Reinsch's widening-circles metaphor is relevant once again. Patterns of representation and participation by nation-states will be analyzed here, and the analysis must be extended to the role of non-state actors, in accordance with suggestions offered by Mitrany, Lyman C. White, and others.[44]

[44] Besides the writings by Mitrany and White cited previously, see White, "Peace by Pieces—The Role of Nongovernmental Organizations," *The Annals of The American Academy of Political and*

Representation and participation are understood here as instrumental elements within the functional mechanism: as receptors and communicators of needs, and effectors of their fulfillment. The functionalists seem to understand these elements as providing double service—even as they aid in need-fulfillment they become the intermediaries through which attitude change ramifies outward. The tentative proposition that increased representation and participation indicate ipso facto an unalloyed strengthening of the function must be reviewed later. For the moment we leave aside this question and look to positive indicators. What is the record of representation and participation by member states through the years? Is there evidence of representation and participation by non-state actors?

The basic information needed to begin this assessment is an over-all picture of the status of state membership in the several agencies through the years. Membership data for the IBRD triad are presented in Figure 8.[45]

It will be apparent that the IBRD-IFC-IDA membership complex has not come to include state actors of all ideological hues. The Soviet bloc is not represented therein.[46] On the other hand, the Special Fund's Governing Council, for which the Economic and Social Council is directed by the General Assembly to include an equal representation of more and less developed states among its appointments, includes representatives from across the political spectrum, as well.[47]

Social Science, No. 264 (July 1949), 87-97; White, "Non-Governmental Organizations and Democracy," *NGO Bulletin*, V (November 1953), 437-41; Jusuf Buch, "The Role of Non-Governmental Organizations in the Implementation of the Principles of the United Nations," *idem*, V (October 1953), 375-78; and issues of *International Associations, passim*.

[45] Figure 8 includes data from IBRD, Press Release No. 64/2, 4 February 1964, p. 2.

[46] See Chapter V, Vignette #1.

[47] General Assembly res. 1240 (XIII), paras. 11, 13, 14. On 11 December 1963 the General Assembly voted to enlarge the SF Gov-

FIGURE 8

NEW FINANCING AGENCY MEMBERS (BY FISCAL YEAR)

	1946	47	48	49	50	51	52	53	54	55	56	57	58	59	60	61	62	63	64
Afghanistan											B		C			A			
Algeria																			B, A
Argentina												B			C			A	
Australia			B									C				A			
Austria												C				A			
Belgium	B											C				A			
Bolivia	B											C				A			
Brazil	B											C				A			
Burma							B					C							
Burundi																		A	B, A
Cameroon																		A	B, A
Canada	B											C				A			
Central African Republic																			B, A
Ceylon					B							C				A			
Chad																			B, A
Chile	B											C				A			
China	B															A			
Colombia		B										C				A			
Congo (Brazzaville)																			B, A
Congo (Leopoldville)																			B, A
Costa Rica	B											C				A			
Cuba	B											C			Bx, Cx				
Cyprus																	B, C, A		
Czechoslovakia	B								Bx										
Dahomey																			
Denmark	B											C				A			B, A
Dominican Republic	B											C			Bx, Cx	Bx, Cx		A	

FIGURE 3 (continued)

Country	1946	47	48	49	50	51	52	53	54	55	56	57	58	59	60	61	62	63	64
Ecuador	B											C					A		
Egypt	B											C		**			A		
El Salvador	B											C				A			
Ethiopia	B											C				A			
Finland			B									C				A			
France	B											C				A			B, A
Gabon																			
Germany								B					B, C						
Ghana													C						
Greece	B															A			
Guatemala	B											C					A		B
Guinea																			
Haiti									B			C				A			
Honduras	B											C				A			
Iceland	B											C				A			
India	B								B			C				A			
Indonesia												C					Cx		
Iran	B											C				A			
Iraq	B											C				A			
Ireland										B			B			A			
Israel		B										C		C		A			
Italy		B										C							
Ivory Coast																		B, C, A	C
Jamaica																		B	
Japan								B				C				A			
Jordan								B				C				A			
Kenya																			B, C, A
Korea											B					A			C
Kuwait																		B, C, A	A
Laos																	B		A
Lebanon																	A		
Liberia		B										C					B, C, A		

FIGURE 8 (continued)

	1946	47	48	49	50	51	52	53	54	55	56	57	58	59	60	61	62	63	64
Libya	B													B, C			A		
Luxembourg												C							A
Malagasy Republic																			B, C, A
Malaysia‡													B, C			A			
Mali																			B, A
Mauritania																			B, A
Mexico	B											C				A			
Morocco													B			A		C	
Nepal																	B	A	
Netherlands	B											C				A			
New Zealand																	B, C		
Nicaragua	B											C				A			
Niger																		B, A	
Nigeria	B											C				B, C	A		
Norway	B											C				A			
Pakistan				B								C				A			
Panama	B											C					A		
Paraguay	B											C				A			
Peru	B											C					A		
Philippines	B											C				A			
Poland	B				Bx											B			
Portugal																			
Rwanda																			B, A
Saudi Arabia													B			A			
Senegal																		C	
Sierra Leone																		B, C, A	
Somalia																		B, C, A	
South Africa	B											C						B, C, A	
Spain															A				
Sudan														B	C	C, A			
Syria	B													**		B*	C, A		

FIGURE 5 (continued)

	1946	47	48	49	50	51	52	53	54	55	56	57	58	59	60	61	62	63	64
Sweden							B					C				A			
Tanganyika																		B, C, A	
Thailand			B									C				A			
Togo																		B, C, A	
Trinidad & Tobago																			B
Tunisia													B			A		C	
Turkey		B										C				A			
Uganda																			B, C, A
United Arab Republic														**		A			
United Kingdom	B											C				A			
United States	B											C				A			
Upper Volta																		B, A	
Uruguay	B																		
Venezuela	B											C				A			
Vietnam												B				A			
Yugoslavia	B																		

Symbols indicating beginning of membership:
  B—International Bank for Reconstruction and Development
  C—International Finance Corporation
  A—International Development Association
  x indicates termination of membership
  r indicates resumption of membership
** The governments of Egypt and Syria merged as the United Arab Republic. On 18 July 1958
  United Arab Republic was substituted for Egypt and Syria on the Bank's records.
* Syrian Arab Republic resumed separate membership.
‡ Malaya until 1964.

If "participation" is construed to include monetary contributions, the circle is further widened by the Special Fund. By 1963, 105 governments had contributed.[48] Participation in Special Fund operations by way of *reception* of direct benefits had enlarged the SF circle to 121 countries and territories by early 1964.[49] Both contributors and recipients included Soviet bloc countries.

Membership has expanded and participation by state actors increased, though the over-all pattern is uneven in the important respect noted. In the interpretative chapter this question must be followed, if only in indirect fashion: How, if at all, does the functionalist thesis explain this unevenness?

In several respects the enhanced operative status of non-state actors is a more important functionalist contention than a widened circle of nation-state participants. State actors may be the initiators and signatories of those limited liability associations to which Mitrany refers; certainly the nation-state is the physical medium through which the products and by-products of functional activity must move. But the state, in its functional association with other states, provides only a necessary condition for the ramification of these benefits. In a sense, state membership is the façade behind which developments more important to the functionalists are held to take place. The factors in this more significant process are experts and non-governmental organizations (NGOs).

---

erning Council to twenty-four states. (GA res. 1945 [XVIII].) Five days later ECOSOC elected Denmark and India to one-year terms, Sweden and Tunisia to terms of two years, Nepal and the Federal Republic of Germany for three years each. Other members of the Governing Council at its Eleventh Session, 13-20 January 1964, were Argentina, Brazil, Canada, France, Ghana, Indonesia, Italy, Japan, Mexico, Netherlands, Norway, Philippines, Poland, Senegal, Union of Soviet Socialist Republics, United Kingdom, United States, and Uruguay.

[48] Special Fund, *Target* . . . , pp. 26-27. This total includes the Holy See.

[49] "New Special Fund Projects," p. 25.

In Mitrany's argument the expert occupies a central position. His expertise assures an appropriate solution to problems which arise in the area of his competence. These areas were chosen by "natural selection" and the binding together of common interests in the first place, and it is the expert's assignment and his special glory to keep his functional domain uncontaminated by politics or controversy. In so doing he acts as the unassuming handmaiden of the functional dynamic. Most important, his expertise and his dedication to technique provide one of the main factors in laying the foundation of obligation which is a necessary implication of the functionalist thesis.[50]

If the functionalist contention is valid, we might expect to witness an increasingly prominent role for the expert in the course of the financing programs. In fact, a rather mixed pattern emerges.

As understood in international parlance, "expert" in its purest form refers to a person selected for a position demanding technical proficiency or skill by virtue of his special competence in that field, and not because of his geographic residence, citizenship in a given nation-state, or political views. He serves in his capacity as an individual. In conjunction with the financing programs, the nearest approaches to a permanent, formalized, and relatively autonomous status for such technicians have probably been the subcommissions which operated for a short time under the Economic and Employment Commission. A more transitory manifestation of expertise is the appearance of groups of experts appointed on an ad hoc basis for specific studies.

Yet both the subcommissions and the ad hoc expert groups provide a rather perverse outcome for the functionalist prophecy. The subcommissions were absorbed into their parent body, which itself disappeared in the early fifties—a fate which would seem not only to breach the

[50] See above, Chapter II.

functionalist promise but also, in view of the rather considerable activity of those particular subcommissions, to
fly in the face of the Lamarckian law of organic development.[51]

The ad hoc experts' conclaves have lost ground to intergovernmental committees in recent years. What would
otherwise seem to be simply a wayward trend by functionalist lights attains the status of paradox when we observe,
with Hadwen and Kaufmann, that member states which
might have seemed most eager for functional development
along financial lines were precisely the ones whose representatives hailed the changeover to an inter*governmental*
committee to study the SUNFED proposals as a "big step
forward in comparison with previous resolutions under
which groups of experts had made reports."[52]

Finally, it must be noted that approaches to an unadul-
terated status of appointment-for-expertise generally have
been tarnished by the exercise of "representative" criteria,
even though the overtones of recruitment from the great

[51] That which was said by the French delegate of the 1951 report
entitled *Measures for the Economic Development of Under-Developed Countries* (*op.cit.*) might well have been the earlier thought
of certain others when the Subcommission on Economic Development made its recommendations: "the experts had compiled a
document in which technical considerations played their part, but
which appeared, in more than one respect, to be little more than a
manifesto. It seemed, indeed, like a sign of the times—men of
science venturing to encroach on the field of political action."
Quoted by Asher, *op.cit.*, n. 73, pp. 621-22. See also Harold Karan
Jacobson, *The USSR and the UN's Economic and Social Activities*,
pp. 220-21, 225.

[52] Hadwen and Kaufmann, *op.cit.*, p. 92. NB that the Committee
on a United Nations Capital Development Fund is similarly of the
intergovernmental genre.

The ad hoc expert has to a certain extent found his way toward
the field. IBRD, e.g., makes use of him on its survey missions; it
also appoints him to serve on panels such as the one which reviewed
tenders submitted by manufacturers for a proposed nuclear power
station in southern Italy. See IBRD, *Fourteenth Annual Report*,
1958-1959, pp. 8-9. Figures on SF use of experts in the field appear
below.

powers and from across the political spectrum are generally muted by the customary homage paid "geographic" selection.

What muddles this picture is the extent to which expertise has been institutionalized in the UN secretariat—at UN headquarters, in the field, in the regional commissions, and on the IBRD-IFC-IDA Staff. Certain quantitative aspects of this phenomenon will be assayed in the final section of the present chapter.[53]

If there is a bridge between expertise and representation in the functionalist scheme, that bridge is provided by "the relevant non-governmental organisations."[54] They bear certain attributes of both the expert and the representative. The assumption of an increasingly important position for NGOs in the course of the given programs would, if borne out, indicate a growth in structural support for functional action. What *is* the record?

One widely used text in international organization disposes of the question for some of the agencies in a single sentence: "The Bank, IFC, and the [International Monetary] Fund do not maintain official relationships with NGO's."[55] The absence of such relationships is raised to the level of principle in the Report of the Committee on Site (for IBRD) tendered at the inaugural meeting of the Bank's Board of Governors. That report offered as one reason for its choice of Washington over New York the

[53] See also IBRD, *Fifth Annual Report, 1949-1950*, p. 17; Asher, *op.cit.*, p. 1044; Hadwen and Kaufmann, *op.cit.*, pp. 19ff.; Gunnar Myrdal, *Realities and Illusions in Regard to Inter-Governmental Organisations* (London: Oxford University Press, 1955), especially pp. 21ff.; Stephen S. Goodspeed, *The Nature and Function of International Organization* (New York: Oxford University Press, 1959), p. 385.

"Representative" criteria are certainly not absent in the Bank's recruitment. IBRD annual reports point with pride to the number of nations represented on the Bank Staff. In June 1964 this figure stood at 62 nationalities for the regular staff.

[54] Mitrany, "International Cooperation in Action," p. 647.

[55] Goodspeed, *op.cit.*, p. 403.

nature of the International Bank, which, "as an intergovernmental institution, should be free of any possible influence from economic, financial, or commercial private
interests."[56]

The lack of influence that is offered as a sort of moral
imperative by the Committee on Site is made a generalization on the actual potency of NGOs by two astute UN
participant-scholars: "Much will depend on the importance of the organization in question but the direct influence of NGO's on decision-making at the U.N. is relatively
small since governmental representatives are not in a position to alter radically the instructions they receive. It is
possible that the NGO's are more influential in the social
and human rights fields than they are in the economic
field where financial considerations place the emphasis on
specific governmental decisions rather than on general attitudes towards problems discussed in the U.N."[57]

This thesis, NGO impotence throughout the UN system
and double impotence in economic affairs, does appear to
provide an explanation for one sequence of events concerning IBRD. That agency's Articles of Agreement direct
"an Advisory Council of not less than seven persons [to
be] selected by the Board of Governors including representatives of banking, commercial, industrial, labor, and
agricultural interests, and with as wide a national representation as possible," and the Articles specify that for
the "fields where specialized international organizations
exist, the members of the Council representative of those
fields shall be selected in agreement with such organizations."[58] The first members were to advise the Bank in
1948.[59] This panel met at the Bank in 1948 and again in

[56] IBRD, Inaugural Meeting of the Board of Governors, Savannah,
Georgia, 8-18 March 1946, *Selected Documents*, p. 62. Emphasis
added.

[57] Hadwen and Kaufmann, *op.cit.*, pp. 23-24.

[58] Article V, Section 6.

[59] It included Sir Arthur Salter (United Kingdom), chairman;
Edward E. Brown, Chicago banker, and former President Herbert

1949, after which the chairman advised the Bank's President and Board of Governors that in his opinion and that of the majority of Advisory Council members no such group was likely to have a value commensurate with its cost in time and money. The Bank's Executive Directors recommended that selection of Advisory Council members for the next two year term be deferred pending a study of all matters relating to the body. On September 16, 1949 the Board of Governors endorsed the recommendation. No Advisory Council members have been appointed since. This budding functional assembly has, in effect, withered away.[60]

We have been seeking evidence of the participation of non-state actors in the financing programs. The initial

---

Hoover, from the United States; S. K. Albert Sze, Chinese diplomat; Lionel C. Robbins, British economist; Michal Kalecki, Polish economist; Leon Jouhaux, French labor leader; Col. R. Dickson Harkness, Canadian industrialist; Sir C. Venkata Raman, Indian scientist; and Pedro Beltran, Peruvian financier.

[60] IBRD, *The International Bank for Reconstruction and Development, 1946-1953* (Washington: IBRD, 1954), pp. 22-23; IBRD, Fourth Annual Meeting, *Proceedings*, p. 24.

On the other hand, IFC now has a panel of advisers—five bankers who periodically offer "the benefit of the private investor's judgment on investments." Present experts are Hermann J. Abs, Director, Deutsche Bank A.G., Frankfurt; Viscount Harcourt, Managing Director, Morgan, Grenfell & Co., London; Dr. Raffaele Mattioli, Chairman, Banca Commerciale Italiana, Milan; Andre Meyer, Senior Partner, Lazard Freres & Company, New York; and Baron Guy de Rothschild, a partner in de Rothschild Freres, Paris. George D. Woods, while Chairman of The First Boston Corporation, New York, served as an IFC adviser prior to his presidency. IFC, *Sixth Annual Report, 1961-1962*, p. 5; *Seventh Annual Report, 1962-1963*, p. 9. Furthermore, the Bank's Economic Development Institute is counseled from time to time by a Universities Advisory Committee composed, in September 1963, of Simon Kuznets, Professor of Economics, Harvard University; Edward S. Mason, Professor of Economics, Harvard University; Max F. Millikan, Director, Center for International Studies, Massachusetts Institute of Technology; Theodore W. Schultz, Chairman, Department of Economics, University of Chicago; Robert Triffin, Professor of Economics, Yale University; and C. A. Curtis, Professor of Economics, Queens University.

inquiry led to an unproductive examination of the formalized relationship between NGOs and the primary financing agency—IBRD. An expectation shared by persons who espouse such relationships is the application of expertise by groups or their representatives; Mitrany's desire for "a functional assembly . . . composed of people who really know something about the task in hand"[61] is reasonably typical of the NGO school of thought. In this circle, little attention is given the articulation of private interests. Select NGOs were summoned into the tribunal and assigned advisory status: they were not expected to work their way into the corridors to press their own specific demands. This appears to be the conception behind formalized NGO arrangements in the UN system.

Modern scholarship shows that interest groups on the domestic scene are related to the political apparatus in ways infinitely more subtle and complex than that nexus symbolized by the legislative chamber, the legislature's lobby, and the legislator's buttonhole. By extending the notion of participation, we may find that non-state actors have played a greater part in the financing programs than a first view would suggest.

The inquiry might be prefaced by recounting facets of various financing operations which engage the private sector. Two operations immediately catch the eye. One is the sale of securities from IBRD and IFC portfolios to institutional investors. A comparable transaction, the commitment of private funds to the project at the time the agency's loan agreement is consummated with the borrower, is called a "participation." The other financial operation is the sale of IBRD's own debentures in the capital market. Part of the Bank's bonds are placed with public or quasi-public holders—central banks and government special accounts, for instance. Many are placed with commercial banks, insurance companies, or other private

[61] Mitrany, "International Cooperation in Action," p. 647.

corporations, or sold to them in the securities market.[62]

The magnitude of Bank borrowing and sales from portfolios has been noted.[63] To what extent has the over-all secular increase been matched by an extension in the circle of private holders of Bank or local securities?

One obvious trend is an internationalization of Bank bondholders. The early Bank bond issues were placed in the United States; by mid-1961, however, 53 percent of the Bank's outstanding funded debt was held by investors in approximately forty countries other than the U.S. The Bank's $100 million bond issue of August 28, 1961, alone was placed with fifty-three institutional investors in thirty-two countries, not including the United States.[64]

---

[62] See, e.g., "U.S. Plan to Increase I.M.F. and World Bank Funds," *The Times* (London), 27 August 1958, p. 12; "International Bank Lent $711m. Last Year," *idem*, 7 October 1958, p. 15; IBRD, *Eleventh Annual Report, 1955-1956*, p. 16; *Seventeenth Annual Report, 1961-1962*, p. 13; *Eighteenth Annual Report, 1962-1963*, pp. 14-15.

[63] See figures 4 and 5.

[64] IBRD, *Sixteenth Annual Report, 1960-1961*, p. 13; "U.S. Plan to Increase I.M.F. and World Bank Funds," *op.cit.*, p. 12; IBRD, *Seventeenth Annual Report, 1961-1962*, p. 13.

In at least one case the placement of dollar bonds seems to have aroused a certain amount of antagonism within purchasing countries. Note this *New York Times* dispatch of 11 October 1956 under the title "Europe Dubious on World Bank":

"The World Bank has been almost too successful in raising capital outside the United States, in the opinion of influential European financial circles. There is nothing but admiration for the bank's success, as a technical operation. But there is beginning to be a good deal of doubt as to whether, by this success, it is making the contribution it should to a better balance in the world economy. . . . Of . . . $850 million [in Bank] bonds about $695 million are payable in dollars. And of these dollar bonds, about 36 per cent are held outside the United States. The non-dollar bonds are mainly sterling, guilder and Swiss Franc securities. This means that a substantial part of the dollars given to the bank for relending is furnished by West European investors. It is a sign of West Europe's economic strength that this is now possible. . . . [but] there is a feeling . . . that Europe ought not to be contributing dollars to the rest of the world, or even, so to speak, to itself. Putting it the other way around, Europeans feel that while they may well be able to contribute their own currencies for relending by the World Bank,

The incidence of buyers from Bank and IFC portfolios shows a similar trend. IBRD's *Eleventh Annual Report* states that non-U.S. buyers "have become increasingly interested," and it offers a chart to show that in fiscal year 1954 United States purchases became a minority of the total. By mid-1956 the percentage of sales from Bank loans made to purchasers outside the U.S. had mounted to 58 percent of the total. During the year ending June 30, 1964, IFC sold securities to financial institutions in Europe, the United States, and the Middle East; Corporation investments reportedly were joined by direct financing from forty institutions domiciled in France, Germany, Hong Kong, India, Italy, Japan, the Netherlands, Sweden, Thailand, the United Kingdom, and the United States. There is some evidence that the circle of participants has advanced into areas local to the respective projects.[65]

But the relationship with the private sector does not exist solely on the input side of financing operations. IBRD's charter allowed it to make loans to private enterprise, and the Bank has gone about as far as it could go in this direction.[66] More striking in a constitutional sense is

---

dollars ought to come from the United States. There is [a] particular grudge against the bank now in Switzerland because it just borrowed $50 millions from the Swiss Government, at a rate of interest considerably more favorable than the rate it would have had to pay on the Swiss capital market." (p. 61.)

In this instance the widening circles of functional participation may be regarded as a questionable instrument of cooperation.

[65] IBRD, *Eleventh Annual Report,* 1955-1956, p. 15; cf. *Thirteenth Annual Report,* 1957-1958, pp. 12-13; *Sixteenth Annual Report,* 1960-1961, pp. 7f.; "International Bank Lent $711m. Last Year," p. 15. More specifically, see the listings of purchasers and participants in IFC annual reports, participations by individual project in the annexes to IBRD annual reports, and references to participants in IBRD and IFC press releases, e.g., IFC Press Release No. 64/9 of 4 May 1964.

[66] Paul Heffernan, "World Bank: New Look," *New York Times,* 30 September 1957, p. 41. But cf. the comments of George D. Woods at the 1963 meeting, in *Summary Proceedings,* pp. 11f.

IFC. One of the chief arguments invoked on behalf of its establishment was the awkwardness of situations compelled by the Bank charter's state-guarantee requirement. The Bank's placement of state-guaranteed loans for relatively autonomous projects and IFC's investments directly into the private sector thus represent two steps in the direction of substantial relationships with non-state actors on the output side of the financing programs. IFC's authorization to draw upon IBRD resources no doubt will make the latter step even more significant.

Finally, an extension in the locus of expenditures from Bank disbursements has taken place. There was a time when these funds were spent almost altogether in the United States; at least one Bank president has had to deny that loans were tied in fact if not in principle. By mid-1961, however, over 50 percent of the Bank's disbursements had been spent outside the United States. Countries whose firms have received major portions of these orders include the U.S., the U.K., Germany, France, Italy, Canada, Japan, Belgium, Switzerland, Sweden, and the Netherlands, in the order listed. The same eleven countries are the primary recipients of expenditures from IDA credits, although their rank order is different. The magnitude of expenditures in Japan was almost twice that of the U.K., which was second as of mid-1964.

Several phases of the financing operations with a close relationship between financing agency and private economic sector have now been outlined. What has this to do with the representation and participation of non-state actors? Are not these financial relationships a rather tenuous basis for concluding that there has been an increase in non-state representation and participation?

The question is an important one. In Chapter VI we shall return to it in order to give closer attention to the implications of certain specific aspects of this relationship. The point pertinent to the present inquiry is established: there has been an increase in structural support for these operations by way of an expansion in financial participation by non-state actors on both the input and output sides of financing programs.

Field Capacity

A third structural support development implied by the functionalist argument is an extension of the capacity for field action. If functional activity is propitious, that argument implies, it will be crowned with new patterns of organization and activity in the field. The functionalist contention suggests that widening circles of state membership and non-state participation will be accompanied by an extension of the functional arm itself.

Structural aspects of this outstretch will be considered under three headings: (1) indications derived from a survey of administrative expenditures; (2) relevant administrative reorganizations; and (3) the personnel gap and prospects for coordination.

ADMINISTRATIVE EXPENDITURES

An overview of the magnitude and growth of field operations may be gained from the analysis of relevant administrative costs through the years. IBRD expenditures are the subject of Figure 9. In fiscal year 1950 a new category was included in the Bank's annual accounting—"Special Technical Services." This category was carried the next year and showed a moderate increase. The report for 1951-1952 initiated an amended version, "Special Services to Member Countries," which was derived retroactively for the previous year and remained the designation for three subsequent reports. Since 1956 the category has been simply "Services to Member Countries." Items during recent years include the following: general survey missions, project and sector studies, resident representatives, missions, cooperative programs with FAO and UNESCO, Economic Development Institute, training programs, set-

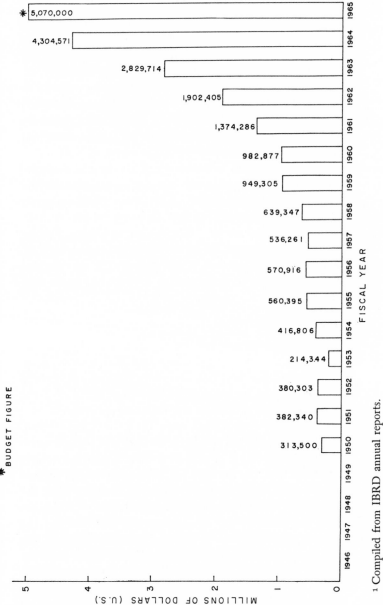

tlement of investment disputes, and other services, whether advisory or of an unspecified nature.

Only circumstantial evidence of the development of field capacity comes from records of administrative expenditures by IFC and IDA. The two largest categories in the respective administrative expense columns, "personal services" and "travel," probably include the amounts relevant to this inquiry. (See Figure 10.) Both categories show a substantial increase over the years.

Figure 11 presents a breakdown of Special Fund administrative costs. "Operational Services"—in particular the Technical Assistance Board (TAB) subvention—suggests a tremendous expansion of field capacity. Additional indicators are buried under "Administrative Costs." For instance, the allocation for travel, "essential to the development and operation of sound projects in an efficient manner," as one budget message stresses, has more than tripled.[67]

STAFF REORGANIZATIONS

One Mitranian use of the organismic analogy is the suggestion that functional efforts will bear a series of organizational modifications, including "mitosis" of existing elements, so as to better serve emergent needs. Is there evidence of this process in the financing programs?

It might be argued that since IFC, the Special Fund, and IDA all followed IBRD chronologically, their *seriatim* appearance signals a process of structural growth wrought by productive functioning. To be germane to the present inquiry this would demand a further showing: that the appearance of the newer organs indicates an extension toward the field. In this connection it is sufficient for the moment to note that IFC and IDA were to share the Bank's facilities, while the Special Fund's small staff was to rely heavily upon existing UN units for the execution

[67] SF/L.24, p. 9. Actual travel figures are included under "Other departmental costs" in Figure 11.

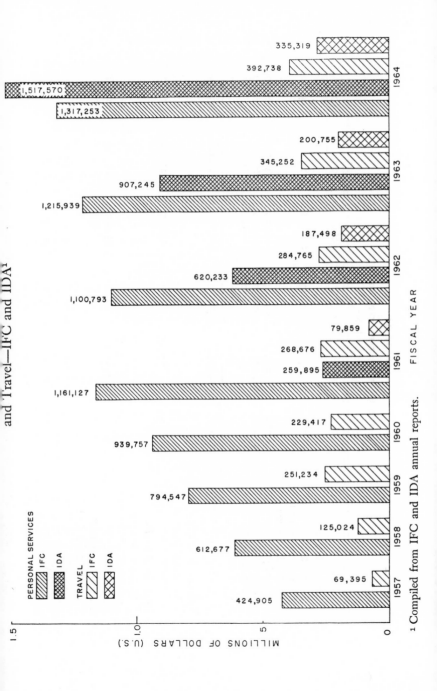

and Travel—IFC and IDA[1]

PERSONAL SERVICES
IFC
IDA

TRAVEL
IFC
IDA

FISCAL YEAR

MILLIONS OF DOLLARS (U.S.)

1.5
1.0
.5
0

1957
424,905
69,395

1958
612,677
125,024

1959
794,547
251,234

1960
939,757
229,417

1961
1,161,127
259,895
268,676
79,859

1962
1,100,793
620,233
284,765
187,498

1963
1,215,939
907,245
345,252
200,755

1964
1,317,253
1,517,570
392,738
335,319

[1] Compiled from IFC and IDA annual reports.

FIGURE 11

SPECIAL FUND STAFF EXPENDITURES

(in U.S. dollars)

	1959	1960	1961	1962	1963*	1964†
Administrative costs						
Salaries & wages	186,267	324,742	405,223	599,428	881,700	1,247,000
Other departmental costs & common services	32,731	82,549	68,294	82,139	140,500	203,500
Common staff costs	58,372	104,953	169,677	210,422	367,200	383,600
Hospitality	91	80	70	154	1,000	1,000
Contingencies	—					
TOTALS	277,461	512,324	643,264	892,143	1,390,400	1,835,100
Subvention to UN for central financial services	—	—	—	14,555	22,500	22,500
Operational services						
Managing Director's costs for preliminary investigations	#	#	2,648	13,983	10,000	10,000
Subvention to TAB for SF-related field services	—	150,000	410,000	771,200	1,504,100	2,814,000
TOTALS	277,461	662,324	1,055,912	1,691,881	2,927,000	4,681,600

* Approved estimates. † Budget figures. # Included under *Administrative costs.*

Compiled from "Administrative Budget Estimates," 1959 through 1964, UN docu-

of SF projects. These comments on the field capacity of post-Bretton Woods agencies relate to the significance of their genesis, not the question of their development. The status of IBRD field capacity is rendered all the more important as an object of inquiry by the Bank's expanded assignment as facilitator of IFC and IDA operations and executor of certain SF projects.

Several organizational changes during the lifespan of the IBRD Staff suggest an extension of the Bank's field capacity—as well as that of the other three agencies, insofar as they utilize the same facilities. Recent announcements also indicate developments with regard to the IFC Staff.

(a) On November 1, 1951, the Bank's Staff Office was redesignated the Technical Assistance and Liaison Department. To the previous responsibility for liaison with other international organizations and the development of "policy recommendations with respect to matters not falling within the jurisdiction of any of the other departments"[68] was added an assignment of responsibility for "the Bank's technical assistance activities."[69] While not a structural subdivision, this marked the advent of formal organizational status for the technical assistance activities already undertaken by IBRD.

(b) In September 1952 the Bank reorganized its operational arm, "primarily to provide for more systematic and continuous contact between the Bank and its member countries."[70] The Loan and Economic Departments were made over into four new operating departments, three of them territorial in focus. These were designated the Departments of Operations for Asia and Middle East, for Europe, Africa and Australasia, and for the Western Hemisphere. The fourth unit was named the Department of Technical Operations. It was assigned the duty of "assessing the economic, financial and technical merits of

[68] IBRD, *Second Annual Report, 1946-1947*, p. 22.
[69] IBRD, *Seventh Annual Report, 1951-1952*, p. 40.
[70] IBRD, *Eighth Annual Report, 1952-1953*, p. 42.

projects proposed to the Bank for financing, and of following the progress of projects financed by the Bank."

The Bank reported at the end of its next fiscal year that the reorganization had "contributed to improved liaison with member countries and borrowers, and . . . had a generally beneficial effect on Bank operating methods."[71]

(c) In its annual report for 1956-1957, IBRD announced a division of geographic responsibilities in the best functionalist style: "In April a new Department was formed in the Bank to assist in handling the growing volume of work in Asia. Over the last two years, the total lent in that region has more than doubled and a corresponding increase has taken place in the Bank's advisory work. Responsibility has therefore been assigned to a separate Department of Operations, Far East. . . . Relations with the remaining countries that were formerly the responsibility of the Department of Operations, Asia and the Middle East . . . are now handled by the Department of Operations, South Asia and the Middle East. . . ."[72]

(d) The Bank established a special staff unit in fiscal year 1960 to "study the development of the capital markets of various member countries. . . ." At the end of the year it reported that several country studies had been launched and others were planned. One objective of these studies was to determine "whether and how the Bank might provide further technical assistance in the creation and expansion of such markets."[73]

(e) A Department of Operations for Africa was created in fiscal year 1962 by splitting the Department of Operations for Europe, Africa, and Australasia.

(f) In the same year, the Bank organized a Development Services Department; this "absorbed the Technical Assistance and Planning Staff."[74] To judge from name

[71] IBRD, *Ninth Annual Report, 1953-1954*, p. 43.
[72] IBRD, *Twelfth Annual Report, 1956-1957*, p. 26.
[73] IBRD, *Fifteenth Annual Report, 1959-1960*, p. 16.
[74] IBRD, *Seventeenth Annual Report, 1961-1962*, p. 9.

alone, the headquarters-field department bespeaks a development more comprehensive in scope and more systematic in execution.

(g) IFC set up a Development Bank Services Department during 1962, and directed this department to take the lead in considering "all proposals for financial and technical assistance to industrial development banks by the World Bank and its affiliates. . . ."[75] It was later redesignated the Department of Operations—Development Finance Companies.

(h) IFC's engineering group has recently become the IFC Engineering Department, suggesting a strengthened organizational base for field operations.

In the beginning the staff of the Special Fund grew larger without growing noticeably more complex, as though preformed at conception. For several years the Office of the Managing Director, the Bureau of Operations, and the Joint Administrative Division were the major organizational units. The Bureau of Operations was functionally subdivided for Research and Agriculture, Engineering, and Training in keeping with the original pre-investment trinity. As the pace of SF project-contracting quickened, personnel were added to the Operations Bureau. Here rested the responsibility for evaluation of project requests and follow-up investigation of project implementation, both of which involve intimate contact with conditions in the field. A Reports unit was created in the Bureau of Operations to collect and systematize information on the status of project execution.[76] In 1963 the Bureau of Operations was reorganized. Research, Training, and Surveys were given divisional status and joined by a "Special Projects Section."[77] These changes in the organi-

[75] IFC, *Sixth Annual Report, 1961-1962*, pp. 3, 5.

[76] John B. Edwards, "The Politics of the United Nations Special Fund," unpublished M.A. thesis (Berkeley: University of California, 1963), pp. 46-47.

[77] UN doc. SF/L.73, p. 15. Today the Special Fund lists nine major headquarters units: Office of the Managing Director, Bureau

zational pattern imply an increased capacity for communication with the field.

PERSONNEL AND COORDINATION

The definitive interpretation of technical assistance activities via multilateral channels is yet to be written.[78] When this full accounting does appear, it may well include among its themes the pragmatic or, better, the groping, stop-gap nature of early measures, and a survey of the divers activities swept under the rubric "technical assistance" through the years. Here the functionalist claim of creative evolution seems well substantiated, at least at the level of description.

Technical assistance is related to the financing of economic development in respects vastly more complicated than it is possible to explore here. One very direct relationship is the increasing assistance in the field by the financing agencies themselves. An idea of the development and diversification of IBRD practice, for instance, may be conveyed by statements made at various times through its history.

As early as 1947 the Bank acknowledged a need exceeding its current task: "The less well developed nations need international assistance for full realization of their potentialities. They need not only financial assistance but technical assistance. Because they lack the advanced technology and skills which characterize the more highly developed nations, the Bank may well be requested to exercise more initiative in considering their problems and to participate more actively in the formulation of their plans. While the Bank cannot undertake to furnish technical assistance from its own staff on any large scale, it can help

---

of Operations, Research Division, Surveys Division, Training Division, Special Projects Section, Reports Section, Financial Management Section, Joint Administration Division. SF/L.90, p. 10.

[78] He who undertakes this assignment will find valuable information in Walter R. Sharp's work, *Field Administration in the United Nations System* (New York: Frederick A. Praeger, 1961).

its member nations to select and procure the necessary private technicians. The Bank stands ready at any time to consult with member governments on this matter."[79]

Two years later the Bank sent a 14-member survey mission to Colombia, thus demonstrating its own willingness to "offer its members technical assistance which transcends individual loans."[80] The Colombian mission was the first in a series of comparable undertakings which had reached a total of about twenty-five by 1963.[81]

The survey mission proved to be "the forerunner of other forms of developmental assistance, especially . . . resident representatives in selected member countries to assist governments in the programming and execution of measures for economic development." It was a "logical outcome of [IBRD] interest in the formulation of development policies" for the Bank to establish, in 1955, an Economic Development Institute to train senior economic management personnel. Junior officials are trained by the Bank itself.[82] In mid-1964 the IBRD "staff college on economic development" had 317 alumni.

[79] IBRD, *Second Annual Report, 1946-1947*, p. 14.

[80] Eugene Black, "The World Bank at Work," p. 409.

[81] Black, "Financing of Economic Development," p. 22. See IBRD, *Eleventh Annual Report, 1955-1956*, pp. 24-25, for a description of the types of missions dispatched to that date. In addition to survey missions of various kinds, the Bank sends out "end-use" missions to check on use of loan resources. See Sharp, *Field Administration . . .*, p. 30. In his Paris address of 4 June 1964, IBRD Vice President Wilson indicated that Bank missions sometimes "recommend measures and help carry them through on the spot; a written report has been only an incidental product of their work."

[82] "A Note on the World Bank," in Black, *The Diplomacy of Economic Development* (Cambridge: Harvard University Press, 1960), pp. 67-68; Black, "Financing Economic Development," p. 22; "New Training Program of International Bank," *United Nations Bulletin*, XIV (1 February 1953), 121; "Two World Bank Training Schemes," *United Nations Review*, II (March 1956), 51; Dana Adams Schmidt, "Men of 18 Nations Attend School for Money Managers," *New York Times*, 4 December 1957, pp. 59f.; IBRD, "The Economic Development Institute," September 1963. The special access of IBRD resident representatives to governments in a few cases is briefly described by Andrew Shonfield in *The Attack on World Poverty*, pp. 119-20.

It would seem these programs extended the Bank's reach. Yet despite efforts to provide its own personnel and train local officials for service far from IBRD headquarters, a rising demand prompted the Bank to seek other responses. Eugene Black announced a "major innovation" in his address to ECOSOC on April 5, 1962:

"In recent years, we have been receiving an increasing number of requests from our member countries to provide resident advisers to help in resolving the major policy problems which inevitably arise in preparing and carrying out development problems. Although we have done our best to meet these requests, we have found it difficult to do so. . . .

"Our aim is to establish a new career service of highly qualified persons willing to undertake repeated assignments of this kind in the developing countries—a pool of experienced talent upon which the Bank will be able to draw, in appropriate cases, to meet requests for assistance when they are received."[83]

The Development Advisory Service (DAS) had been brought forth in November 1961 as a division of the Bank's Development Services Department; by 1963 its pool of experts numbered about twenty persons.[84] While this and the earlier measures demonstrate the remarkable verve of IBRD, the task grows apace.

The shortage of qualified local personnel has been both a major focus for some Special Fund pre-investment and a negative factor in the implementation of other SF projects. By January 1964, "advanced education and technical training" projects totaled 143.[85] At the same time, the belated local allocation of suitable counterpart personnel had hampered the fulfillment of some SF contracts,

---

[83] Black, "Greatest Immediate Challenge Facing Mankind," p. 27.
[84] IBRD, *Eighteenth Annual Report, 1962-1963*, p. 16.
[85] Governing Council of the Special Fund, *Report on . . . Eleventh Session*, 13-20 January 1964, E/3854, Table 3, p. 20.

prompting Paul Hoffman to comment on this bottleneck in his statement to the Food and Agriculture Organization Conference of 1961. "In some cases governments have not recognized that the Special Fund means business. . . ."[86]

Like IBRD and its affiliates, the Special Fund has made growing use of experts in the field. Relatively free-floating consultants—mostly from Western nations—have played a major role before and during project implementation. The Special Fund claimed 1,300 international experts in the field in 1963, a thirteenfold increase over 1960. About 2,000 will be serving by the end of 1964.[87]

Resident representatives of the Technical Assistance Board, already actively involved in SF matters, gained a new hat in 1961, adding a designation as "Directors of Special Fund Programmes."[88] Hoffman reported that 76

[86] Hoffman, "Principles of U.N. Special Fund Assistance," 13 November 1961, as quoted by Edwards, *op.cit.*, p. 56. FAO had been given contracts for 146 SF projects as of January 1964. By way of comparison, IBRD held 18 during the same period. See Special Fund, *Target . . .* , pp. 32-47, 50-52, and "New Special Fund Projects," pp. 26-30.

A scarcity of qualified personnel and the related implication, by the SF Managing Director, of a failure of national will in allocating this scarce resource are not the only reasons offered for tardy project implementation. In the same address Hoffman cited delinquent local financial contributions and inadequate provision of "the promised buildings, facilities and use" for expensive equipment. Another explanation was offered at the Eleventh Session of the Governing Council, where "several members" expressed the view that implementation had been slow because "Executing Agencies had not yet sufficiently adjusted their internal organization to cope with the steadily increasing work-load in carrying out Special Fund projects." E/3854, p. 8.

[87] "New Special Fund Projects," pp. 25, 27.

[88] SF/L.54, p. 17, as cited by Edwards, *op.cit.*, p. 49. More recently, Hoffman has proposed "a high-level consultant, appointed by the [SF] Managing Director" with the agreement of the government concerned, to advise that government on possibilities for investment follow-up of SF projects. While General Assembly resolution 1715 (XVI) provided some of the impetus for this proposal, it received less than universal acclaim among UN member states. Edwards puts it well: "some governments are wary of having the Special Fund provide advice on the sources of investment capital

field offices were manned by 150 international officers in 1963; a joint EPTA-SF establishment of 83 offices was proposed for 1964.[89] The SF budgetary component for these offices rose from 9 percent in 1960 to 45 percent in 1964.[90]

Resident representatives assist SF operations by

(a) advising Governments on Special Fund criteria and policies, receiving and forwarding to Headquarters Government requests for assistance, obtaining such clarifications and amplifications of questions emerging from requests as may be required by the Managing Director or the Government, and negotiating revisions in requests; . . .

(b) participating as the Managing Director's representative in negotiations of Plans of Operation for approved projects and working with Executing Agencies and the Government to develop detailed arrangements for the implementation of projects; and

(c) providing administrative support on behalf of Executing Agencies for projects in operation, and reporting to the Managing Director on the progress of field operations.[91]

In pre-SF days, A. D. K. Owen observed that among "the principal functions given the [resident] representative" was that of advising the local government "with respect

rather than becoming one of those sources itself." See Edwards, op.cit., pp. 75-77; SF/L.64; SF/L.64/Add. 1; SF/L.64/Add. 2.

[89] SF/L.73, p. 24; E/3854, p. 4; E/TAC/131, p. 37. For a list of established posts, see ibid., table 2, pp. 48-51. According to Target . . . , op.cit., p. 11, more than 900 local persons have also been recruited.

[90] SF/L.90, p. 5.

[91] SF/L.37, pp. 2-3. See also SF/L.54; Sharp, Field Administration . . . , p. 412, passim; Sharp, "Trends in United Nations Administration," pp. 395, 404-05; C. Hart Schaaf, "The Role of the Resident Representative of the United Nations Technical Assistance Board," International Organization, XIV (Autumn 1960), 548-62.

to the preparation and co-ordination of its requests for assistance. . . ."[92] There is little evidence this type of technical assistance has diminished with the appearance of the Special Fund.

In his outline of the progression of functionalism, Mitrany suggests that, as individual functional activities flourish, a stage of inter-functional coordination may be expected, followed by the development of international planning.[93] It may be conjectured that the virtual absence of Special Fund operative machinery has stimulated not only the field capacity of executing agents but also the coordination of their activities. Substantiation of the hypothesis demands a much closer look at both the headquarters and field levels than this analysis can offer. Pending such an investigation, Walter Sharp has provided some notes:

"The range of inter-secretariat cooperation [between units in the UN system] has been noticeably extended as a consequence of the establishment of the Special Fund. . . . Not only does the Special Fund management call upon the UN and specialized agencies to execute projects, but they frequently participate by request in the tasks of evaluating project applications before any decision is taken on them by the Managing Director of the Fund. It is significant that virtually no new machinery was created to serve the Special Fund.

.   .   .   .

"The advent of the Special Fund has brought the International Bank . . . into a closer relationship with the United Nations in two different ways. First, by agreeing to serve as the executing agent for Special Fund projects in the engineering field, the Bank is involved in types of staff

[92] A. D. K. Owen, "The Technical Assistance Programme of the United Nations," *The Political Quarterly*, XXII (October-December 1951), 327.
[93] See above, p. 13.

contact with the UN both at headquarters and in the field that scarcely existed earlier. More important still are the arrangements for periodic consultation between the management of the Special Fund and the President of IBRD relating to the 'pre-investment' potentialities of Fund projects under consideration. In order to encourage such consultation, the General Assembly in 1958 authorized the establishment of a 'Consultative Board' composed of the Secretary-General, the Executive Chairman of TAB, and the Bank's President. The Board's function, in the strict sense, is to advise the Managing Director concerning program proposals and project requests, and in this capacity the Board normally meets about two months prior to each meeting of the Governing Council of the Fund. But it is not improbable that the Board may come to play a more significant role once the new International Development Association gets under way. One can conceive of this channel of UN-Bank-IDA collaboration being gradually extended to the over-all evaluation and coordination of economic development programs in given areas. . . ."94

"Coordination" is a word of many moods. From one perspective, the need for coordination of the financing programs is wrought by a rising demand for scarce resources—men and money. As such, coordination may be extolled as a device to render more rational the allocation of resources, or on the other hand it may be prescribed as a substitute for further allocations. From another perspective, coordination is a problem bound up with the conflict of institutional loyalties among international entities, a neglected focus in an age of Cold-War, state-actor analysis. It may be that functional coordination will develop through—not merely despite—inter-agency jurisdictional disputes, shielded in part by the walls of the Con-

94 Sharp, "Trends in United Nations Administration," pp. 404, 405; see also primary sources cited. Cf. Shonfield, op.cit., pp. 108-09; George D. Woods, address to ECOSOC, 18 December 1963, p. 9 of reprint.

sultative Board meeting-room, unheralded largely because on-site altercations are dispersed to the southern corners of the earth. Already a certain amount of peaceful competition among prospective SF executing agents has occurred. One suspects there is an intimate relationship between such tensions, fruitful tensions, as they may prove, and Hoffman's plea for the appointment of country-level directors of United Nations Development Assistance programs recognized by host governments and UN agencies alike "as having general responsibility for the planning, administration and operation of all United Nations technical assistance and pre-investment activities."[95] The recent EPTA-SF "merger" proposal is bound up with these tensions, too; its coming treatment and its subsequent fate may well serve as prime examples of the process of "coordination" and its products.

Perhaps Mitrany foresaw just this process. In his projection of the functional dynamic he puckishly observes that coordination "may in some cases amount almost to arbitration of differences between functional agencies. . . ."

With some relatively minor exceptions, the functionalist contentions about structural support seem to be borne out for the agencies and indices followed here. Yet these claims, after all, are the less important ones. Functional efforts are dedicated to the solution of problems, not the raising of organizational monuments. The efficacy of functional efforts is to be gauged less by quantitative indications than by the *solutions* for these problems, and by the closely related consequence which is to accompany participation in the problem-solving process: the change of attitudes by participants. These variables will hold our attention in the next chapter.

[95] E/AC.49/R.2/Add. 12, as quoted by Edwards, *op.cit.*, p. 50.

V

Functional Consequences: Problem-Solving and the Change of Attitudes

WE SHIFT now from an assessment of structural change in the course of the financing programs to a consideration of other consequences suggested by the functionalist argument. In doing so, we move nearer the central contentions advanced on behalf of the functional approach to international organization. Structural manifestations may strengthen and consolidate ongoing functional activity, but they are distinctly subordinate to the goal of attitude change and the ubiquitous claim of problem-solving.

The analysis will be modified for the present undertaking. In the last chapter most indicators were positivistic: relative to the evidence now to be ordered, at least, those inquiries would be easily replicable. Here we venture into the shadowy realm of subjectivity. This analysis will use as a framework for investigation the functionalist claim of problem-solving; attitude-change by participants will be drawn in within the interstices of the discussion, where it is pertinent to the problem-solving leitmotif.

In an earlier chapter the functionalist argument was criticized for apparent weaknesses in its treatment of problem-solving. At that point the issue was the argument's intrinsic adequacy. Here we wish not only to inquire about the extent to which problems have actually been solved but also to test whether the application of "problem-solving" as a conceptual overlay leads toward insights otherwise unexploitable in an investigation of the programs financing economic development. Answers must emerge from the investigation. First, however, it may be well to draw a more complete picture of what would seem to be involved in two sharply divergent problem-solving situations.

When the solution of problems was discussed before, a "problem" was held to imply at least an observer and that which is observed. The relationship between these elements necessary to a problem situation involves an indeterminate kind and degree of tension. The tension may be asymmetrical; that is, it may be felt only by the observer toward what he observes. On the other hand, tension may be symmetrical, which suggests a further aspect of some problems: the "observed" may itself prove to be an *observer* of its own self-styled problem, and this second problem may include observer #1. The "observed," that is, may be human, may be plural, may indeed be adjudged a problem in part or in whole because of its "inner" conflict. From the archangels' viewpoint, at least, "observer" and "observed" in such circumstances rapidly tend to lose any distinction beyond that applicable as an analytical exercise, for to add to the complexities already mentioned, the *observer* too may be plural, may disagree as to the nature of the problem, may even be in open self-antagonism.

This, however, is not the expectation of the functionalists. This hodge-podge is just what a functional approach avoids; it is avoided through the "functional" or "natural" selection of "those interests which are common, where they are common, and to the extent they are common." Common interests converge at the point of commonly felt needs; to say that the need is met is to say in effect that the problem has been solved. One further point must be reiterated. The functionalist contention is generalized by pointing to economic and social sectors as the most promising areas for initiating efforts to bind together common interests; problems in other sectors will be all the more easily solved by approaching them circuitously. One reason for the ease of this progression is the spirit of cooperation generated among participants by joining and pulling together in solving the initial problems.

In investigating the solution of problems through the financing programs we must be prepared to find either of these patterns, but also it is well to prepare for the appearance of capricious configurations wavering between the extremes of this continuum. To provide a means for assessing change, the problem-solving process may be stretched and analytically divided into several phases in order to provide general guidelines for this inquiry: (1) recognition that a problem exists; (2) definition of the problem; (3) finding and agreeing on a solution to the problem; (4) application of the solution; (5) acceptance of the solution, as manifested by a general acknowledgment that the problem has been or is being solved by the solution tendered and applied.

It may readily be admitted that problem-solving in everyday experience tends to be a seamless web of activity, not a series of phases. Problem-solving for the functionalists is conceived in much the same manner. We do not want or intend to do violence to actuality by this construct. However, it would seem that even the simplest problem-solving cases would register in some of the categories. The most complex, intractable problem would make a sharp impression in the earlier analytical phases—if perforce falling short of leaving its mark in the latter ones. The fullest validation of the functionalist contention would demand that phase #5 be completed.

Part of the foundation for assessing problem-solving and change of attitude has been laid in the preceding chapters. Thus, an introduction to "economic development" as a problem is provided by reference to the origin and status of economic development financing agencies, their membership, and participation therein. But it is necessary to press the inquiry further to ascertain the extent to which this problem has been recognized and met. We shall move closer and reorient our view.

Two foci seem especially promising in this quest. One is the perspective provided by viewing the evolving situation in terms of the current—perhaps the changing—"problem" seen by those responsible for the management of the financing agencies: by attempting to look over their shoulders, as it were. The second focus embraces the context of certain major decisions made in the course of the financing programs. Where a shift in position by an important participant has occurred, understanding of problem-solving and the change of attitudes alike may be enhanced by scrutinizing this process more closely. This will be done by three vignettes, slices of functional life taken from the circumstances surrounding crucial junctures in the financing programs. Hopefully these excursions may augment the perspective for a concluding assessment of the functionalist contention on problem-solving.

The Perception of Institutional Tasks

Statements of purpose in the basic instruments or other relevant official documents of the agencies selected for study give some feeling of the clarity and single-mindedness with which economic development has been authoritatively acknowledged to be a problem over this time-span. These statements of purpose have not changed for any single agency, but the establishment of the several agencies covers the period fairly well.

At a general level, indicating recognition that a problem exists, these documents demonstrate some change of goal, but hardly more than would be expected from their names. As set forth in the Articles of Agreement of IBRD, the Bank's purposes center upon "the reconstruction and development of territories of members," and "equitable consideration" is to be given "projects for development and projects for reconstruction alike." Twelve years later, reconstruction has been dropped as a purpose, but of course development remains: the International Finance Corporation is directed by its charter "to further economic development. . . ." In October 1958, the General Assembly resolution establishing the Special Fund calls for a similar orientation: "The Special Fund is envisaged as a constructive advance in United Nations assistance to the less developed countries which should be of significance in accelerating their economic development. . . ." And the International Development Association's purposes are "to promote economic development, increase productivity and thus raise standards of living in the less-developed areas of the world. . . ."

If these statements of purpose are approached at a slightly less general level, however, an interesting shift in language appears.

Article I of IBRD's charter calls for the Bank's basic purposes to be realized by "*facilitating* the investment of capital for productive purposes, including the *restoration* of economies destroyed or disrupted by the war, the *reconversion* of productive facilities to peacetime needs and the *encouragement* of the development of productive facilities and resources in less developed countries." The words emphasized here sound a tone of optimism and testify to high expectations for short-run measures designed to restore and reconvert some economies and to facilitate and encourage others. The mood of optimism toward reconstruction is again evident in the latter part of Article I, which calls on the Bank, "in the immediate postwar years, to assist in bringing about a smooth transition from a wartime to a peacetime economy." The facilitation and encouragement of growth elsewhere is to be accomplished through the promotion of private foreign investment, and Article I (ii) of the Bretton Woods document seems to indicate that this may be accomplished primarily by means of "guarantees or participations in loans and other investments made by private investors." Thus, "finance for productive purposes out of its own capital, funds raised by it and its other resources" was seemingly perceived as being an exceptional measure, necessary only "when private capital is not available on reasonable terms," and then only "to supplement private investment."

The facilitation and encouragement of growth through measures to promote the flow of private capital is again the proximate objective in IFC's statement of purposes. The Corporation is directed to "seek to stimulate" and to "help create conditions conducive to" this flow of private capital.

General Assembly resolutions concerned with the Special Fund, however, exhibit a different emphasis. The assumption of a more active approach to economic development is evident in two respects:

1. There is an endorsement of the need to develop foundations of economic growth. For instance, both General Assembly resolutions 1219 (XII) and 1240 (XIII) take note of "the particular needs of the less developed countries for international aid in achieving accelerated development of their economic and social infrastructure."[1] The latter resolution sets forth as one of the Special Fund's guiding principles the provision of "systematic and sustained assistance in fields essential to the integrated technical, economic and social development of the less developed countries."

2. The resolutions express a determination to move toward economic development both deliberately and with dispatch. For instance, the objective is no longer merely to facilitate or even encourage growth, but "to promote social progress and better standards of life in larger freedom." More important is the resolve to "employ international machinery" in this promotion of social and eco-

[1] The term "infrastructure" has seen a great deal of usage in recent years. For purposes of this study, the definition offered by Sir Robert G. A. Jackson is satisfactory. In *The Case for an International Development Authority*, edited with an introduction by Harlan Cleveland (Syracuse: Syracuse University Press, 1959), p. 39, Jackson states that the term "covers such basic needs as ports, transportation, urban housing and power development which are the preconditions of more varied economic advance." Jackson adds that he would include the human element: "education, technical training, health, and social services. . . ."

nomic advancement. This determination is supported by a rather tentative reference to the need for public capital investment, and to a somewhat greater extent by the reference to "systematic and sustained assistance."

The two resolutions are filled with a sense of immediacy. These phrases are symptomatic: "accelerated development"; "urgent needs"; "a rapidly achieved enlargement in . . . financial resources and . . . technical assistance"; "assistance . . . of immediate significance"; "early results."

The Preamble to IDA's Articles of Agreement is a veritable functionalist creed:

"The Governments on whose behalf this Agreement is signed, *Considering*:

"That mutual cooperation for constructive economic purposes, healthy development of the world economy and balanced growth of international trade foster international relationships conducive to the maintenance of peace and world prosperity;

"That an acceleration of economic development which will promote higher standards of living and economic and social progress in the less-developed countries is desirable not only in the interests of those countries but also in the interests of the international community as a whole. . . ."

Thus, the IDA Preamble would seem to add to official statements of urgency whatever support might be implicit in the authoritative acknowledgment of rapid economic development as a common interest.

While a rapid-fire comparison of purposes embedded in basic instruments conveys a sense of change from founding to founding, we need conceptual modes nearer to actual operations to arrive at even the most tentative conclusions regarding modifications in definition of the problem and solutions perceived.[2] A. D. Lindsay's notion of "operative

[2] Cf. James D. Thompson and William J. McEwen, "Organiza-

ideals" provides a clue,[3] though his notion must be tailored to our own objectives. Insofar as possible, we want to make explicit the tasks perceived for their agencies by individuals significant in the formulation of financing policy. For shorthand purposes these can be called "perceived tasks," and their comparison will aid an analysis of the expansion or contraction of the assignment assumed on behalf of each agency by its management.[4] In terms of the previous problem-solving model, this should reveal something further about how an acknowledged problem has been defined and what "solutions" have been selected.

The aura of optimism in IBRD's statement of purposes was to fade with a subsequent realization of the magnitude of European dislocation during the war. For the first years of the Bank's existence, however, this mood permeated the statements of its officials and informed the operations which they perceived to be that institution's assignment. The Bank's proclaimed duty during this period might be

tional Goals and Environment: Goal-Setting as an Interaction Process," *American Sociological Review*, XXIII (February 1958), 23: "In the analysis of complex organizations the definition of organizational goals is commonly utilized as a standard for appraising organizational performance. In many such analyses the goals of the organization are often viewed as a constant. . . . It is possible, however, to view the setting of goals (i.e., major organizational purposes), not as a static element but as a necessary and recurring problem facing any organization. . . ."

[3] A. D. Lindsay, *The Modern Democratic State* (London: Oxford University Press, 1943), I, 3, 43, 45. "[W]hile an association can only be understood in the light of its purpose, no association is entirely inspired by its purpose; that is, is never entirely what it is supposed to be. . . . [T]o understand human associations it is as necessary to take into consideration their falling short of the purposes which inspire them as to remember that they are actually inspired by these purposes. . . . Political theory . . . is concerned with fact, but with fact of a particular kind. Its business is to understand the purposes or ideals actually operative in sustaining a political organization. These purposes or ideals may vary from time to time. . . ."

[4] Cf. Ernst B. Haas, "The Comparative Study of the United Nations," *World Politics*, XII (January 1960), 309; Haas, "International Integration: The Regional and the Universal Process," *International Organization*, XV (Summer 1961), 368.

called a "guaranty task." Its clearest formulation was offered by Henry Morgenthau, Jr., U.S. Secretary of the Treasury and President of the United Nations Monetary and Financial Conference, in his closing address at Bretton Woods: "The chief purpose of the International Bank for Reconstruction and Development is to guarantee private loans made through the usual investment channels. It would make loans only when these could not be floated through the normal investment channels at reasonable rates."[5]

With the early groundwork laid by the Articles of Agreement and this statement, the Bank's official representatives continued to render pronouncements that could be viewed as deductions from the basic proposition. John W. Snyder, a later U.S. Secretary of the Treasury and Chairman of the IBRD Board of Governors, stated in his opening address at the first session of that board in 1946 that the Bank's tasks were "assisting in the restoration of war-devastated areas [and] . . . stimulating the flow of international capital for development purposes." The Bank's first President, Eugene Meyer, looked back over a brief history to his institution's founding for the guiding principle he pronounced in presenting the First Annual Report. "The International Bank," he said, "was created to assist in the reconstruction and development of the territory of its members by facilitating the investment of

[5] "Analysis by Morgenthau of Monetary Agreements," *New York Times*, 23 July 1944, p. 25. Cf. Russell Porter, "Diplomatic Gains Credited to Soviet in Monetary Move," *New York Times*, 24 July 1944, p. 11: "The 'final document' on the International Bank . . . showed that the 'bank' is no bank at all, but primarily an institution for the guaranteeing of international loans, like the function performed by a New York title company in guaranteeing mortgages. Only 20 per cent of its assets would be useable for making direct loans, and there were few conference delegates who felt that the direct lending function would be exercised." U.S. Under Secretary of State Dean Acheson told Congressmen that the IBRD "function will be to investigate the soundness of . . . projects . . . and, if it agrees they are sound, . . . guarantee the loans made by private banks."

capital for productive purposes. This is the only sound basis on which any international lending institution can be conducted."[6]

The Bank's Second Annual Report develops approximately the same argument in the context of a cause-effect diagnosis and prescription: "The Bank cannot . . . do the whole job [of development in Latin America, Asia, Africa, and the Middle East]; it cannot by itself do even a substantial portion of the job. Development on the scale that is within the range of practicability needs financial assistance in amounts which only established credit and the consequent free flow of private capital can provide."[7]

Yet in truth the Bank never undertook the guaranty task contemplated at Bretton Woods and implied or expounded afterwards. To guarantee loans involving varied lenders and borrowers would breed chaos in the market, it was decided. The more passive Bank role as guarantor was rejected in favor of an IBRD task as lender.

Assumption of the task of direct lending did not mean an end to the quest for a "free flow of private capital"; it simply implied a Bank role as pump-primer. And to its role as lender the Bank added a "removal-of-obstacles" task. "There exist today a number of deterrents to the free flow of private capital, and with it of foreign technical, managerial and administrative skills, to the underdeveloped nations. If the Bank, by use of its resources, its influence and the technical specialists on its staff, can help to remove some of these deterrents, it will have achieved an important task in the development field."[8]

[6] IBRD, First Annual Meeting of the Board of Governors, *Proceedings and Related Documents*, pp. 6, 9.

[7] IBRD, *Second Annual Report*, 1946-1947, pp. 12-13, 14.

[8] *Ibid.*, p. 13. As if to keep its new assignment in perspective, the Bank, in the next paragraph of the same report, reminded some of its members of the scale of priorities in loosing this flow of private capital: "The first step is the improvement of the credit position of many of the countries concerned. There are several things which those underdeveloped nations with a poor credit standing can do

Though the task had been expanded, the premise remained the same. The basic problem was still seen to be the drying up of the flow of private international capital which had made possible the lush economic growth of another day. The solution, clearly, was the restoration of that flow. And the Bank's role was to titillate the keepers of the well-springs and clear the channels, where necessary.

During the next few years the Bank became more aware of the "job" of development, and its official statements reflect a shifting emphasis in this concern. On his retirement from the Bank presidency, John J. McCloy emphasized that the "reconstruction phase" was "largely over" and the "development phase" at hand.[9] Development loans by the Bank initially were advanced in accordance with a guideline of direct productivity. As a minimum, lending for productive purposes meant screening requests so as to assure an excellent chance they could and would be repaid. Eugene R. Black wrote in April 1952 that the Bank's lending rate was "being increased as fast as possible—subject always to the limitation that more will not be loaned than the borrowing country can utilize effectively and has a reasonable prospect of repaying."[10] "Productivity" implied primarily that the project involved would itself rapidly become capable of carrying repayments.

But if repayment was the minimum objective, something more was implied. As Black wrote in the same article, the Bank was seeking "to finance those projects which will bring the most important benefits to the borrowing country in the shortest time."[11] A list of the "most important benefits" a borrower could realize would certainly have continued to include near its top that in-

---

to improve their position. Perhaps the most effective would be for them to clear up their external debt records."

[9] IBRD, Press Release No. 136, 18 May 1949.
[10] Black, "The World Bank at Work," *Foreign Affairs*, p. 403.
[11] *Ibid.*, p. 404.

creased rate of private investment to be induced by productive loans. But Black emphasized a more far-reaching aspect of productivity, as well, and offered as specific examples certain of the projects the Bank had already aided. "Through lending," he wrote, the Bank "assists in raising productivity *and providing basic facilities* on which further investment can be built. . . . A major test of any project the Bank is asked to finance is whether, directly *or indirectly*, it will increase production."[12] "Productivity" was gaining a broader meaning.

An increased flow of private capital was given renewed emphasis by the International Finance Corporation after its establishment in 1956. The Corporation's investment selection criteria, as set forth in a booklet issued under the signature of the IFC President, Robert L. Garner, provide a scale of priorities which is all the more striking because of its explicit effort to distinguish Corporation criteria from the International Bank's:

"In choosing among various investment opportunities, IFC's decisions will be largely influenced by (i) the extent to which IFC participation would bring about the investment of private capital by other investors; (ii) the estimated profitability of the investment both to IFC and to its associates; and (iii) the prospective contribution of the investment to IFC's objective of building up a reasonably diversified portfolio. . . . Unlike the World Bank, IFC, when satisfied that the enterprise is productive in character, will customarily *not* investigate its developmental priority as against other possible investments in the same country."[13]

The freer flow of private capital sought by both IBRD and IFC was to be encouraged by the newer agency through a demonstration effect. In Garner's words, the

[12] *Ibid.*, pp. 403, 404. Emphasis added.
[13] IFC, *The International Finance Corporation* (Washington: IFC, 10 August 1956), p. 5. Emphasis added.

Corporation would "demonstrate in concrete form that soundly conducted investment in the less developed areas can be highly profitable, and by that demonstration . . . stimulate the flow of private management and capital into such investment." So conceived, the institution's task followed rather naturally. As Garner put it in the same address, "IFC operates as an investment fund, taking the risks and seeking the rewards of enterprise, and plays the role of the investor rather than merely a lender of money."[14]

Garner also drew on a physical analogy to convey his sense of IFC's task, or role, as he phrased it:

"This role seems to me rather well set forth in the dictionary definition as 'the acceleration of a reaction produced by a substance, called the *catalyst*, which may be recovered. . . .'

"The reaction in which the IFC is involved is accelerating the spread of private enterprise, and we seek to recover our catalytic funds (naturally with appropriate rewards for their use) so that we can participate in more and more reactions."[15]

The Corporation's description by its management still reflects the task Garner envisaged. Today, however, IFC is portrayed by its management as an agent more mortal and even more active. In Garner's introduction, IFC was analogized to a substance directed to propitious existing

[14] Address by Garner to First Annual Meeting of the Board of Governors of IFC.

[15] *Ibid.* Emphasis in original. IFC's *raison d'être* reaches a loftier level in the closing paragraphs of Garner's address: "All of our member countries—those economically most advanced and those which comprise the new frontiers of economic growth—have a mutual self-interest in the full development of their human and natural resources. It is my deep conviction that this mutual interest can be most fruitfully promoted by the export, by those countries in which it has most fully developed, of their free private enterprise—not merely its capital and its machines and its techniques, but its concepts, initiatives and experience."

situations with the immediate and uncomplicated effect of precipitating desirable change. Now the Corporation is touted as a recruiter of capital on an international basis, a financial actor in the role of trustee for future local investors, an organizer of local institutional development adjuncts, a *banque d'affaires.*

The International Development Association has been in operation a relatively short time, and its spokesmen have not been loquacious. Nevertheless, official statements, taken in conjunction with the early pattern of IDA loans, provide a measure of the mission perceived for this youngest agency.

IBRD Executive Directors circulated an amplifying report along with IDA's Articles of Agreement as approved for submission to prospective member states. Their interpretation indicates that "the Association is authorized to finance any project which is of high developmental priority, that is, which will make an important contribution to the development of the area or areas concerned, *whether or not the project is revenue-producing or directly productive.*"[16]

That the Association's actual range of projects is to be wider than the Bank's is evidenced by more specific official statements of intention. For instance, in their clarification accompanying the IDA Articles of Agreement, the IBRD Executive Directors stated that "projects such as water supply, sanitation, pilot housing and the like are eligible for financing." More recently IDA President Eugene Black broadened the Association's project scope even more: "In the economic sector, our financing will not be confined to so-called infrastructure projects—we have already in view, for example, projects to finance an industrial development bank, an industrial estate, and irrigation and

[16] IDA, *Articles of Agreement as Approved for Submission to Governments by the Executive Directors of the International Bank for Reconstruction and Development and Accompanying Report of the Executive Directors,* p. 7, para. 14. Emphasis added.

other agricultural projects. And we expect to be active in other sectors: in the field of water supply, for example, where the projects are often designed for both productive and public health purposes; in the challenging field of education and technical training; and in several other fields as well."[17]

With the expanded scope of Bank financing and advisory operations, an increasingly effective pursuit of IFC's special concern with "widen[ing] the areas where private membership can flourish and the profit motive can awaken dormant energies," and the additional flexibility sought and obtained with IDA and its financing terms, the IBRD triad came to be viewed by its management as a "unified group of institutions offering a comprehensive service . . . to economic development."[18]

Earlier ideals remain operative. Black and his successor, George D. Woods, have continued to seek the untrammeled movement of private capital; proposals for a multilateral assurance system for investments and IBRD-sponsored facilities for conciliation and arbitration of disputes between governments and investors have been under discussion, the latter formulated as a draft convention. The Bank previously undertook settlement of financial disputes on an ad hoc basis; now it seeks to institutionalize settlement procedures. Now—as then—the objective is to remove potential "obstruction[s] to the international flow of private capital."[19]

[17] IDA, *Articles of Agreement . . . and Accompanying Report of the Executive Directors, op.cit.,* p. 7, para. 14; Black, comments on the discussion of the Annual Report, Annual Meeting of the Board of Governors, 1961, *Summary Proceedings,* p. 14. See also IDA, *First Annual Report,* 1960-1961, pp. 3, 5; address by Black to Annual Meeting of the Board of Governors, 1961, *Summary Proceedings,* p. 10.

[18] George D. Woods, address to the Investment Bankers Association, Hollywood, Florida, 5 December 1963; IBRD, *Seventeenth Annual Report,* 1961-1962, p. 5.

[19] IBRD, *Seventeenth Annual Report,* 1961-1962, p. 8; *Eighteenth Annual Report,* 1962-1963, p. 7; *Summary Proceedings,* 1963 . . . ,

But the "comprehensive service" conception also implied new tasks for individual agencies and for the group. President Woods, speaking March 25, 1964, before the United Nations Conference on Trade and Development, affirmed that the Bank, in order "to go on being a dynamic agent of economic progress," would "adapt itself to the changing development environment and respond to the changing needs of its membership." IBRD terms would be framed with an eye to the debt-burden status of the borrower. Investment possibilities in agriculture, industry, and education would draw increased attention; all three agencies were involved. Comprehensive service suggested an even more vigorous role in formulating development programs, in providing and training personnel qualified in planning and project evaluation.[20] And, at Geneva, Woods announced the willingness of the IBRD family not only to continue the long-run alleviation of monoculture difficulties through investment for diversification, but also "to join actively in the search for answers to the vexing question of how to stabilize income from commodity exports."

The tasks envisaged at Bretton Woods had been remarkably expanded.

One account of the early days of the Special Fund reported that it was "still evolving, and neither governments nor agencies have as yet a complete understanding of its aims and procedures."[21] This is still a rather apt comment. The legislative history of the Special Fund, surveyed in Chapter III, had stressed the need for accelerated development of economic and social infrastructure and established as a guiding principle the "systematic and sustained assistance" of technical, economic, and social development. Furthermore, General Assembly resolution 1240 (XIII)

---

p. 14; address by Geoffrey M. Wilson, Vice President, IBRD, to the Institute of Banking and Financial Studies, Paris, 4 June 1964.

[20] See Chapter IV.

[21] "Issues Before the Fourteenth General Assembly," *International Conciliation*, No. 524 (September 1959), p. 114.

had encouraged the selection of "relatively large projects" and specified that these Special Fund projects could "be implemented by the provision of staff, experts, equipment, supplies, and services, as well as the establishment of institutes, demonstration centres, plants or works, and other appropriate means." On the face of it, these objectives and directives would have seemed to establish an expansion of task considerably beyond that of either IBRD or IFC, the existent agencies in 1958.[22]

However, this inference must be substantially qualified. The key to the Special Fund's task, and perhaps to the ambiguities in the perception of that task, is to be found in the words of Managing Director Paul G. Hoffman.

In the alluring Hoffman article which appeared in 1957 while its author was a member of the U.S. delegation to the General Assembly, the Fund's Managing Director-to-be had stressed the importance of assistance in building basic facilities and indicated the form such assistance should take:

"A number of great institutions have been actively financing international development for several years—notably the World Bank, the United States Export-Import Bank and more recently the International Finance Corporation. Their creative financial efforts, however, are bound and limited by charter. Their loans must be sound; that is, financing must be restricted to countries which can use it directly to boost their own production and then repay the loans out of income from new production.

"But the catch is that few of the countries we are concerned with have reached that stage. . . . If a country has

[22] This presumption is supported by the provisions in General Assembly resolution 1240 (XIII) which authorized SF "to build up gradually a reserve fund" and gave its Governing Council permission to "consider allocating part of the resources of the Special Fund for assistance on a refundable basis. . . ." See also Kaufmann, "From Concept to Reality," *United Nations Review*, VI (February 1960), reprinted in "Extending Aid Activity in the Developing Lands," pp. 7-8.

neither an expanding economy *nor* the basic facilities which such an economy needs and can support—transport, communications, schools, hospitals, etc.—it cannot build those basic facilities by borrowing money, because it has too little income from production to repay the loan. Such a country is trapped in a vicious circle.

"This means that for most underdeveloped countries we need something which no existing program offers. Therefore, an important share of aid for economic development must go in grant aid rather than in repayable loans."[23]

Hoffman stressed the same need in a pamphlet published well after he had assumed his position with the Special Fund. There he scored the failure to invest enough in "basic public improvements" in the underdeveloped countries during the 1950's, and called for "$20 billion in new money" during the 1960's, largely for non-revenue-producing but productive public facilities and services.[24]

Another plea runs through Hoffman's writings, and it probably offers a more accurate image of the initial task visualized for the Special Fund by its Managing Director. It was in the same pre-SF article that Hoffman suggested "a United Nations experimental fund . . . to be used for surveys of mineral, water and soil resources, and for a limited number of pilot projects."[25] This theme, stressing commitments far less demanding upon financial resources, likewise runs through subsequent Hoffman comments, both official and private.[26]

[23] "Blueprint for Foreign Aid," *op.cit.*, pp. 38, 40. The emphasis is Hoffman's.

[24] Hoffman, *One Hundred Countries, One and One Quarter Billion People: How to Speed Their Economic Growth and Ours in the 1960's* (Washington: Committee for International Economic Growth, 1960), pp. 31, 12, 48-49.

[25] "Blueprint for Foreign Aid," *op.cit.*, p. 43.

[26] See, e.g., *One Hundred Countries*, pp. 11, 42; United Nations, *United Nations Special Fund*, 1960, UN Pub. Sales No. 60.I.8, p. 7. For a further comment on the divergent views of SF, see Kaufmann, "From Concept to Reality," p. 8. See also Chapter III, above.

As its Managing Director, Hoffman soon improvised the word "pre-investment" to herald the Special Fund's role and activities.[27] The early quest for a defensible SF role appears to have been influenced by the pattern of activities already undertaken by multilateral development-assistance institutions, and by the expectation—quickly substantiated —that a deluge of requests would far outstrip available resources of the fledgling agency. SF was to provide neither capital investment nor technical assistance in the manner of existent programs, although from the outset it could be inferred that pre-investment shared some attributes of both.[28] Among its ground rules governing pre-investment, the Fund's management established an "absolute minimum" of $250,000 for SF support to a project, to this extent distinguishing SF undertakings from EPTA offerings. On the other hand, Hoffman first declared preinvestment would include "surveys of resources, technical training, and industrial research," and perforce exclude investment-preparatory but resource-absorptive programs such as development planning, non-technical education, and community development. SF support for a project was to be limited to five years.[29]

This working definition of pre-investment did not prove to be immutable. On May 26, 1960, Hoffman intimated forthcoming changes when he told the Fourth Session of the SF Governing Council that "it is not possible to spell out . . . all the possible situations in which assistance might be desired and requests for it considered eligible."[30]

[27] Edwards, op.cit., p. 33.

[28] Hoffman, One Hundred Countries, pp. 25, 45, 60; Kaufmann, "From Concept to Reality," p. 8. In United Nations Special Fund, 1960 (p. 19) it is suggested that UN programs in technical assistance (presumably including the Expanded Programme of Technical Assistance) "might . . . be described by the awkward term 'pre-investment.' . . ." The same SF brochure reaffirms the Fund's authorization "to make its grants to less-developed countries on a reimbursable basis. . . ."

[29] Edwards, op.cit., p. 35, citing "The Form and Content of a Request to the Special Fund," SF/4, p. 7, and E/3270/Rev. 1, p. 3.

[30] SF/L.35, p. 2, as quoted by Edwards, op.cit., p. 34.

At the Seventh Governing Council session, project criteria were implicitly broadened, as signified by the Council's approval of proposals for SF participation in economic development planning, training institutes for secondary teachers, services to small industry, and "the pre-investment aspects of the development of industrial estates."[31] The following session endorsed its first regional project and two feasibility studies costing less than $250,000 "of the kind that the Managing Director had informed the [UN] Committee for Industrial Development that the Special Fund would welcome." SF "longer range" commitments were also affirmed.[32] Hoffman encouraged "more pre-investment projects in the industrial field" and indicated that SF "would also consider sympathetically requests for additional pre-investment studies with respect to housing, building and urban planning" at the Tenth Session of the Governing Council.[33] In June 1964, the Governing Council approved Hoffman's request for "the establishment [in India] of a station to train operators in the use of modern satellite training and communications techniques," along with "a pre-investment survey for the reconstruction of . . . Skoplje, Yugoslavia," badly damaged by an earthquake in 1963, and forty-seven other projects.[34]

A Special Fund report issued in 1963 promises that the Fund "will always remain sensitive to changing Government needs."[35] That promise rests upon a substantial record of new endeavors.

The argument for pre-investment takes note of a present dearth of information on resources available in most underdeveloped countries, offers the judgment that this lack of information is a major reason for the "underutilization of physical and human resources" necessary to development, and suggests that pre-investment activities will

[31] E/3576, pp. 8, 11-12, 2.   [32] E/3646/Rev. 1, p. 3.
[33] E/3789, p. 5.
[34] UN Monthly Chronicle, I (July 1964), 53.
[35] Target: An Expanding World Economy, p. 23.

remedy the lack of information and thereby facilitate employment of these resources.[36]

A second claim for pre-investment goes further. This activity not only reveals resources already "available" but prepares others for utilization, as well. This is the role of pre-investment vis-à-vis the present "shameful neglect of . . . human resources."[37] Pre-investment's aim is partly revelation, partly training.

The justification of this Special Fund task might seem at first to indicate an instrument of economic development complete in itself. But Hoffman did not regard it thus. Skills and resources are not sufficient. The word "pre-investment" indicates a third factor.

We have already noted how the tasks perceived for the Bank and IFC were seen as contributing to the achievement of an increased rate of investment; for the most part this investment was to come from private sources, whether through international or local channels. How is pre-investment related to investment? What form of investment is it meant to presage?

To a certain extent the Special Fund's objective, as interpreted by Paul Hoffman, is the same. This would seem to be the thought behind his prediction that "pre-investment work can attract billions of dollars of highly productive investment in the crucial decade ahead [viz., the 1960's]."[38] But Hoffman relates pre-investment to public as well as private investment. His 1960 pamphlet draws the connection in a manner suggestive for this inquiry. "Our aim is to raise production and productivity, particularly in the low-income countries. This requires investment. But investment, public as well as private, will not venture into

[36] Hoffman, "Blueprint for Foreign Aid," p. 43; *One Hundred Countries*, p. 11.

[37] *Ibid.*, p. 11.

[38] *Ibid.*, p. 43. Cf. Hoffman, "Bootstrap Statesmanship," *Bulletin of the Atomic Scientists*, XVII (December 1961), 412.

the dark. On the other hand, it is attracted by possibilities for its fruitful use."[39]

If public investment "will not venture into the dark," precisely how will the dispelling of darkness by pre-investment lead to its expansion? What are the steps by which this capital will be "attracted"? These perplexing questions merit attention when a better position has been attained.

Attitude-Change Vignette #1: A "Banker's Bank" and the Soviet Bloc

The Soviet Union was one of the forty-four nations participating at the Bretton Woods Conference in July 1944. This conference ended on a note of optimism: after receiving an eleventh-hour cable from Moscow, the Soviet Union actually agreed to increase its Bank subscription by $300,000,000. Wrote a *New York Times* reporter of the Bretton Woods atmosphere: "The dramatic change of position announced by the Russian delegation late last night was interpreted as a good omen for future international cooperation for collective security, peace and prosperity."[40]

Months passed without the Soviet government's ratification of the Bretton Woods agreements. It was assumed during the latter part of 1945 that Russia *would* join: she had "more to gain and less to lose . . . than any other nation in the world . . . because her totalitarian system so completely isolates her domestic economy from the rest of the world," as one analyst put it. Furthermore, "her representatives [had] signed the agreements at Bretton Woods."[41]

[39] *One Hundred Countries*, p. 11.

[40] Porter, "Diplomatic Gains Credited to Soviet in Monetary Move," *op.cit.*, p. 1.

[41] John H. Crider, "British Loan Opens Way to Economic Peace," *New York Times*, 9 December 1945, p. 10E; Crider, "14 Nations Invited to Consider Easing of Trade Barriers," *New York Times*, 14 December 1945, p. 1. See also Crider, "Fund Established," *New York Times*, 28 December 1945, p. 1; "Expect USSR

Reports from the Moscow conference of the Big Three Foreign Ministers ending toward the close of 1945 noted, however, that "while Foreign Commissar Molotoff at first responded warmly to American suggestions that Russia act quickly to preserve her rights as a first member of the institution, he suddenly cooled to the subject."[42] The end of the year passed without Soviet ratification; in Moscow, the U.S. Ambassador was told that more time was needed to study the proposals.[43]

The Soviet Union sent observers to Savannah in the spring of 1946, but not to the Board of Governors conference which met in October of the same year. The Associated Press observed that "Soviet interest in economic collaboration has dwindled as her diplomatic relations with Britain and America have worsened."[44]

From the Soviet viewpoint such "economic collaboration" appeared to be full of dangers. A *London Times* Moscow correspondent's analysis brings this out well, and thus bears extended quotation:

"Examinations of American foreign policy, revealing some of the reasons for the Soviet suspicion, published in Soviet newspapers the last few days are cast in terms so cogent and uncompromising as to command special attention. . . .

"Writers in the *New Times* and the *Bolshevik* examine their subject with the premise that the American industrial and financial monopolists are wedded to a new course in American policy deliberately opposed to the Stalin-Roosevelt policy of mutual respect, and that they are succeeding in imposing this policy on the State De-

---

Action on Bretton Pacts," *New York Times*, 29 December 1945, p. 4.

[42] "Expect USSR Action on Bretton Pacts," p. 4.

[43] "Russia and Bretton Woods," *The Times* (London), 7 January 1946, p. 4.

[44] "World Fund, Bank Writing Russia Out," *New York Times*, 7 October 1946, p. 8.

partment. The aim of this policy, they assert, is to maintain the high rate of productivity and profit achieved in America during the war by establishing United States world hegemony—a *pax Americana*; and attention is drawn to America's far-flung bases, her diplomatic intervention all over the world, and the Nelson plan for maintaining strategic industry in a state of preparedness. The instigator of this policy is considered to be Mr. Herbert Hoover, and one of its most powerful instruments the Bank for International Reconstruction [sic], whose plans, in the Moscow writers' view, are based on the assumption that all belligerents in the late war are losers except the United States."[45]

Soviet rejection of the international financial institutions was accepted by some members, perhaps cherished increasingly by others. All seemed to be sweetness and light within the Bank's own councils until the annual meeting of 1948. In a closed session the Bank governors from Czechoslovakia, Poland, and Yugoslavia charged that Bank policy had "deferred too much" to the European Recovery Program, and they attacked the "political considerations" attendant upon a lending policy which denied aid to Eastern Europe. Bank President John J. McCloy's rebuttal, at a news conference after the session, was that ERP was too important and germane to be slighted, that the present situation in Eastern Europe made it "impossi-

[45] "Soviet Views of U.S. Aims," *The Times* (London), 18 October 1945, p. 4. Klaus Knorr concludes from comments in the Soviet press that its hostility toward the Bank and IMF was based on three considerations during this period: the absence of a veto, along with U.S.S.R. relegation to third place in terms of quotas and votes, behind the U.S. and U.K.; the detailed information exacted of IMF members and IBRD borrowers; the nature of the objectives of both institutions—increased "foreign investments by private capitalists, relatively free and multilateral trading, and in general a world economic environment within which free-market and free-enterprise countries are apt to thrive." Knorr, "The Bretton Woods Institutions in Transition," *International Organization*, II (February 1948), p. 35; see also p. 36.

ble to determine where economics ends and politics begins."[46]

The next spring these issues and others were carried into the Economic Committee of the Economic and Social Council. On March 2, 1949, McCloy answered a bitter attack by Dr. Juliusz Katz-Suchy of Poland. To the latter's charge of a sinister denial of loan funds to Poland and Czechoslovakia the Polish delegate added the further contention that the Bank had helped finance military actions in Vietnam and Indonesia through its loans to France and the Netherlands, and that in these and other actions the Bank had proved itself subservient to the political aims of the United States. McCloy denied that the Bank was "making any loans for warlike preparations anywhere," expressed regret that the Bank had not yet found it possible to aid East European countries, and added that he himself had not "by any means" written off financial assistance to Poland. At a press conference prior to this meeting the Bank's president had told reporters that his institution did not regard Communist countries as prima facie bad risks, and he emphasized that the Bank was already moving toward loans to Finland and Yugoslavia.[47]

In March 1950, Poland withdrew from both the Bank and International Monetary Fund. The Polish letter of notification included the charge that the two institutions had departed from their original purposes and become mere tools of United States foreign policy. The U.S. State Department remarked that the Polish move seemed but another element in the Soviet policy of withdrawal from international organizations so as to deprive the satellites of contact with the West. Bank President Eugene Black's written response to the Polish Ambassador cited the

[46] Felix Belair, Jr., "World Bank Calls for Unity in West," *New York Times*, 30 September 1948, p. 9. As noted in Chapter III, the Bank had by this time come under fire in other UN organs.

[47] "M'Cloy Denies Aim to Bar East Loans," *New York Times*, 3 March 1949, p. 16.

Bank's official records as sufficient evidence of its conformity with the Articles of Agreement.[48]

Bank lending policy was the object of criticism as well as compliments during the Economic and Social Council's consideration of the IBRD report in June 1952. The most general dissent came from Czechoslovakia's Jiri Nosek, who decried not only meagre credit activities, but what he referred to as a discriminatory loan policy and the imposition of Bank decisions on underdeveloped countries. The charge of subservience to U.S. foreign policy was once again raised: Nosek claimed that seventy-five percent of loans had gone to the "aggressive North Atlantic bloc and their allies" or had been directed to the increased output of strategic raw materials in the colonies and dependent territories. He indicated that it was well known that a $50 million loan to South Africa had been extended to increase uranium production.[49]

Another issue made prominent by the annual meetings of 1950, 1951, 1952, and 1953 had similar overtones, although in form it was a question of accreditation to membership. Czechoslovakia, the sole remaining Soviet bloc country after Poland's withdrawal, sought unsuccessfully at these meetings of the Boards of Governors to unseat the Chinese Nationalist delegation and to extend representation to the Peking government.[50] Shortly after the Czech proposal was tabled at the 1953 annual meeting, Czechoslovakia's membership was itself put in jeopardy at the

[48] IBRD Press Release No. 178, 16 March 1950; Felix Belair, Jr., "Poles Quit World Bank and Fund," *New York Times*, 15 March 1950, p. 1; "World Fund Scoffs at Polish Charges," *ibid.*, 16 March 1950, p. 16; "U.S. Denies Ruling World Fund, Bank," *ibid.*, 17 March 1950, p. 3.

[49] "Council Reviews World Bank Progress," *United Nations Bulletin*, XIII (1 July 1952), p. 57.

[50] "Fiscal Stability Held World Need," *New York Times*, 7 September 1950, p. 47; "President Scores Barriers to Trade," *ibid.*, 11 September 1951, p. 1; "World Bank Bids Free Nations Call Upon it For Help," *ibid.*, 6 September 1952, p. 1; "U.S. Fully Supports World Fiscal Aims," *ibid.*, 10 September 1953, p. 12.

instigation of the Bank's Committee on Finance and Organization, which voted, in executive session, to recommend to the Executive Directors that Czechoslovakia be suspended if her capital subscription arrears of $625,000 were not paid by December 31 of the same year.[51] The Board of Governors approved this ultimatum, and with the passage of the deadline Czechoslovakia was automatically suspended.[52]

Charges by the Soviet bloc did not cease with Czechoslovakia's suspension from Bank membership. In 1955, for instance, the Soviet Union raised some of the same accusations in the Economic and Social Council. Georgi F. Saksin charged the Bank with "flagrant violations" of the UN Charter, said it had been "transformed into an instrument of United States monopolies," and held its loan policies to be "guided entirely by strategic-political considerations, especially in nations around the periphery of the Soviet Union." This barrage followed Black's report, in which the Bank was shown to have reached a new record in the magnitude of its 1954 operations.[53]

Cuba later became the third original member to leave the Bank's charter circle. On October 18, 1960, a Presidential decree stated that there was no reason for Cuba to belong "since the economic policy of that institution is far from being effective in regard to the development and expansion of the Cuban economy, which the Revolutionary Government is carrying out according to a definite

[51] *Ibid.*, p. 12.

[52] Paul P. Kennedy, "World Bank Votes '54 Meeting in U.S.," *New York Times*, 13 September 1953, p. 1; "Suspension of Czechs From World Bank Is Likely as Nation Defaults on Payments," 2 January 1954, p. 19; "Czechs Are Ignoring World Bank Ouster," 5 January 1954, p. 37.

Those who sense here a precedent for exclusion of a non-paying member state might ponder the contemporaneous IBRD arrearage of China. In fiscal years 1951 through 1955 Taiwan owed over $2.7 million on its IBRD subscription.

[53] "Russia Denounces Bank Policy," *New York Times*, 8 April 1955, p. 3.

plan."[54] Stronger words were uttered at Geneva in March 1964 by Ernesto Che Guevara. In an address before the UN Conference on Trade and Development, the Cuban Minister of Industry labeled IBRD and IDA "instruments of imperialist exploitation." At the same conference it was reported that Rumanian delegates had "made preliminary soundings about possible membership in the World Bank and the International Monetary Fund."[55]

Attitude-Change Vignette #2: A "Bank for Private Enterprise" and U.S. Domestic Politics

One student of events leading up to the establishment of the International Finance Corporation has noted that the idea of an international agency to make equity investments was entertained in the U.S. Department of the Treasury prior to Bretton Woods, and in the Department of State at least as early as 1949.[56] Such a proposal, part of the informal agenda of more than one international forum in the interim, was given substantive expression and a name by the U.S. International Development Advisory Board in March 1951.[57]

Nonetheless, the "Bank for private enterprise" proposed by this Rockefeller Report was not given United States governmental support during these years.[58] Primary source

[54] "Cuba Withdraws From World Bank," *New York Times,* 19 October 1960, p. 21.

[55] Philip Shabecoff, "World Bank Head Urges Debt Shift," *New York Times,* 26 March 1964, p. 55; Richard E. Mooney, "Plan Formulated to End Trade Rift," *ibid.,* 12 June 1964, p. 52.

[56] Matecki, *op.cit.,* pp. 47, 49, and references cited.

[57] United States International Advisory Board, Partners in Progress, *A Report to the President* (Rockefeller Report), March 1951; see also Matecki, *op.cit.,* on the international arenas involved.

[58] See, e.g., IBRD, *Report on the Proposal for an International Finance Corporation,* April 1952; *Report on the Status of the Proposal for an International Finance Corporation,* May 1953; *Second Report on the Status of the Proposal for an International Finance Corporation,* June 1954. The final report stated that "some of [the countries on which IFC would necessarily have to depend for

of opposition within the administrations of the early 1950's was the Treasury Department; one later account described Secretary of the Treasury George M. Humphrey as the IFC's "most adamant foe."[59] Harold Linder, then Assistant Secretary of State for Economic Affairs, testified before a House subcommittee on March 10, 1953, that while his own department "would be sympathetic to the 'idea of creating'" a small agency along the lines of the IFC proposal, he would add "perfectly frankly that the idea has met with considerable resistance in the private banking community."[60]

The anti-IFC ideology in the United States during this time, according to B. E. Matecki, included a defense of the separation of private enterprise and state activity in general, and emphasized in particular the proscription of governmental participation in equity investments.[61] At its 1952 convention, the National Foreign Trade Council concluded that "the use made of such [public] funds would, to a large extent, be dominated by selfish, short-sighted, and politically motivated considerations which would pervert the avowed intent. Fundamentally . . . the injection of a governmental or intergovernmental agency into the field of equity financing would be subject to grave abuse, and may have vicious consequences." The 1954 convention of this association added that U.S. participa-

---

the greater part of its funds] doubt the soundness of the idea in principle." *Second Report* . . . , p. 2, as quoted by Matecki, *op.cit.*, p. 75.

[59] John Crider, "Lots of Lenders," *Barron's*, 29 November 1954; quoted by Matecki, *op.cit.*, p. 77. Matecki states that the Treasury Department during the Truman years following the Rockefeller Report was opposed to IFC, as well. The Board of Governors of the U.S. Federal Reserve System and the U.S. Export-Import Bank likewise opposed the proposal. See pp. 77-80, especially the quotations from Matecki's interviews with administration officials.

[60] Quoted by Matecki, *op.cit.*, p. 76. Besides the State Department, the Securities and Exchange Commission, the Mutual Security Agency, and the Commerce Department favored the plan with varying degrees of intensity. See Matecki, p. 81.

[61] *Ibid.*, pp. 79-80.

tion "in any scheme involving such intentions would stand in conflict with the fundamental concepts of our private enterprise system. . . ."[62]

Other portions of the non-governmental sector, however, favored or acquiesced in the proposal. At hearings on the IFC establishment bill before the House Committee on Banking and Currency, representatives of the American Farm Bureau Federation, the Committee for a National Trade Policy, the Washington Board of Trade, the American Bankers Association, the Investment Bankers Association of America, and the United States Council of the International Chamber of Commerce either testified or submitted letters and statements supporting the measure. The Chamber of Commerce of the United States did not take a stand either in favor or in opposition to the IFC; Matecki lays this to "a division within its ranks."[63]

The United States government's ultimate decision to support the IFC proposal was announced by Secretary of the Treasury Humphrey, in his capacity as Chairman of the National Advisory Council, on November 11, 1954. In his analysis of this decision, Matecki emphasizes the division of opinion toward the proposal in private and governmental circles, the growing pressure from underdeveloped countries for new multilateral sources of economic assistance, concurrent Soviet trade overtures to these countries, friendly persuasion by IBRD, and changes of attitude encouraged by the exposure of individual U.S. representatives at international conclaves. More specific factors included the "Black Plan," in which the Bank's President proposed a compromise reducing the initial capital of the IFC and denying it the authority to make equity investments; the impending Inter-American Economic Conference to be held in Rio de Janeiro, at which Secretary Humphrey was shortly to represent the U.S. and defend

[62] *Ibid.*, pp. 86, 87-88.
[63] *Ibid.*, pp. 88, 90, and n. 153, p. 173.

its prior decision to turn thumbs down on the recommendations contained in the Prebisch Report; and the face-saving formula implied in the invariable designation of IFC among members of the Eisenhower Administration as an "experiment."[64]

This was the background. One unnamed high U.S. official, skeptical if not hostile to the end, is reported to have said that he had gone along with the decision "not because I became convinced about the economic merits . . . but because the issue was too insignificant in my judgment to stand in the way of what others considered to be important on political grounds."[65]

These are some of the elements in the story of how the International Finance Corporation came to be supported as well as proposed by the United States, as told by B. E. Matecki. And as Robert Asher adds, "the real issue was always the willingness of the United States to participate": thus it is, as well, the story of how IFC came about.

But the story does not end with IFC's beginning. At the Fourth Annual Meeting of its Board of Governors in 1960, Robert Garner proposed a change in the Corporation's charter to enable it to invest in capital stock. The proposal was "favorably received" at the meeting[66] and

[64] *Ibid.*, pp. 92-151. The Prebisch Report, so named after Raúl Prebisch, then Executive Secretary of the Economic Commission for Latin America, proposed to state members of the Inter-American Economic and Social Council of the Organization of American States several measures to aid the economic development of Latin America. One recommendation was to establish an Inter-American Fund for Industrial, Agricultural and Mining Development. This international financing agency would have had a capital base somewhat like that of IBRD: 20% paid in, 80% constituting a guaranty fund. The United States would have been the major subscriber. In certain respects the later Inter-American Development Bank bears a resemblance to the previous idea. See United Nations, *International Co-Operation in a Latin American Development Policy* (Prebisch Report), UN Pub. Sales No. 1954.II.G.2, especially pp. 131-33, 136-37.

[65] *Ibid.*, p. 135.

[66] IFC, *Fifth Annual Report, 1960-1961*, p. 10.

submitted for formal consideration in February 1961. By August 1 the proposed amendment had received the support of 60 percent of the governors with 56 percent of the voting power of IFC, a percentage sufficient for approval in terms of the former but lacking in the latter. The impending United States government decision was crucial. Previously there had been considerable opposition in the U.S. to an IFC because of the proposed equity investment authority; Humphrey had reportedly argued that this would "encourage state intervention in private enterprise rather than the opposite." Opponents to IFC establishment had been assuaged by dropping the equity authorization. But no serious opposition developed to the subsequent shift. Kennedy Administration Treasury officials sounded out key Senate members, and a subcommittee of the House Banking and Currency Committee took just two minutes to reach a 9-0 accord on the bill after hearing the new Treasury Secretary, Douglas Dillon, testify on behalf of U.S. backing for the amendment. *Business Week*'s prediction that the charter change would be endorsed "since Congress tends to look with favor upon anything designed to strengthen private enterprise" was fulfilled. The amendment was announced by Garner in September 1961.[67]

[67] "Socialist Policy Upheld by Ghana," *New York Times*, 30 September 1960, pp. 35, 40; Robert L. Garner, "International Finance Corporation Should Invest in Equities," *The Commercial and Financial Chronicle*, CXCII (November 1960), 18-19; "World Bank Seeks to Buy Stock in Firms in Poorer Countries," *Wall Street Journal* (Eastern Edition), 24 February 1961, p. 4; "IFC's Bid for Bigger Job Abroad," *Business Week*, 25 February 1961, pp. 59ff.; "World Bank Arm May Widen Role," *New York Times*, 26 February 1961, p. 42; "House Unit Votes Bill to Ease IFC's Aiding of Poorer Countries," *Wall Street Journal* (Eastern Edition), 11 May 1961, p. 10; "International Finance Corp.," *Wall Street Journal* (Eastern Edition), 28 August 1961, p. 10; IFC, *Fifth Annual Report, 1960-1961*, p. 10; Garner's address to 1961 Annual Meeting of IFC Board of Governors, 21 September 1961.

Attitude-Change Vignette #3: A "Bank for the Unbankable" and the Atlantic Alliance

Senator A. S. (Mike) Monroney's IDA proposal was met by unusually wide support from the United States press. Beyond a general affirmation of the need to support economic development, two themes run through the collection of articles and editorials reprinted with the Senate subcommittee hearings: the need for new weapons to meet the Soviet economic offensive, and the desirability of enlisting greater participation by others so as to lighten the U.S. burden of international assistance.[68] The first objective was to be pursued by establishing an agency which could complement bankable loans from other sources with low-interest, long-term loans repayable in local currencies. IDA quickly gained the nickname "second mortgage bank" to go with *Fortune*'s label—"bank for the unbankable." The second objective, that of burden-sharing, was initially heralded by IDA backers as being aided both by other capital subscriptions to be paid in hard currencies and by the use of local counterpart currencies.

Although Monroney's plan was favorably received by a large segment of the press, it met with a rather cool response from individual members of the Administration. E. W. Kenworthy of the *New York Times* wrote that "Secretary of State Dulles was reported chilly to the idea." Dulles apparently was "firmly wedded to bilateral loans, believing them to be more . . . useful diplomatic tools," according to Kenworthy.[69]

In truth this was but one part of an extended dialogue. Monroney had already been highly critical of bilateral pro-

[68] See U.S. Senate, *International Development Association: Hearings* [on S. Res. 264] *Before a Subcommittee of the Committee on Banking and Currency*, 85th Congress, 2nd Session, 18-20 March 1958, pp. 24ff.

[69] "World Fund Proposed to Aid Weak Nations," *New York Times*, 2 March 1958, p. E5.

grams, and he later referred to the U.S. Development Loan Fund (DLF) as "Mr. Dulles' bank" and the "State Department bank."[70] Secretary of the Treasury Robert Anderson supported Dulles' argument during the hearings, stating that "the national interest requires the capacity for bilateral financing."[71]

The DLF did not suffer from Monroney's attacks, and much Administration opposition evaporated. After some relatively minor changes in wording, the resolution was approved by the Senate, though not without some difficulties, as noted in Chapter III.

Now the International Development Association proposal belonged to the Administration. Secretary of the Treasury Anderson carried the plan to New Delhi for the annual meeting of the Boards of Governors in early October 1958. There he indicated that the United States wished the IDA proposal to be the subject of informal discussion.[72] Arthur Bonner, special correspondent for the *Wall Street Journal*, reported that Anderson "referred to the International Development Fund [sic] with a noticeable lack of enthusiasm," denied he was proffering any blueprint, and merely stated his hope that other countries would give "thought to the matter" to match the U.S. government's own studies of the "feasibility and desirability" of forming an IDA. If informal studies should lead to "encouraging results," Anderson said, more formal studies might follow.

It was Bonner's observation that there was a rather obvious disinclination to favor the general idea. "Unofficially, western delegates make it plain to any one who asks that they are dead set against the suggestion and view it only as a way of turning good currency into bad." Bonner

[70] Robinson, *op.cit.*, p. 7.
[71] E. W. Kenworthy, "Anderson Is Cool to 2d World Bank," *New York Times*, 19 March 1958, pp. 1f.
[72] "World Bank Told of Asia's Dire Need for Aid," *The Times* (London), 7 October 1958, p. 8.

singled out as his example the German delegation, headed by Ludwig Erhard.[73]

Negotiations concerning IDA were carried on by the United States over the next months, in particular with the countries of West Europe, Canada, and Japan. The proposal seemed to gain increasing U.S. favor. By December it could be reported that United States officials believed the proposed IDA, which had been "considered a few months ago to have dim prospects," now to be "very much alive" and in fact to have a better than even chance of coming into being. The report by Edwin L. Dale, Jr. in the *New York Times* went on to note that this "change [had] come gradually over the last two months, beginning with conversations at New Delhi and shortly thereafter." And by the next May the same writer announced that the U.S. was "now confident that its proposal for a new billion-dollar International Development Association" would be "ready for approval in principle by the world's finance ministers in September."[74]

One factor involved in the increasing warmth toward the IDA proposal by the Eisenhower Administration may be surmised in part, and in part confirmed. The United States balance of payments deficit, by no means an abnormal situation of itself, was accompanied in 1958 by a sharp rise in the outflow of gold which left the United States with a $2.3 billion drop in gold reserves for the calendar year.[75] The gold flow occasioned no great im-

[73] Arthur Bonner, "Plans for Development Fund Greeted Coolly at World Bank Meeting," *Wall Street Journal* (Western Edition), 7 October 1958, p. 8.

[74] Edwin L. Dale, Jr., "New World Bank for 'Soft' Credit is Gaining Favor," *New York Times*, 8 December 1958, pp. 1f.; "U.S. Hopes to Get World Aid Board Approved in Fall," *ibid.*, 19 May 1959, pp. 1f.

[75] "Martin Not Concerned By Dip in Gold Reserves," *New York Times*, 1 May 1948, p. 49; Edward H. Collins, "The Gold Exodus," *ibid.*, 15 September 1958, p. 31; Collins, "The Gold Movement," *ibid.*, 1 December 1958, p. 45; "Outflow of Gold at Record High," *ibid.*, 12 January 1959, p. 57; "High Flow of Gold from U.S. Halted After Thirteen Months," *ibid.*, 5 March 1959, p. 43.

mediate concern among most economists and financial experts.

By the middle months of 1959, however, the outflow—which had persisted—began to cause more raised eyebrows.[76] In early September, Dale reported that the "big deficit in the United States balance of international payments . . . has begun to have a major impact on Administration thinking about foreign aid." His further comments help illuminate the reasons for the increasing support extended to IDA by U.S. officials in negotiations and subsequently at the annual meeting of the Board of Governors.

"In a sense, [Dale wrote,] the Administration is torn between two powerful emotions. One stems from acceptance of the basic idea that the under-developed countries must be helped in the interest of the United States as well as for the good of those nations that get aid.

"The other is a growing fear for the future stability of the dollar. . . .

"European countries have been running strong surpluses in their balance of payments while the United States has been in deficit. To United States officials this means only one thing; Europe should become a much bigger exporter of capital and the United States a smaller one. . . .

"[One] reflection of the [Administration's] line of thought, paradoxically, is United States support for the new International Development Association, even though this will cost the United States $330,000,000. Such a new institution . . . puts Europe in the lending picture for the first time on a formal, multilateral scale . . . [and since] it will be equipped to make 'soft' loans . . . [IDA]

[76] Edwin L. Dale, Jr., "Heavy Gold Flow From U.S. Causes Global Concern," *New York Times*, 3 May 1959; "Economists Warn on Gold Outflow," *ibid.*, 1 July 1959, p. 20; "Our Payments Deficit," *ibid.* (editorial), 9 September 1959, p. 40.

should eventually ease the pressure for a larger and larger Development Loan Fund in the United States."[77]

Read in this light, Anderson's comments at the annual meeting are especially pointed. He captured in a single sentence the two major concerns of his own government: "What we must recognize is that we are confronted today not with a dollar shortage, but with a capital shortage." This situation perhaps goes a long way toward explaining why the United States, initially a reluctant advocate, was led to support IDA wholeheartedly in adversary proceedings involving its own North Atlantic allies and a partner across the Pacific.

The Problem-Solving Process

With these ventures as background we can return to the question raised at the beginning of this particular inquiry: To what extent have problems been solved in the course of the financing programs?

Perhaps no word or phrase finds more general acceptance today as a symbol for nations and mankind alike than "economic development": this level of verbalism brings virtual unanimity. Furthermore, there is general implicit agreement on *whose* economic development is involved. In its broader sense, of course, economic development (or better, perhaps, economic growth) is a universal domestic concern of the present day. But "economic development" usually is reserved for application to those areas variously referred to as "backward," "poor," "impoverished," "underdeveloped," "less developed," or "developing." The application of terminology in the UN provides a handy measure of agreement on the problem-area's scope: as Hadwen and Kaufmann remark, "a country is less developed [for UN purposes] if it considers itself less developed and . . . applies for economic assist-

[77] Edwin L. Dale, Jr., "Big Trade Deficit [sic] Generates Move to Cut Aid Funds," *New York Times*, 6 September 1959, pp. 1f.

ance."[78] This pragmatic delineation has generated little discord.

Moreover, there is rather general agreement that some form of international action is desirable in dealing with the problem of economic development. That is one implication of the establishment of international organizations for both general and specific purposes, in the first place, and of authoritative subsequent acceptance of the principles and provisions set forth in their basic instruments —including the UN Charter—by way of ratification on the part of individual nation-states. The international contracts perused earlier invariably include a reference to economic development.

"Economic development" may pass the test as a verbal abbreviation for a commonly accepted problem. But what is the depth and extent of the consensus involved? What have been the implications in terms of the solution of this problem, particularly regarding the financing programs?

The time-span surveyed opened with a rather monolithic image of the problem, insofar as it was recognized at any level more specific than the IBRD Articles of Agreement. To speak of economic development at the time of Bretton Woods was to speak of the international flow of private capital. This was the problem; this, the solution. It would seem that the Latin American participants as well as the victorious allies of the North Atlantic area agreed on this combined definition of problem and solution.

To say this was the early operative formulation does not imply that it has been superseded. Indeed, one of the most striking aspects of this period is the extent to which the goal of enhancing private capital movements has been made to serve as a justificatory substructure for development of the entire financing-program complex. In 1963 the *Wall Street Journal* defined the problem for the IBRD group in much the same way it had been posed a decade

[78] Hadwen and Kaufmann, *op.cit.*, p. 53, p. 142.

earlier: "What new wrinkles can be devised for spurring the flow of investment from industrial nations to the underdeveloped areas of the world?"[79]

What has happened is that alternate definitions of the problem have entered the field on a competitive basis. One alternate definition sharply distinguishes a measurable local outcome from the means to that outcome. More specifically, the developing nations refer to the higher per capita real income and rising standards of living in a manner which shows they regard these as supplying both the meaning and the indices of problem-solving in the realm of economic development. So defined, economic development is perceived as a difficult problem indeed, even without considering metaeconomic variables such as demographic and political factors. As a source of indices on progress toward the objective, this conception of the problem sets a considerably harder task than an increased international flow of private capital.[80]

[79] "World Bank, IMF Officials Face Three Big Problems at Joint Conference This Week," 30 September 1963, p. 8.

[80] The theses posted by representatives from the developing nations have gained sustenance from the writings of Gunnar Myrdal and Raúl Prebisch, among other economists. Besides the sources already cited, see Myrdal, *An International Economy* (New York: Harper & Brothers Publishers, 1956); Myrdal, *Rich Lands and Poor* (New York: Harper & Brothers Publishers, 1957); Prebisch, *The Economic Development of Latin America and Its Principal Problems,* published under the auspices of the UN Economic Commission for Latin America in 1950; and *Towards a New Trade Policy for Development,* UN Pub. Sales No. 64.II.B.4, a report by Prebisch in his capacity as Secretary-General of the United Nations Conference on Trade and Development (UNCTAD). In essence this argument might be said to center upon Myrdal's notion of a vicious circle which, without deliberate and substantial offsetting measures, restrains the development of backward areas in its operation. The economic argument is chiefly directed at claims of the sufficiency of free trade as an engine of development; as applied by spokesmen for the southern tier, it is sometimes utilized also to call into question the sufficiency of autonomous international private capital movements for development. For an excellent summary statement of the economic element in the problem of development as seen by underdeveloped UN members, see Hadwen and Kaufmann, *op.cit.,*

This definition of the problem is not restricted to economic variables. Development is held to be both condition and concomitant of a peaceful world. It is also identified time and again with the problem of justice: the justice of the oppressor toward the newly independent, as it is often formulated. But increasingly the hard indices—principles honed to the requisites of quantitative analysis—are brought to bear.

"Juridical independence without economic independence is a new type of dependence, it is worse than the first because it is less obvious. Therefore, the United Nations has a duty. If it wishes to obtain peace and achieve true decolonization it must organize economic assistance from the developed countries to the underdeveloped.

.   .   .   .

"[A]id is a duty insofar as it is agreed that underdevelopment is primarily the consequence of colonial expansion. It is also a measure of justice insofar as the exploitation of these countries' resources and the trade derived from such exploitation have been achieved at the expense of the communities ruled. Such aid, supplementing the efforts and sacrifices necessarily made by the newly independent peoples themselves, will give to the phenomenon of decolonization its full meaning, by opening for our countries the way to a rapid and harmonious restoration of their economic and social structures.

.   .   .   .

"The injustice and neglect of centuries needs to be redressed.

.   .   .   .

---

pp. 72-80; cf. Raymond F. Mikesell, "Economic Doctrines Reflected in U.N. Reports," *American Economic Review*, XLIV (May 1954), 570-82. For recent accounts of the status of the debate among economists, see Gerald L. Meier, "Development Through Trade," *International Trade and Development* (New York: Harper & Row, 1963), pp. 151-91, also sources in Selected Bibliography; John D. Powelson, *Latin America: Today's Economic and Social Revolution* (New York: McGraw-Hill, 1964), *passim*.

"[C]onditional and meager assistance offered by the developed countries from the surplus of their accumulated wealth will not solve the problems of the underdeveloped countries. Accordingly, we believe we are justified in urging that all assistance to the poor countries should be channeled through the United Nations and its specialized agencies. At the same time, the developed countries should be urged to increase the amount of their assistance.

.   .   .   .

"The General Assembly . . . [d]esignates the current decade . . . the United Nations Development Decade . . . with each country setting its own target, taking as the objective a minimum annual rate of growth of aggregate national income of 5 per cent at the end of the Decade. . . . [Emphasis omitted.]

.   .   .   .

"The [Cairo Conference of representatives from thirty-six developing states] notes that despite universal acknowledgement of the necessity to accelerate the pace of development in less developed countries, adequate means of a concrete and positive nature have not been adopted to enable the developing countries to attain a reasonable rate of growth."[81]

There is a third major definition of the problem of economic development, that of the Soviet Union. Alvin Z. Rubinstein traces its roots most succinctly:

[81] Leopold S. Senghor, President of the Republic of Senegal (General Assembly, Sixteenth Session, A/PV.1045, 31 October 1961); Mongi Slim, Chairman of the Tunisian Delegation and President of the Sixteenth Session of the General Assembly (General Assembly, Fifteenth Session, *Official Records*, 10 October 1960); "Joint Declaration by 77 Nations [at UNCTAD]," as quoted in *UN Monthly Chronicle*, I (July, 1964), p. 50; Ibrahim Abboud, President of the Republic of Sudan (General Assembly, Sixteenth Session, A/PV. 1036, 13 October 1961); General Assembly res. 1710 (XVI) of 19 December 1961; Cairo Declaration of Developing Countries, E/3682, 27 July 1962, Annex, p. 2. The Senghor, Slim, and Abboud quotations are from "Africa Speaks to the United Nations," edited by Norman J. Padelford and Rupert Emerson, *International Organization*, XVI (Spring 1962), 326, 315-16, 311.

"The logic is clear: political and economic independence depend upon military strength, which in turn can be developed only through heavy industry. The sinews of military power emanate from the steel, mining, electrical, and chemical industries of a nation.

.   .   .   .

This [heavy industry] approach, confirmed by the developmental experience of the USSR, has been made an unquestioned tenet of the Marxist-Leninist formula for economic development and modernization. Soviet proposals in the UN maintained that economic liberation could proceed only if technical assistance were used to promote the expansion of heavy industry, which alone represents the key to economic development of backward areas."[82]

This monolithic conception has been modified through the years, as Rubinstein shows; the problem is no longer as clearly defined even in ideological terms. At a working level Soviet practice has long demonstrated that its response to the problem of economic development—however defined—is Soviet bilateral arrangements and those UN projects which can be made to exhibit an unmistakable Soviet brand.

Soviet contributions to the Special Fund and EPTA have been bound at the outset. During the 1959 Pledging Conference, for instance, the Soviet delegate stated that 75 percent of his pledge to the Special Fund would be in rubles "earmarked for exploratory and planning work by Soviet organizations, the provision of fellowships in the Soviet Union and the purchase of Soviet equipment," and the remaining 25 percent might be used "to defray expenses arising in connection with sending Soviet experts abroad, and supplying educational and laboratory equipment and machinery."[83] When these contributions are

[82] Alvin Z. Rubinstein, *The Soviets in International Organizations: Changing Policy Toward Developing Countries, 1953-1963* (Princeton: Princeton University Press, 1964), p. 14.

[83] General Assembly, 1959 United Nations Pledging Conference

employed at all, Soviet spokesmen proclaim the projects with top billing for the U.S.S.R.

"The Soviet Union has contributed to the U.N. Technical Assistance and Special Funds [sic] substantial amounts of currency. The U.S.S.R. uses this money to deliver to the underdeveloped countries modern technical equipment; it has sent experts there and has provided scholarships for the training of members of these countries in Soviet educational institutions and to set up installations in these countries. . . . On the basis of Soviet funds contributed to the United Nations, the U.S.S.R. has trained hundreds of specialists from various countries. It may be noted in this connection that the Soviet assistance channelled through the United Nations could have been considerably greater if the Western representatives in leading positions in this international body had not placed obstacles in its path."[84]

It has been suggested that at least three images of economic development have been displayed in and about the international arenas with which this study is concerned. Economic development was first perceived and acted on as a combined end and means—the encouragement of private capital movements. This definition of the problem

on the Expanded Programme of Technical Assistance and the Special Fund, *Summary Record of the First Meeting*, A/CONF. 18/SR.1, p. 7. For commentary on Soviet "tied" SF and EPTA contributions and attendant difficulties somewhat euphemistically dubbed "currency utilization problems" see Robert Loring Allen, "United Nations Technical Assistance: Soviet and East European Participation," *International Organization*, XI (Autumn, 1957), 620ff., or Allen, *Soviet Economic Warfare* (Washington: Public Affairs Press, 1960), pp. 149ff.; Hadwen and Kaufmann, *op.cit.*, 1962 edition, pp. 115-24; Harold Karan Jacobson, *The USSR and the UN's Economic and Social Activities* (Notre Dame: University of Notre Dame Press, 1963), 239ff.; Rubinstein, *op.cit.*, pp. 40ff., 63ff.

[84] V. Rimalov, *Economic Cooperation Between the U.S.S.R. and Underdeveloped Countries* (Moscow: Foreign Languages Publishing House, n.d.), pp. 60-61.

was joined later by two others. Like the initial perception, one of the subsequent viewpoints defined economic development in operational terms to mean an increase in certain bilateral transactions between less and more developed nations. The other separated end from means and posed a set of hard indices.

Hypothetically these definitions of the problem of economic development might seem to complement one another. However, this is hardly apparent along the plane at which international economic development measures are publicly assessed.

Soviet spokesmen say private investment capital deters development either by Western design or simply because of its consequences: it makes or keeps governments subordinate to Western interests exploiting local resources, rendering these countries "agrarian and raw-material appendages," and brooking no escape from "non-equivalent exchange" with the West for primary commodities. Public Western aid is directed mainly to quashing local "liberation" efforts; it has the additional effect of sucking scarce local skilled personnel and material resources from economically productive occupation. The small non-military balance of Western aid goes not for "industrialization" but for infrastructure to support the local Western-controlled interests or as an indirect subsidy to Western exporters. IBRD loans, IFC investments, and IDA credits fall within approximately the same Dantean circle. The Special Fund alone has received qualified Soviet endorsement; even this acknowledgment is related and limited to the fact and incidence of Soviet participation.[85]

[85] Rimalov, op.cit., passim; V. Aboltin, "The U.N. and Industrialization," New Times, 5 June 1963, pp. 9-13; Alexander Dallin, The Soviet Union at the United Nations (New York: Frederick A. Praeger, 1962), p. 64; Jacobson, The USSR and the UN's Economic and Social Activities, pp. 252ff.; Rubinstein, op.cit., pp. 130ff.; Richard E. Mooney, "Khrushchev Scores West As U.N. Trade Talks Open," New York Times, 24 March 1964, p. 1; "U.S. Aid Policy Is 'Slippery,' Russian Says at Geneva Talks," New York Times, 4 April 1964, p. 5.

Conversely, Soviet measures, through multilateral auspices or outside them, have been decried in the West as diversionary at best, likely to prove gifts from the Greeks rather than assets to development. Soviet aid is designed for maximum psychic and political impact, not economic development. The bilateral arrangements by which the Soviet Union extends credits repayable in barter fashion with local primary products are not only measures to enslave the borrower (which should be sufficient reason to avoid them), they are also cruelly deceptive: showpiece industries erected with Soviet assistance misuse local resources that would be more productively utilized otherwise; repayment in commodities discourages economic diversification.[86]

This is the most audible dissonance, but it is not the only one. The earlier Western consensus has splintered; mutually exclusive Western solutions to the problem of economic development confront each other today. As long as the international financing programs went no further than bankable loans which private enterprise would not itself extend but with which it could and did associate, there was little quarrel with the efficacy of these measures in solving the problem. The flow of private capital was quite obviously being encouraged.

More recently, public measures, acclaimed by their advocates as conducive to the flow of private investment, have become less directly connected with the movement of private capital, and hence less necessary to it in the eyes of other observers. Public measures have become more expensive, also. Today a significant portion of the private sector is disgruntled by public financing, especially though not exclusively multilateral financing. U.S. enterprise today enjoys a smaller proportion of the total Western benefit from untied IBRD loans, as noted in Chapter IV.

[86] Besides the American studies and commentaries already cited, see Joseph S. Berliner, *Soviet Economic Aid* (New York: Frederick A. Praeger, 1958), especially pp. 163-67.

When this discontent is given public expression, the charge often leveled is precisely that the proffered means vitiate the chosen end. In his comments "as an individual [and] not . . . as an official of an international organization" upon retiring as President of IFC, Robert Garner added a new interpretation to the old problem:

"I . . . maintain that an immense reservoir of private capital exists throughout the world which can be tapped for expanding production in the less developed areas. . . .

"However, there are several forces which are damming this potential flow. . . .

"[One such force is] the low subsidized rates at which funds of both national and international institutions are loaned to some private business."[87]

The economic aspect of this line of criticism is sometimes interwoven with an analogy characterizing the UN as a vast and permissive extended family composed of a few grown-ups and many adolescents. The *Wall Street Journal*, for instance, has editorialized under the title "Why Grow Up?" in this fashion: "If the emerging countries of Asia and Africa seem to behave irresponsibly in the United Nations, it is not always their fault. They are often led to folly by those who ought to know better. . . . African, Asian and Latin American politicians wish to

[87] Garner also singled out these other damming forces in his valedictory: the threat of confiscation of property and rights; nationalism, "which in varying degree obstructs the import of foreign capital"; and "the jealousy of local business men who prefer their monopolies, and resent the appearance of foreigners who may supply the country with better products at lower prices." Cf. this passage from p. 9 of IFC's *Third Annual Report*, 1958-1959: ". . . it appears that in many instances public credit at cheap rates substitutes for and tends to dry up the flow of private investment capital." The charge is sometimes leveled at IDA. See, e.g., "Mr. Black's Two Hats," *The Economist*, 23 September 1961, p. 1181.

A comment by the Soviet delegate to ECOSOC in 1955 probably did little to allay such fears: "A reduction in the Bank's rate of interest caused by the operations of SUNFED would . . . be a welcome development. . . ."

water their schemes with all the money they want—on their own terms. And this illusion, at odds with any sound and practical program of development, goes unchallenged by U.N. economists; indeed, it is encouraged. Is it any wonder, then, that some new nations are reluctant to grow up?"[88]

However formulated, the point behind these charges is that public financing does not complement private international investment. This "non-complementarian" view of public financing operations confronts the newest in a long line of justificatory arguments by Western supporters of such programs. Edwin M. Martin, Assistant Secretary of State for Economic Affairs, took note of public international investment as "the main source of capital for most of the developing areas of the world," and added: "Its wise use in providing . . . economic and social infrastructure is a basic prerequisite for successful private investment. Without this, . . . private investment is well-nigh impossible on any scale." More recently, Paul Hoffman has written that "[i]nvestments in infrastructure provide the underpinnings of self-perpetuating economic advance" through private investment.[89]

In such a debate, it might be assumed that verbal tactics would dictate an attempt at re-definition of ancient and honored words on the one hand and a defense of their traditional substance on the other. With this understanding, the vagaries of usage which accompany hallowed adjectives such as "productive" and "sound" are more easily fathomed. For instance, Hoffman argues that "[s]ound business practice requires . . . [expanded] preinvestment

[88] "Why Grow Up?" (Western Edition), 13 December 1960, p. 12. Cf. "Global Mischief: UN Economics Points the Way to Poverty, Not Progress," *Barron's*, XL (22 February 1960), 1; "Teething Trouble," *Wall Street Journal* editorial, 23 January 1964, p. 10.

[89] Edwin M. Martin, "International Investment and the Problems of Economic Growth," *United States Department of State Bulletin*, XLV (30 October 1961), 714; Hoffman, *World Without Want* (New York: Harper & Row, 1962), p. 133.

programs"; the *Wall Street Journal* takes note of a similar Hoffman plea and retorts: "We'd like to know what this veteran aid-giver means when he speaks of seeking out 'sound' investments."[90]

Nor has the solution tendered by the Soviet Union remained above criticism from within the Sino-Soviet bloc(s). A Chinese critique touches familiar themes in its economic thrust no less than in the expected denunciation of Soviet political aims. "Instead of sincerely helping these [African and Asian] countries develop an independent national economy," charged the head of the Chinese delegation at the second Asian Economic Seminar in Pyongyang, North Korea, the Soviets "demand that some of these countries serve them as suppliers of raw materials, and they even establish control over the economies of other states. They do not trade at reasonable prices but cut down prices of imports while raising those of exports."

The Soviets counterattacked by measuring Chinese assistance by standards true to the heavy-industry premise. "Enterprises of heavy industry account for less than 20% of the projects being built in the developing states with the aid of the C.P.R., while such enterprises account for approximately 50% of the projects being built with the as-

[90] Hoffman, *One Hundred Countries*, p. 43; "Why Grow Up?," p. 12.

Another example of the breakdown of consensus is the war of words between Edward H. Collins of the *New York Times* and an editorialist for an unnamed newspaper who has taken IFC to task for its low initial rate of investment. Collins quotes and responds thus: " 'Perhaps at this early stage . . . ,' conceded this journalistic critic, 'caution is necessary. But a flexible attitude ought to prevail, especially with respect to the needs in those Asian and African areas where private enterprise is on trial, and where communism is often, if not always, the alternative.' Why is it, [Collins asks,] . . . that persons whose concept of the perfect government lending institution is one that is prepared to make loans to any would-be borrower for any purpose at any time don't say just that? Why is it that they invariably resort to such locutions as 'a more flexible policy' when what they really mean is no policy at all?" "Investment Catalyst: A Defensive Study of the 14-month-old International Finance Corporation," *New York Times*, 7 October 1957, pp. 35ff.

sistance of the U.S.S.R." But the Soviet answer also complains of Chinese irregularities in terms strikingly similar to those one might expect from a Western observer. "The sets of equipment delivered by the C.P.R. in many cases do not conform to world standards. It has also been reported that the plywood mill built in Cambodia with C.P.R. aid is unprofitable and that there is now even a question of closing it. Last year the C.P.R. was compelled to renege on the construction of a metallurgical plant in Cambodia because of the low technical level of the prospecting work, which was carried out by Chinese specialists. . . . During the years of the 'great leap' the C.P.R. tried to force its aid on Nepal in the construction of primitive blast furnaces, which, as is known, turned out to be completely unsound."[91]

Measurement of the extent that the problem is being solved thus requires specification of *whose* problem is to be analyzed. For the West in general and the U.S. in particular, the basic problem is still seen to be the movement of private investment capital. In quantitative terms there has been an increase in this flow over the years, although this is uneven as to geographic and sectoral destination, and subject to considerable secular fluctuation.[92] Participa-

[91] Seymour Topping, "China Tells Poor Nations Not to Take Soviet Aid," *New York Times*, 22 June 1964, p. 1; K. Dontsov, "Peking's False Tone: Fact and Fancy About Aid to Developing Countries," *Izvestia*, 12 July 1964, p. 4, as translated in *The Current Digest of the Soviet Press*, XVI (5 August 1964), 7. For a lucid analysis of Soviet and Chinese strategy and tactics in one consequential southern corner of the globe, see Robert A. Scalapino, "Sino-Soviet Competition in Africa," *Foreign Affairs*, XLII (July 1964), 640-54, especially p. 653. See also Richard Lowenthal's essay in Zbigniew Brzezinski (ed.), *Africa and the Communist World* (Stanford: Stanford University Press, 1963), pp. 147ff.

[92] See United Nations, Department of Economic Affairs, *International Capital Movements During the Inter-War Period*, UN Pub. Sales No. 1949.II.D.2; *The International Flow of Private Capital, 1946-1952*, UN Pub. Sales No. 1954.II.D.1; *The International Flow of Private Capital, 1958-1959*, E/3369; United Nations Bureau of Economic Affairs, *The International Flow of Long-Term*

tions and sales from the portfolios of the Bank and IFC have increased, as noted in the previous chapter. For those who define the problem in this manner there have been other heartening signs: the legal circumvention of government guarantees (and the consequent avoidance of government meddling, as it is said) through establishment of IFC; the trend away from Bank guarantees on sales from its portfolio in recent years; IBRD's recent bid to devise a conciliation and arbitration scheme to lessen noncommercial risks; the prospective infusion of IBRD funds into IFC.

In regard to other measures, Special Fund pre-investment and IDA credits in particular, disagreement has increased within the West as to whether the problem is being solved or exacerbated. Some see these programs as conducive to private investment; others think public and private investment are engaged in a kind of zero-sum game.

On the other hand, the growth of international capital movements induced in part by UN system programs can hardly be taken as progress toward development by Soviet standards. With regard to non-Sovietized Special Fund undertakings, the U.S.S.R. in effect sides with the Western "complementarians": the SF mechanism, according to an ECOSOC delegate from the Soviet Union, is "used for work profiting private credit institutions and commercial undertakings." The Soviet proportion of total SF contributions, 4.5 percent in 1959, had fallen to 1.6 percent by 1963.[93]

Capital and Official Donations, 1951-1959, UN Pub. Sales No. 62.II.D.1; *The International Flow of Long-Term Capital and Official Donations, 1959-1961,* UN Pub. Sales No. 63.II.D.2; "Apartheid of Rich and Poor," *The Economist,* 10 August 1963, pp. 493ff.; Richard E. Mooney, "Money Aid Flow Steady for Year," *New York Times,* 25 July 1964, p. 32; Andreas Freund, "Flow of Funds to Poorer Lands Is Termed Inadequate to Need," *ibid.,* 15 January 1965, p. 47.

[93] Rubinstein, *op.cit.,* pp. 130-31, citing Economic and Social Council, *Official Records,* 30th Session, p. 145. For Soviet criticism

For the developing nations, economic development as a process is subordinated to economic development as a product. Little has been achieved. The reason is not a conflict among alternative actions being taken; it is their cumulative paucity. Responding to the Secretary-General's call for proposals to meet the aims of the Development Decade, the government of Ghana rated capital the question of first magnitude. "The fact is that countries like Ghana and many others could have economically absorbed far more capital in the 1950's than was available to us. . . . [F]oreign private capital has been offered all conceivable types of inducement. . . . Until recently the failure of Ghana to attract *either public or private* foreign capital on any scale was not due to any particular disinclination to come to Ghana, but merely to the fact that the total of such funds available to all the countries in need was very small."[94]

Lack of agreement is evident on the specific operative definition of the problem itself. Some "solutions" contradict others, at least on the verbal level. Paradoxically, one actor—or congeries of actors—manifests both a basic acceptance of the substance of *all* solutions and a lack of satisfaction with over-all results.

Certainly this is less a paragon of problem-solving than a cacophony bearing some affinity to Alice's croquet game in Wonderland. That famed contest took place on a field of ridges and furrows, with uncooperative flamingoes for mallets, reluctant hedgehogs for balls, and independent-minded soldiers for wickets. "The players all played at

---

of SF projects, see Aboltin, *op.cit.*, p. 9; Tania Long, "Soviet Criticizes U.N. Special Fund," *New York Times*, 13 January 1965, p. 4. For analyses of U.S. criticism of a Cuban project by the Special Fund, see Rubinstein, "Soviet and American Policies in International Organizations," paper prepared for delivery at the 1963 American Political Science Association, pp. 5-6; John G. Stoessinger, *The UN and the Superpowers*, forthcoming.

[94] "United Nations Development Decade: Proposals for Action; Replies from Governments," E/3613/Add.2, p. 19. Emphasis added.

once, without waiting for turns, quarreling all the while, and fighting for the hedgehogs. . . ."

And yet, as we found in Chapter IV, it moves. How are we to explain this? To what extent does the functionalist argument offer sustenance? To these questions we now turn.

PART III. THE FUNCTIONALIST THESIS REEXAMINED

VI

An Essay in Interpretation

THE PRIOR chapter ended with a question. This chapter begins with the same question. Some elements within the functionalist prophecy are validated in the case of the financing program, yet in certain important respects—notably with regard to problem-solving—the functionalist prediction seems to have gone badly astray. The previous analysis bequeaths a legacy of unanswered questions which fall into two general categories. There are, first, the questions as to why certain developments did or did not take place in the course of the financing program. A second range of questions concerns the functionalist argument itself. Why did it succeed as a prophecy in some respects, and fail in others? Unifying these two orders of questions is a general query, indicated earlier. Did the developments foreseen in the functionalist argument transpire *for the reasons suggested* by it?

In gauging the interpretative power of the functionalist argument our initial focal point will be the "consequences" on which that argument may most appropriately rest its claim to prescience. The interpretation will begin by viewing some of the more successful projections through what might be called the "functionalist overlay" —that conceptual apparatus, implicit within the functionalist argument, which purports to explain *why* functional activity has brought these consequences. This discussion provides a springboard for further explanatory efforts. But the pursuit of understanding may be aided by a scrutiny of prophetic failure as well as prophetic success, in particular that paradoxical discontinuity singled out at the end of the last chapter. Thus functionalist failures in the role of seer will receive attention, also.

I

The functionalist interpretation of the financing programs might go somewhat as follows. A long-term process of social and political change in the less-developed areas of the world accelerated in the years after World War II, bringing with it a common awareness of the need for economic development of these areas. To deal with this problem there appeared an international organ, which adjusted its functioning by technical self-determination so as to fulfill the changing aspects of the need. In the course of solving the problem other facets of the same general need developed which were filled by a structural subdivision of the original organ—again with the aid of technical self-determination.

More specifically, the functionalist mode of interpretation could well produce such observations as these on the financing program. The International Bank for Reconstruction and Development arose to meet a common need. Its evolution in terms of function, structure, and offspring mirrors the development of the need itself since the Bank's origin—the need, that is, plus the technical self-determination which the Bank's management has exercised. Technical self-determination guided the shift in emphasis from reconstruction toward development loans, steered the organ toward the bond market as a major source of sustenance for its activities, expanded the meaning of phrases such as "productive purposes" and "specific projects" by its interpretative skill so as to allow for the satisfaction of emergent needs.

When barriers appeared which the Bank found insurmountable, so the functionalist interpretation might continue, the IBRD management directed its expertise to the conception of new structural forms. As Eugene Black has written, "quite early in the Bank's operations it became obvious that the requirement of a government guarantee for all its loans must limit its lending for private industry."[1] In a period of fluctuating primary commodity prices on the world market, moreover, it was found "desirable that a considerable part of the foreign capital employed for development purposes be in the form of equity investments in order to avoid an undue burden of fixed charges which might impair the credit of the borrowing country or intensify its balance-of-payments problems. . . ."[2] For these reasons the International Finance Corporation was born, and the Bank's Vice President became the new agency's head. When practice revealed that certain technical attributes of IFC's structure made difficult its capacity to fully meet these needs, its authority was extended, at the instigation of President Robert Garner. This enabled the Corporation to make equity investments in the first place instead of having to create them by means of sales to private investors from its portfolio.

The Bank's management subsequently found and made use of an interlocutory device by which it could partially overcome the paralysis it had experienced due to the requirement for governmental guarantee of its loans. This structural adjunct allowed the Bank to predestine a single loan for ultimate distribution among a large number of small projects including light industry and, more recently, agriculture. More and more the Bank and its affiliates extended credits to these development companies, and it trained their experts as well. Eugene Black has observed that "there exists a very sizeable guild of artisans in economic development in the underdeveloped world today,

[1] Eugene R. Black, "Financing Economic Development," p. 21.
[2] Matecki, *op.cit.*, p. 41. See also pp. 36-37 for a discussion of two other "pressing needs" cited in the Rockefeller Report which the Bank was presumably unable to fill adequately—*viz.*, the need for a means to bring together foreign and domestic investment in undertaking local projects, and the need to draw forth for more productive use the local capital presently invested in land or in dwelling-places, or held as hoardings.

and within the guild a very healthy exchange of information on the state of our trade goes on all the time."[3]

The Bank and IFC, guided by technical self-determination in their evolution, progressed toward solution of the problem of economic development. Shortly it became apparent that yet another gap existed in the apparatus. The Bank and IFC were investing in projects which gave promise of fairly immediate economic benefits; various technical assistance programs in and outside the UN system were helping to prepare the way for others. But in between a need appeared for longer-term, more expensive undertakings than existing technical assistance programs could handle—for "pre-investment," as Paul Hoffman called it. The Special Fund arose to fill this niche. Its management sought to meet the interstitial need by arranging skilled appraisal leading to the appropriate allocation of resources for training, research, and surveys.

With the addition of this newest member to the financing family, the program as a whole was better able to handle the needs of those in all stages of development. But now another need appeared. Those countries which had earlier been extended IBRD loans and credits from elsewhere were moving rapidly toward the limits of their debt-servicing capacity. Payments were falling due; at the same time new public investment was needed. These countries could not increase their hard currency earning capacity at the same rate that new investment was needed. Yet certain other countries were accumulating a backlog of counterpart soft currencies, in part from sales of agricultural surplus. It was said that these currencies would prove to be a useful supplement to loan resources by covering local and some foreign procurement costs. None of the existing agencies could handle this aspect of the problem. The International Bank, however, was having to turn down loan requests which might have been approved in

[3] Black, "Newly Developing Nations: Economics and the Cold War," *General Electric Forum*, V (January-March 1962), 36.

slightly altered circumstances: if the Bank "did not believe the applicant able to repay the whole loan and meet the interest payments in hard currency," it said no, even though IBRD "often regarded 50 to 80 percent of a loan request as 'bankable.' "[4] Clearly a new organ was needed to function in this area. The result was the International Development Association, with separate funds but the same body and head as the Bank. The Association has extended long-term, long-grace-period, no-interest loans; often these have been in conjunction with Bank credits.

With comparable sagacity the functionalist interpretation looks to the future: if there is a need for a capital development fund, a capital development fund will appear. If, on the other hand, an existing agency can extend its functioning and multiply—or divide—its functionaries so as to cover such a need, *that* development will be the outcome.

In the meantime, such indices as Bank lending, the increase in participations and sales from Bank and IFC portfolios, and the extension of collateral services demonstrate both the continuing need and a continuation of need-fulfillment.

Admittedly, the functionalist interpretation sheds some light on these developments. But its adequacy is disappointing. The functionalist interpretation neither brings nor encourages a grasp of the context or the specificities of these developments. It enfolds everything in a vague formula: need, functional response, modified need, functionally modified response. We see an agency and assume, in *post hoc* fashion, a prior or concurrent need; we sense a need and presume an agency or a structural extension will be along shortly. This is an exaggeration, of course. But it suggests the very general type of answer to which the functionalists would be pressed in demonstrating the

[4] E. W. Kenworthy, "Monroney Urges a 2d World Bank," *New York Times*, 23 February 1958, p. 25.

explanatory efficacy of their approach to understanding. We would like to be afforded new purchase on old puzzles; we *wish* to be able to see potential events taking shape, insofar as it may be possible through a combination of human wit and conceptual machination. As it is, the functionalist interpretation appears to do little to move toward either goal.

The chief explanatory implement in the functionalist tool-house is "technical self-determination." Its very composition is conducive to uncritical acceptance. What could be more appealing to the analyst of international organizations in an age of science and democracy than the elements in this little organon? The new follower of the functionalist school may sense that he has gained a key to the mysteries of that universe which embraces all international activities in the social and economic sectors: it unlocks everything, he may say after a few quick turns at the interpretation of change in such programs. Yet one may wonder whether such conceptual parsimony is not pound foolishness—whether much understanding has really been purchased at so slight a cost.

Mitrany's "technical self-determination" is not very different from William E. Rappard's "administrative self-determination." In noting the "increasing autonomy of the [League] technical organizations," Rappard in 1931 ascribed this process in part to the fact that "administrative convenience and efficiency demand that an expert body be not unduly hampered in its investigations by the necessity of constantly awaiting new instructions and authorizations."[5] By whatever name, the exercise of this administrative discretion is proffered as an explanation both of changes in substantive policy and of emergent procedural patterns, or "structure." There is an immanence of the function qua administrative discretion within the need, which is to say that the need itself consists in

[5] Rappard, *The Geneva Experiment*, p. 63.

part of "administrative convenience and efficiency" or similar values.

In other words, certain agencies are born with or achieve what Mitrany calls "functional autonomy" by virtue of the desirability of such an autonomous status for working their art or science. But "desirability" presumes desire, and desire presupposes a desirer. It is all well and good to say that program A's functional autonomy is due to the desirability of such an arrangement, but how—if at all—are we to know in *advance* that it will prove to be desired as well as desirable? And how may we go about explaining why other programs are *not* functionally autonomous, by birth or by breeding, in terms more meaningful than simply saying it was not a desirable arrangement from the standpoint of convenience, efficiency, or the like? This particular criterion of distinction, exercised alone, might lead us to cast into the same analytical category programs concerned with the control of disease and the control of armaments—a patently nonsensical gesture from the standpoint of understanding.

Mitrany's answer is that certain substantive sectors are propitious for this functional autonomy and, consequently, for the exercise of administrative discretion. The case for generalized applicability of the functionalist mode of interpretation (as well as the prescriptive argument for a functional approach to the creation of international community) is made to rest upon the implicit contention that certain qualities are common to all "economic" and "social" sectors of international relations, and that these same qualities are either alien to or initially missing from the residual sectors. Chief among the harbingers of functional success is the *non-controversiality* surrounding and accompanying the venture. This is the climatological region in which the functional seed is planted in the first place; this is the atmosphere in which it grows and bears its fruit.

The questions now to be raised and pursued are these:

If the exercise of administrative discretion is assumed as the key factor in explaining the success of functional activity (and likewise in explaining the success of the functionalist prophecy), what *conditions* does administrative discretion presuppose? Are they, in the case of the present empirical investigation, adequately described by the notion of non-controversiality suggested by the functionalist argument?

There is a great temptation at this point to let the latter question stand as its own answer, particularly with the support of a reference to some of the vignettes in the previous chapter. This concluding criticism would place us in good company.[6] But the purpose here lies less in exposing so obvious a shortcoming than in working the materials at hand with any conceptual apparatus that can appropriately be borrowed or created. If an analytical application of "technical self-determination" does not reveal all that the present study intimates about administrative discretion, do other approaches yield additional insights?

I I

In regard to no facet of the financing program has the functionalist prediction been more "right" than with respect to the International Bank for Reconstruction and Development and its activities. By most indices the Bank's actions have substantiated functionalist contentions. Furthermore, the Bank's experience is probably as fine an example of "technical self-determination" as could be chosen. Do alternative approaches supplement—or supplant—the functionalist thesis regarding the conditions under which this exercise of administrative discretion has operated?

One means of explaining the latitude within which "technical self-determination" operates would be to look at the legal framework which has been set by the parties to an original contract, as amended and augmented by sub-

[6] See, e.g., Claude, *op.cit.*, especially pp. 396ff.

sequent conclaves of these members or their representatives, perhaps in more or less continuous session. Using this approach, one school of interpreters would regard the building of pockets of autonomy into the law as a necessary and sufficient explanation of an exercise of administrative discretion—insofar as they would, indeed, recognize the existence of such a phenomenon as other than anachronism or tyranny. This interpretation takes international organizations to be potential or actual products of constituent conventions for casting and for revision of the norms controlling all significant action, and consequently regards these organizations as adequately explicable by means of a geological probing of the strata of legal documentation laid down over time. This general manner of interpretation and prescription was labeled "apocalypticism" earlier, following Inis Claude, Jr.'s language of appraisal.[7] Here the specific concern is with the light such an approach might shed upon the exercise of "technical self-determination" by IBRD.

It may be noted that the International Bank's Articles of Agreement set general provisions which relate to loans and guarantees and direct the Bank to conduct its operations with due regard to certain procedures which are expressed partially in permissive terms, partially in mandatory terms. The Articles of Agreement cast the basic organizational structure of the Bank, specifying a Board of Governors, Executive Directors, and a President, who is to be "chief of the operating staff," to conduct "the ordinary business of the Bank," and to "be responsible for the organization, appointment and dismissal of the officers and staff," subject to the general control of the Executive Directors.[8] Article V, Section 2 (b) authorizes the Board of Governors to delegate its powers to the Executive Directors, with certain exceptions as specified; this the Board

[7] See pp. 24ff.
[8] IBRD, Articles of Agreement, Article V, Section 5 (b).

of Governors has done in Section 15 of the IBRD By-Laws.

Article VIII, the amendment provision, specifies that proposed modifications must achieve approval by the Board of Governors and by three-fifths of members having four-fifths of the total voting power. The next article provides for a "question of interpretation of the provisions of this Agreement arising between any member and the Bank or between any members of the Bank" to be submitted to the Executive Directors, and to the Board of Governors upon appeal.

These are the portions of the Bank's basic instrument and supplementary codified rules which might be expected to provide insights as to the successful "technical self-determination" behind the evolution of Bank operations and Bank organization. It can be said with justice that these explicit and fundamental norms have provided an amply flexible framework within which both developments of function and structure could take place, and thus have been a *sine qua non* of Bank success—a point which the functionalists would denigrate, if not ignore. But it need hardly be emphasized that these legal "do's," "don't's" and "may's" scarcely explain the developments of major significance in the Bank's history—the magnitude, variety, and distribution of loans and collateral services, and the expanded capacity for field operations. These patterns *could* have been quite different without violating a single article. This line of inquiry is a necessary step in explaining such developments; it is far from being a sufficient means to understanding, at any rate in the case of IBRD. As Edmund Burke once said, "the laws reach but a very little way. Constitute government how you please, infinitely the greater part of it must depend upon the exercise of powers, which are left at large. . . ."[9]

[9] Cf. Asher's comment on the Bank's technical assistance activities, in *The United Nations and Promotion* . . . , p. 318. The Bank Staff makes the following observation as part of the appendix to

I I I

Another mode of interpretation starts from a quite different vantage point. "Men make history," it begins, "and great men make great history." We have become less accustomed to this approach in the present age, perhaps in part for the reasons suggested by Alexis de Tocqueville.[10] A considerable segment of contemporary political science has a vested interest in approaches which relegate the role of great men to epiphenomena. How is one to incorporate *sui generis* data into the nomothetic desire and design of modern social science, into the "frigid theories of a generalising age," to borrow Disraeli's words?

The great-man approach, which defies the constitutional categorical in its interpretation no less than it transcends nomothetic social science, enjoys a strange compatibility with the functionalist thesis at several points. Both the present approach and the functionalists would emphasize in their analysis of cases demonstrating the fruitful conse-

---

Eugene Black's *The Diplomacy of Economic Development*, p. 65: "Once the Bank moved from reconstruction into development lending, the guide lines of the Articles [of Agreement] were only the beginnings of paths into new territory. Moving carefully from problem to specific problem, the Bank had to elaborate its own policies and mark out its own trails."

[10] In that section of his penetrating analysis entitled "Some Characteristics of Historians in Democratic Times," Tocqueville states: "Historians who write in aristocratic ages are inclined to refer all occurrences to the particular will and character of certain individuals; and they are apt to attribute the most important revolutions to slight accidents. They trace out the smallest causes with sagacity, and frequently leave the greatest unperceived. Historians who live in democratic ages exhibit precisely opposite characteristics. Most of them attribute hardly any influence to the individual over the destiny of the race, or to citizens over the fate of a people; but, on the other hand, they assign great general causes to all petty incidents." Alexis de Tocqueville, *Democracy in America* (New York: Vintage Books, Inc., 1955), II, First Book, translated by Henry Reeve, revised by Francis Bowen, and edited by Phillips Bradley, p. 90.

quences of administrative discretion those propulsive factors endogenous to the functional unit itself. The functionalists further cite the external need as a triggering mechanism for the dynamics of functional activity; presumably great men are great in part by virtue of an awareness of their times. On the other hand, the functionalists strive to raise to the level of conceptualization those qualities which great-man analysis would hold to manifest a high degree of uniqueness of circumstance. That is, the functionalist argument, in explaining why functional activities will develop, subsumes individual acumen within such notions as expertise, the proclivity of the *function* to determine its own dimensions, organs, and powers, and "technical self-determination" itself.

The interpretation in which an institution's success is determined essentially by way of analysis of its principal leader might be illustrated briefly. In the Bank's brief annals, Eugene Black fills this hallowed niche—"Gene Black [the] political genius," the man of "charm and cool competence," the "creative pragmatist," possessor of the quiet and winning manner, practitioner of development diplomacy par excellence.[11]

The great-man interpretation of the Bank is apt to begin with such personal attributes as these. It seeks initially to explain whence these attributes came. One account of Black's guidance of the Bank, for instance, ascribes the direction of this guidance to Black's firm conviction that economic development is a good thing in and of itself, and sees the "roots of this conviction . . . in Black's [personal] heritage." The account then recalls Black's involvement, as grandson of an early editor of the *Atlanta Constitution*, in the trials and tribulations of Reconstruction in the American South: this experience, "Black concedes, . . . made him sympathetic to the plight of backward peoples

[11] James Reston, "Another 'Georgia Peach' Slides Home," *New York Times*, 18 February 1962, p. 8E.

everywhere."[12] Another analyst states that Black's story "illustrates the flexibility of the American mind."[13]

Having established the genesis of individual ability, the analysis moves on to apply these qualities to an interpretation of specific trends and events. Black's deep conviction "has enabled him to translate a banker's orthodoxy into a gospel of action . . . [and] made Black by degrees an economic planner and even an advocate of land reform."[14] With the pragmatic quality of his culture to nurture and sustain him, "the orthodox conservative American banker out of Atlanta via the Chase National became a kind of international social reformer and managed to do it, not with grants but with sound self-liquidating loans."[15] Black's persuasive salesmanship opened up the U.S. bond market to the Bank;[16] his personal charm and cool competence achieved notable international mediation successes by gaining an agreement for the use of the Indus River waters and settlement of two disputes growing out of the Suez incidents of 1956.[17]

While the functionalist interpretation would see in these developments a happy augury, great-man analysis is likely to show its occasion-motivated initiation and its essentially reportorial objective by way of a melancholy moral. "The weakness of greatness," writes Reston in his tribute to Black as the Bank President's retirement neared, "is that it tends to be irreplaceable."[18]

[12] Douglass Cater, "Eugene Black, Banker to the World," *The Reporter*, XVI (4 April 1957), p. 14.

[13] Reston, *op.cit.*, p. 8E. Cf. Shonfield, *op.cit.*, pp. 145ff.; James Morris, *The Road to Huddersfield* (New York: Pantheon Books, 1963), pp. 55-61.

[14] Cater, *op.cit.*, p. 14.   [15] Reston, *op.cit.*, p. 8E.

[16] Cater, *op.cit.*, p. 14.

[17] Cf. Reston, *op.cit.*, p. 8E, with Black, "Financing Economic Development," p. 22.

[18] Reston, *op.cit.*, p. 8E. But cf. "What Faces New World Bank Chief," *Business Week*, 20 October 1962, pp. 123-24, and "George D. Woods, Bank's Chief, Is Innovator of Policy Changes," *New York Times*, 6 September 1964, p. F1, where the explanatory sequence is more or less repeated.

Great-man analysis is by nature incapable of use for the projection of trends: as the great man is above all predictors, so his choices are above all devices for prediction. For this reason, in part, the great-man explanatory approach has been favored mainly by the historian. Its value is not lessened by the inherent limitation which restricts it to the insights of retrospection, of course. But our present objective, the quest for an understanding of why the Bank's management was able and continues to be able to exercise administrative discretion, directs us to strive to fit individual achievement into a broader schema.

To supplement and put in perspective the insights derived from a biographical reading of events, two aspects of the relationship between individual leadership and its institutional setting will be explored briefly. These would seem fruitful to better understand the conditions surrounding the flexibility of Bank policy. We shall label them the structural legacy of individual achievement and the legitimization of policy.

As noted above, the IBRD Articles of Agreement, augmented by the Bank's By-Laws, delegate to the Executive Directors the authority to make most of the Bank's decisions. In practice the operational decisions appear to be made by the top level of the Bank's management. The roots of this autonomy lie deep; as Douglass Cater puts it, "skillful leadership on the part of successive Bank presidents" has made possible that range of discretion which the present management enjoys.

"The first of them, Eugene Meyer, who opened the Bank's doors in 1946, fought and resigned after six months to force a showdown over the issue of whether the Bank would be run by its officers or by its directors. John J. McCloy, who followed him, succeeded in winning for the president and his assistants a degree of independent authority uncommon in private banks, and even less common in international agencies.

"By the time Black took over as president in 1949, the Bank had firmly eschewed the course of political horse trading among its members that would have quickly led to its demise. In effect, Black and the three vice-presidents are the final judges on every loan."[19]

In other words, the latitude within which Bank "technical self-determination" operates was initiated by an individual determination, but it has subsequently become an attribute of the organization's informal structure.

Another example of this structural legacy of individual achievement involves Eugene Black. Black came to the Bank in 1947 as the U.S. Executive Director. He had been chosen primarily because he was "an extremely persuasive salesman" of bonds. In most states in the U.S. bond sales necessitated special statutes to allow insurance companies, banks, and trusts to hold these securities. This meant the consent of governors and state legislators. Black toured the country, "urging and cajoling." He achieved his objective. Within a year he was able to market the Bank's first offering of $250 million.[20] And the United States market for Bank securities which Black succeeded in opening has remained accessible for these sales ever since.[21]

A second pertinent aspect of the leader-organization relationship, the legitimization of shifts and continuities in policy, bears some resemblance to what Chester I. Barnard calls the "judicial process." Barnard states that this process, "from the executive point of view, is one of morally justifying a change or redefinition or new particularizing of purpose so that the sense of conformance to

19 Cater, *op.cit.*, p. 14.

20 Cater, *op.cit.*, p. 14. One Massachusetts legislator is reported to have responded thus to Black's plea: "I don't know much about banks or bonds, but you look like an honest fellow. I'll support this bill if you'll promise you'll never lend a damn cent to Britain." *Ibid.*, p. 14.

21 The Bank has subsequently looked to the financial market abroad more and more in its bond sales, as noted in Chapter IV. In this as in the earlier security-marketing operations Black seems to have provided initiative, direction, and timing.

moral codes is secured."[22] This conception can best be applied to the Bank by characterizing the general mode by which policy changes and continuities have been legitimized, while at the same time observing the role of IBRD leadership. The earlier discussion of the sequence of tasks perceived for the Bank will not be recapitulated, though it provides additional illustrations of the substance of these choices.[23]

The moral code for the Bank's top leadership is a body of operational rules which partake of a reciprocal relationship with that higher and more general *corpus leges* implicitly acknowledged as the "laws of economics." In the Bank management's perception the latter assumes the status of natural law. Like other natural law systems in human history, the "laws of economics" have provided a flexible foundation for interpretation, application, and justification; like other such systems, they have been excoriated and labeled "unnatural" by the outsider.

Somewhere between higher and lower law is the Bank's charter. More than once it has provided a reference for support of a decision not to undertake a line of action, as when Robert L. Garner, speaking for the Bank in John J. McCloy's temporary absence, answered the criticisms of Bank policy contained in a report of the Subcommission on Economic Development by telling the press that IBRD intended "to stick to making loans on economic rather than 'social and relief grounds.' . . . However 'desirable' it might be, it is not the bank's business—under its charter—'to take care of people who may be poor or even sick.' "[24]

At times the charter has occupied an ambiguous posi-

[22] Chester I. Barnard, *The Functions of the Executive* (rev. ed.; Cambridge: Harvard University Press, 1956), p. 280.

[23] See Chapter IV and pp. 193ff.

[24] As reported in "World Bank to Keep Present Loan Basis," *New York Times*, 26 April 1949, p. 41. The account of Garner's news conference continues: "He also asserted that the present charter of the bank is 'adequate.' "

tion in the hierarchy of laws. On his retirement as President, McCloy emphasized the bearing of IBRD's Articles of Agreement upon its chief decisions. "By its charter," he stated, "the Bank can assist in financing only sound and productive projects." Yet shortly before this, in responding to pressures for an international amendment conference to modify the International Bank's basic instrument, the Bank had supported its findings with an allusion to the higher law: "the obstacles which have thus far prevented a greater volume of investment by the Bank have been imposed by external circumstances and not by charter limitations. . . ."[25]

At other times the Bank's basic instrument has been distinctly subordinate to the categorical imperative which emanates beyond its pale. Article IV, Section 10, entitled "*Political activity prohibited*," states that "The Bank and its officers shall not interfere in the political affairs of any member; nor shall they be influenced in their decisions by the political character of the member or members concerned. Only economic considerations shall be relevant to their decisions. . . ." The distinction between the orders of politics and economics assumed in the section provides a handy enough reference for decisions not to lend: "economic considerations" are always at hand for a reply to the charge of "politics." But more important is the manner in which the "interference" proscription has been skirted in deference to the higher law of economic development. Here logic is apt to be called upon to underwrite an *extension* of institutional responsibility. Eugene Black has stated that the aim of economic aid is to help the underdeveloped countries develop themselves, but adds that "economic aid, if it is to help produce these results, must

[25] IBRD, Press Release No. 136, 18 May 1949; Press Release No. 134, 11 May 1949. See also "World Bank, Fund Hit in U.N. Report," *op.cit.*, p. 41. It may be recalled from Chapter III that the proposal for a second Bretton Woods was made by Emanuel A. Goldenweiser, the U.S. expert on the Subcommission on Employment and Economic Stabilization.

concern itself intimately with the domestic policies of these very sovereign nations." Black continues: "Great resistance from the fractional order to all the many disciplines required for modern economic growth exists in each of these countries. This resistance must be weakened or overcome one way or another. Political and moral choices of the most agonizing sort must be faced as a matter of routine by the leaders of these underdeveloped countries. And through economic aid we will inevitably become involved in these choices. There is no avoiding the hazard; it is in the nature of the exercise."[26]

In one sense, the functionalist interpretation provides relevant terms of reference for discussion of the Bank's rhetoric of action. To take as "given" a universally accepted body of natural law and an authoritative interpreter whose word is at once truth and positive law might well provide an appropriate setting for understanding "the language of economics without the taint of ideology"[27] as just that, nothing more. In such circumstances, the self-determination of a function's dimensions, organs, and powers might indeed prove to be a performance by economic technicians largely veiled by the mystique of expertise.

But such words are presently uttered neither in a traditional society nor a global technocracy. "Laws of economics" come in several varieties these days, and they are apt to be correlated with the non-economic characteristics of their sponsors. Just as the Bank's version of this higher law is not universally accepted, so its edicts are not entirely acceptable—by some because of their heresy, by others simply because of their infrequency.

Viewed from this perspective, these formulations appear to be efforts to gain an ad hoc, instrumental consensus in a world which recognizes a common problem but defines

---

[26] Black, "Newly Developing Nations: Economics and the Cold War," p. 35.

[27] Black, *The Diplomacy of Economic Development,* p. 38.

that problem in divergent, even in mutually exclusive terms. This would seem to provide the plain meaning behind the following statements by Black, prepared essentially for an audience of financiers and industrialists in the United States:

"We must be very careful to isolate from our own experience that which is truly important and relevant from that which is merely sentimental or ideological. We must, in fact, *remove* the taint of ideology from the language of economics so that it can serve to gain agreement from others on the necessary minimum requirements for sound economic growth.

. . . .

"We ask a lot of questions and attach a lot of conditions to our loans. I need hardly say that we would never get away with this if we did not bend every effort to render the language of economics as morally antiseptic as the language the weather forecaster uses in giving tomorrow's prediction. We look on ourselves as technicians or artisans. Words like 'savings' and 'investment,' 'efficiency' and 'productivity' are tools of our trade, and like good artisans we try to develop proper standards for their use."[28]

If this analysis is correct, the Bank's "technical self-determination" implies the ability of its leadership to cultivate and utilize a diversified system of directives to support its practices. And a further aspect of this multiplication of justifications has been the adroit use of the "higher law" to insulate a Bank decision from the debilitating effects of extreme controversy, insofar as is possible, "so that it becomes a question which has the appearance of being merely technical. . . ."[29] This is the significance of

[28] Black, "Newly Developing Nations . . . ," p. 35. Emphasis added. NB the flexibility inherent within a process of developing "proper standards" for the application of such concepts as "efficiency" and "productivity."

[29] Gunnar Myrdal, *Realities and Illusions in Regard to Inter-Gov-*

the aura of expertise in the present case. It is hardly a finding to which the functionalist interpretation would have directed us.

I V

We look now at a clue to understanding offered earlier as part of the functionalist argument. After augmentation from other sources, this functionalist suggestion may provide further understanding of the nature and causes of the "life-space" within which the Bank's management has been able to direct its development. Time and again reference has been made to Mitrany's statement that the function provides its own dimensions, organs, and powers. He adds that the function "determines the executive instrument suitable for its proper activity." The emphasis here will be upon those characteristics of "functions" which distinguish them from one another, and above all upon the implications of this for an understanding of the *why* of IBRD administrative autonomy.[30]

This idea also finds expression in contemporary organization theory. Talcott Parsons, for instance, provides a general definition and rudimentary typology which will serve well in focusing the present inquiry: "An organization is a system which, as the attainment of its goal, 'produces' an identifiable something which can be utilized in some way by another system; that is, the output of the

---

ernmental Organizations, p. 18, as quoted by Asher, *The United Nations and Promotion* . . . , p. 1046.

[30] Walter Kotschnig (in Asher, *The United Nations and Promotion* . . . , p. 67) brings the same style of interpretation nearer our own empirical focus: "Differences in the nature of [the specialized agencies'] functions are responsible, to a considerable extent, for distinguishing characteristics in the structure and organization of the several agencies. They also make for differences in membership and type of representation; they help to determine the position of the chief executive officers and their relationship to the policy shaping and executive organs of the agencies; and they are reflected in variations in budgetary practices and geographical decentralization."

organization is, for some other system, an input. In the case of an organization with economic primacy, this output may be a class of goods or services which are either consumable or serve as instruments for a further phase of the production process by other organizations. In the case of a government agency the output may be a class of regulatory decisions; in that of an educational organization it may be a certain type of 'trained capacity' on the part of the students who have been subjected to its influence."[31]

The distinction between outputs of economic organizations and government agencies which Parsons presents is of theoretical importance, at least.[32] The distinction is somewhat similar to that maintained in the functionalist argument, but the latter bases its typology (or dichotomy) on "controversiality" and the relative need for expertise rather than on the nature of the organizational output. We find Parsons' criterion more suggestive in this respect: the nature of its output may reveal something about the manner and success of an organization in gaining the desired response by those upon whom its decisions impinge. Thus, an organizational unit dispensing purely restrictive outputs (whatever its official designation) would *ex hypothesi* find it more difficult to gain compliance than would an organization distributing a product eagerly sought as an input by "some other system," in Parsonian terms.

[31] Talcott Parsons, "Suggestions for a Sociological Approach to the Theory of Organizations—I," *Administrative Science Quarterly*, I (June 1956), 65; see also *idem* (September 1956), pp. 225-39. Cf. Carl J. Friedrich, "Organization Theory and Political Style," *Public Policy*, A Yearbook of the Graduate School of Public Administration, Harvard University, 1960 (Cambridge: Harvard Graduate School of Public Administration, 1960), p. 60; Amitai Etzioni, *The Comparative Analysis of Complex Organizations* (The Free Press, 1961), *passim*.

[32] But see Marver H. Bernstein, *Regulating Business by Independent Commission* (Princeton: Princeton University Press, 1955), especially pp. 74-102, 250-82.

We might expect to find other differences paralleling this distinction. For example, the outputs by an organization having strictures as its specialized function would in all probability be framed as general commands with wide if not universal applicability. We would be apt to see a rather elaborate supporting mechanism by which such commands were initiated, formulated, adopted, applied, and enforced. We would look for variation in the structural emphasis of organizational systems with restrictive outputs—some having more weight in the initiating and formulating aspects of the process, some in the enforcement sector. In either case, the compass of independent executive action might be sharply circumscribed. For the restrictive-output organization with a highly developed pre-command apparatus we would perhaps find the limitation on the executive emanating from the earlier phases of the process. These limitations might be manifested as "legislative" attempts to restrict the discretion of the executive agent. On the other hand, the executive in a restrictive-output organization with a more highly developed *enforcement* arm would find his personal force dependent upon the coercive potential or the practice of enforcement in gaining actual compliance with his commands. If "decision" is regarded as covering all phases of the process *through enforcement,* the restrictive-output organization would hedge in the executive's decision-making role either by choices made during stages of formulation and adoption (including the choices of those outside the apparatus itself) or simply in the nature of the requirements for enforcement of general restrictive measures.

On the other hand, the organization specializing in the output of highly desired products would, in terms of this hypothesizing gambit, find little difficulty in gaining compliance with its decisions. It would thus neither need nor have an elaborate enforcement mechanism. Insofar as the portion of any organization's apparatus lying anterior to enforcement in the procedure could be said to be purely a device to assist in gaining voluntary "compliance" with the output, that anterior portion of the organizational mechanism too would be unnecessary in the case of the desired-output organization. In the nature of this type of "function," then, the executive (or manager or administrator) might be less restricted in his range of action.

The nature of the primal problem might further distinguish the role of the executive or administrator in organizations specializing in these two types of output. The central concern of the restrictive-output organization is to secure general compliance with its regulations. The organization producing a highly desired output has as its primal problem the mustering and allocation of scarce resources, and toward this end it may assure the conditions, including discretionary latitude, for creative innovation and for making large numbers of choices ostensibly affecting things and not people.

In terms of Parsons' typology, IBRD is best cast as an "organization with economic primacy": it "produces" loans and collateral services and distributes them as its outputs. In any given instance this distribution involves basically two parties, the lending agent and the specific borrower. There is in practice no operative intergovernmental procedure to formulate the Bank's outputs (i.e., to make its specific loan decisions). The Bank's procedure is in distinct contrast to other elaborate intergovernmental parliamentary and consultative mechanisms producing resolutions and draft conventions as outputs. The allocation of loan resources from funds already held by the Bank means that inputs are dissociated from outputs. This acts to further insulate the lending transaction. The Bank has argued with success that a loan to one borrower does not signify the rejection of another applicant because of the lender's limited resources. Apparent acceptance of this Bank pronouncement by potential borrowers, along with the disjuncture between inputs and outputs already mentioned, thus tends to restrict the interest in any given loan transaction to the two parties involved. The output units of the Bank are of specific rather than general interest.

The Bank's *modus operandi* is negotiation; its *modus vivendi*, the bilateral loan agreement. A successfully consummated negotiation is in effect decision, output, and distribution all rolled into one. Failure in negotiation means no loan, and this may have its repercussions; thus far, however, the outcry has been largely restricted to the unsuccessful applicant.[33] Of what he calls "development diplomacy," Eugene Black has written that the International Bank "has had many disputes with its borrowers, but they don't make headlines; there are no ambassadors to recall or armies to mobilize."[34]

In short, the Bank has something that most of its members want very much. Their modal complaint is not that the Bank's outputs are excessive in quantity or repressive in impact, but that they are too few and far between. The Bank's functioning on the output side would therefore seem to provide an additional hypothetical reason for the latitude which its management has enjoyed, and this in turn provides a fuller understanding of the relationship between administrative autonomy and Bank success as measured by the functionalist indices. Substantiation of the more general proposition, however, must await further research. The outputs of international organizations might first be systematically classified. A comparative study of the discretionary latitude of executive arms could then be undertaken by drawing selections from this typology.

We have sought to indicate how IBRD's specific mode of functioning allows or even encourages a management

[33] See, e.g., "World Bank Accused," *New York Times*, 3 October 1961, p. 20.

[34] Black, "Newly Developing Nations . . . ," p. 36. For an indication of the conditions exacted by the Bank, see IBRD, *Some Techniques of Development Lending* (Washington: IBRD, 1960), *passim*; *The World Bank, IFC and IDA*, pp. 30-52.

role with sizeable discretionary interstices. The inquiry leads to a question of exceedingly great importance for further understanding the Bank management's autonomy and the nature of some of its actions. Above it was noted that there are two primary phases in the cycle of Bank operations, "inputs" and "outputs." The discussion then focused on the logic of the Bank's function, which is to say its output—lending. Allocation of resources is the essence of this function, but allocation is only one portion of the primal problem of organizations with highly desired outputs. Equally important for the Bank's operations is the mustering of resources from which its loans can be made.

Given the operative scarcity of resources implicit in the establishment of international organizations to finance economic development, it might be assumed that an elaborate and recurrent ritual involving member state actors would be a primary accompaniment of fund-raising. The experience of other multilateral international organizations certainly has prepared the observer for this type of phenomenon. Such is the case with the Special Fund, whose management witnesses an annual parade of pledgers, long on words and short on promises. Paul Hoffman never avoids an opportunity to enter a plea for larger national contributions to the Special Fund, and his invariable argument is the prospective donor's interest in the matter. The SF management's lines of accountability pass through the contributors' list as well as the roll of those members occupying the formal seats of the councilor.[35] The form of this accounting is not the vote, but the potentiality of a relative deprivation of the substance upon which the Spe-

[35] It will be recalled that the "immediate inter-governmental control of the policies and operations of the Special Fund [is] exercised by a Governing Council" which consists of representatives of twenty-four states, elected by the Economic and Social Council from members of the UN, its specialized agencies, or the International Atomic Energy Agency, and including equal representation of the economically more and less developed countries.

cial Fund is dependent—a deprivation always relative since state contributions are so small in any case. The nature of the Fund makes it difficult if not impossible for a given donor to call the tune, but it must be readily apparent to all concerned that each year presents ample opportunity to refuse to pay the piper. The Special Fund, like the daily paper in its publisher's eyes, undergoes a periodic vote of confidence by its economic benefactors.

With this high ratio of fanfare to output for the Special Fund, one might be led to expect a similar show of ostentatious public soul-searching surrounding the nourishment of IBRD by its nation-state members. Simply to compare the Special Fund and Bank output figures in Chapter IV would ready us for a far grander spectacle at the latter's coffers, for instance at the annual meetings of the Board of Governors. But this is not the case. National soul-searching there is, and international soul-searching, as well, but here the theme is not so much the insufficiency of state contributions to the multilateral financing program as the paucity of Bank lending and the high costs it exacts for those loans it does extend. How may we account for this difference, and what further implications do the findings provide?

One explanation can be called the "redoubt" conception. The Bank was financed by public funds, this interpretation begins, and its capital base was broadened in 1959 by an additional round of member state subscriptions. These subscriptions, which have provided a foundation for the Bank's expansion in operations, are not equal for each state: the United States subscribed far more than any other member, the United Kingdom next, and so on. Just as the schedule of subscriptions was drawn to ask of each according to his ability, so the weight of his vote was assigned according to his actual support. The adequacy of these graduated subscriptions for IBRD operations plus the system of weighted voting has meant that the Bank's leadership can remain sealed off from any serious opposition within the ranks; this elite need look beyond its own inner circle for neither financial nor multilateral parliamentary support. The United States, Britain, Canada, and one or two others provide "an easy working majority."[36] And insofar as this inner circle of leadership consists of persons other than the *de jure* representatives of the leading subscribers, these persons too present no problem in gaining the consensus necessary to operate. The relationship between Bank Staff and the Western bloc's international economic policy, as this interpretative viewpoint sees it, is approximately that of the goatskin to Esau.[37]

The picture we gain from the archangels' viewpoint provided by this interpretation is that of three concentric circles. The innermost is the redoubt, from which the IBRD sponsors hold forth against attacks of various kinds and intensities. Next is a circle containing the underdeveloped members of the Bank. They are not on altogether friendly terms with the occupants in the center, but their belligerence is tempered by a preoccupation with one aspect of Bank policy (the quantity and terms of its lending), and by their realization that Bank procedures would be virtually impossible to change without some danger of cutting off loans altogether. In the outermost ring—beyond the gates, as it were—are those ex-members and non-members with basic hostility toward Bank procedures and the substance of Bank policy. From this perimeter the Soviets and others lay siege with such weapons as they

[36] Cater, *op.cit.*, p. 14. Cf. Morris, *op.cit.*, p. 46; Shonfield, *op.cit.*, p. 113.

[37] For varying views of the extent to which the Bank is an instrument of Western and especially U.S. policy, cf. the following: Cater, *op.cit.*, p. 15; Asher, *The United Nations and Promotion . . . ,* p. 1047, citing Raymond F. Mikesell, "Barriers to the Expansion of United Nations Economic Functions," *Annals of The American Academy of Political and Social Science*, CCXCVI (1 November 1954), 45; Matecki, *op.cit.*, "Subservience of International Bank to United States—a Myth," pp. 162-64; Claude, *op.cit.*, pp. 398f.; "World Bank: The New President," *The Economist*, 20 October 1962, p. 293; Morris, *op.cit.*, pp. 46, 59. See also Chapter V, above.

can train upon the fortress, and intersperse this bombardment with diversionary efforts designed to distract the occupants of the middle region.

The mode of interpretation represented by this illustration is by no means functionalist in its orientation. It is "apocalyptic" in the sense that it interprets a crucial and ineradicable procedure to have been planted in the basic law by the founders of IBRD; it is distinctly political in explaining how this procedure has been raised from paper to practice and in respect to the general dynamics at which it darkly hints.

The redoubt interpretation helps in understanding several aspects of the Bank's activities. Weighted votes are bound to be a factor affecting if not shaping the Bank's every move, whether these votes are cast or remain in the shadows as an ever-present potential. The notion of a redoubt, or citadel, helps fill in the picture of the conditions under which Bank management has been able to achieve considerable autonomy, though the assumptions upon which the metaphor rests must not be accepted uncritically.

The redoubt conception reminds us that it is an *international* organization which we are explaining; it focuses attention on the preeminent roles which the nation-state or its representatives have played in all phases of this dramatic production—as playwright, producer, actor, director, prompter. Yet in so fixing our gaze, this approach to understanding tends to gloss over certain other questions which, though not answered by this approach, promise further insights into the nature of the Bank's general actions and specific choices.

The interpretative formulation which begins and ends its explication of IBRD with references to nation-states in general and certain nation-states in particular assumes the adequacy of member state subscriptions for the Bank's substantial loan operations. The explanation must make this assumption or it would find difficult a showing of why, in their national interest, the borrowing states have subscribed to and remained members of this international organization. Because its conceptual overlay emphasizes other aspects of the topography, this interpretation gives little attention to its assumption. It may, to be sure, note in passing that the Bank's capital base was expanded in 1959 by the decision of member states and their subsequent subscriptions. But it is not likely to raise or pursue the implications of the question—*why* these subscribed resources have been adequate to hold the developing nations in their respective orbits about the Bank.

The Bank has argued that a loan to one borrower does not of itself mean the rejection of a subsequent loan applicant. More generally, the Bank's management has assiduously cultivated the theory that the only quantitative limitation on Bank loans is the readiness of projects which can productively absorb resources. By what token may an international institution so commit its wealthier members?

It is apparent that this state of affairs stands in stark contrast to the kind of statement which could be and has been made by the Managing Director of the Special Fund.[38] We recall, too, that the Special Fund is "subscribed" each year, the Bank but twice, thus far, in its lifetime. And we remember that the Bank gains most of its resources *not* from member governments, but by issuing its own securities. This much is crude fact. More important are the implications that it yields.

Our thesis is that the original lines demarcating the IBRD constituency were drawn, consciously or otherwise, so as to potentially encompass a portion of the international private sector as well as the Bank's nation-state members; and that much of the Bank's subsequent history is enlightened through reading that history as a shift in

---

[38] Paul Hoffman might, of course, seek to justify the raising of the limitation on pre-investment imposed by nation-state contributors by way of a reference to the unlimited resources applicable through the Bank to projects which have been readied by his own agency's allotments. This seems to be very close to his basic theme.

the locus of accountability from state members toward the international financial community.

The IBRD cornerstone relevant to this thesis was laid not at the Bretton Woods Conference, but at the Atlantic City pre-conference caucus. In June 1944 a group of American financial experts was joined by representatives from sixteen countries. John Parke Young has reported the decision relevant to our argument:

"At the Atlantic City meetings, the British experts, headed by Lord Keynes, presented proposals regarding the Bank which involved rather extensive changes from the earlier plan, but which met with almost immediate approval by the experts of the other nations including the United States. According to these suggestions, embodied in the final document, only a small portion of the Bank's capital, namely 20 percent, would be paid in and be available for loans. The remaining 80 percent would constitute a guaranty fund to be used, if necessary, in connection with the Bank's guaranties of private loans or to meet other obligations of the Bank. This proposal meant that the Bank's cash resources would be considerably smaller than originally contemplated."[39]

The immediate supply of loanable funds was further abbreviated by the requirement that only 2 percent of each subscription was exacted in gold or U.S. dollars and freely useable by the Bank. The United States released the remaining 18 percent of its paid-in obligation before the Bank's first major operations. This release, however, left the Bank with considerably less than 20 percent of its total subscribed capital for use in lending operations. The first waves of reconstruction loans mounted to $497 million by July 1, 1948.

Hypothetically, at least, the Bank's officials might have met the need for more loan funds by calling for an im-

[39] John Parke Young, "Developing Plans for an International Monetary Fund and a World Bank," p. 786.

mediate increase in the Bank's capital stock under Article II, Section 2 (b) of the Articles of Agreement. This would have brought member governments' decisions to bear in arriving at the necessary three-fourths of total voting power; if successful, it might have provided a precedent for future replenishment. In fact, the Bank's management had already begun to cultivate alternative sources of funds. That optimistic temper of the Bretton Woods conclave which had impressed itself alike on the Articles of Agreement and the *New York Times* reporter who analogized the Bank to a "New York title company . . . guaranteeing mortgages"[40] had faded with the hard reality of yawning reconstruction needs and reticent private international capital; the peak of the Bank's drive for the release of subscribed funds beyond those made available by the United States was yet to come. But the campaign to open a securities market for the Bank's own obligations had moved into high gear by this time. The 80 percent of subscriptions dead to use as loan money was being activated as collateral for the Bank's borrowings. The fruits of this campaign have been weighed in a previous chapter. What remains is to point up some characteristics and implications of that substantial dependence upon the financial community which the Bank has accepted. For as Douglas Dillon is reported to have stated at the Annual Meeting in 1958, "the World Bank had passed the stage when it could rely for its resources on the paid-in capital subscriptions of member governments. [Dillon] declared the scale of the bank's future lending activities depended 'almost entirely' on its ability to raise funds in the private capital market."[41]

In a general sense, Philip Selznick's conception of the external social base of an organization provides a sugges-

[40] Russell Porter, "Diplomatic Gains Credited to Soviet in Monetary Move," p. 11.
[41] Fund Rise Backed for World Bank," *New York Times*, 10 October 1958, p. 45.

tive lead, particularly if the Bank's input operations are kept in mind. Selznick writes:

"Among the critical decisions facing leadership, closely related to the definition of mission, is the selection of a clientele, market, target, allies, or other segment of the environment to which operations will be oriented. Personnel recruitment, public relations, and many other areas of decision will be affected by this key choice of an external 'social base.' The early phase of an institution's life is marked by a scrutiny of its own capabilities, and of its environment, to discover where its resources are and on whom it is dependent. The achievement of stability is influenced by this appraisal; and the future evolution of the institution is largely conditioned by the commitments generated in this basic decision. Of course, the 'decision' is not always consciously made; and often the outcome is forced upon the organization by compelling circumstances which leave little freedom of choice. . . . [W]hen a political organization bases itself on some special social force, say the labor movement or business interests; when a government agency adapts itself to the influential groups it must please in order to stay alive—there is created an effective and controlling environment of decision. As these commitments evolve, the organization loses its purity as an abstractly or ideally envisioned entity; it assumes a definite role in a living community; it becomes institutionalized. The *design* of that role, insofar as freedom to do so exists, is very largely a matter of choosing the social base upon which the organization will rest. Often this outcome is not designed but simply emerges in an unplanned way, as a precipitant of many short-run decisions."[42]

[42] Philip Selznick, *Leadership in Administration: A Sociological Interpretation* (Evanston: Row, Peterson and Co., 1957), pp. 104-05. Emphasis in original. Selznick distinguishes "organization" from "institution" thus: "The term 'organization' . . . suggests a certain bareness, a lean, no-nonsense system of consciously co-ordinated activities. It refers to an *expendable tool*, a rational instrument en-

More specifically, the implications of the Bank's commitment to the financial community may be treated in terms of two themes: autonomy and accountability.

Several hypotheses have already been advanced regarding the autonomy which the Bank's management has enjoyed. To focus on the relationship between the Bank and its financial clientele guides us toward an even surer understanding of that autonomy. We readily perceive that it is this putative boundless reservoir, coupled with the pump-priming premise that remains a Bank operative ideal, which has prompted the hint of unlimited resources for appropriate undertakings. The contrast between fund-raising efforts by Bank and Special Fund management is better understood, as much in their respective foci as their relative quantitative success. We observe the discretion implicit in the Bank's capacity to initiate and culminate these fund-raising efforts whenever they seem propitious, and to direct them wherever financial or other considerations may dictate.[43] And the obvious is readily noted: it is easier to convince member states' governments that an infrequent recapitalization is in order when those funds

gineered to do a job. An 'institution,' on the other hand, is more nearly a natural product of social needs and pressures—a responsive, adaptive organism. . . . In what is perhaps its most significant meaning, 'to institutionalize' is to *infuse with value* beyond the technical requirements of the task at hand." (*Leadership in Administration*, pp. 5, 17; emphasis in original.) Selznick cites Barnard, *op.cit.*, 1938 edition, p. 73, in connection with his own use of "organization."

[43] In commenting on a 1958 placement of Bank bonds to 40 institutional investors in 26 countries other than the U.S., *The Times* (London) offered this observation: "The bank has always been insistent in stressing that it is an international organization and that, although most of its financial transactions are expressed in United States dollars, to borrow from it is not indirectly to borrow from the United States Government. Thus sales of World Bank bonds, such as this one, are probably so arranged as much for political reasons as to obtain funds from sources outside the United States." From "U.S. Plans to Increase I.M.F. and World Bank Funds," *op.cit.*, p. 12.

are to be pledged for guaranty purposes rather than actually paid in, particularly if influential and interested persons and groups in the major subscribing states lend their support to such a proposal.[44]

There are further implications of the Bank's relatively pecunious position. Primary sources of new funds for lending include earnings from the various investments made by the Bank as well as the raising of funds through issuance of Bank securities.[45] As noted earlier, the Bank realizes a substantial income. No annual contributions by member governments are necessary to support the IBRD administrative budget. This budget, prepared annually by the management and approved by the Executive Directors, is financed from the Bank's own operations.[46]

We shall return shortly to a consideration of the relationship between some of these budgetary expenditures and the new locus of Bank accountability. First we must indicate more precisely what is meant by "accountability" by considering two of its varieties. An example from another realm illustrates this very well.

The legislative representative attains his place as an authoritative participant in the making of public policy through a formal process by which he is endowed with the cloak of legitimacy. He retains this office through a recurrence of the same pattern. His path may be difficult or easy in attaining and retaining this position; the process itself may be all form and no substance, may indeed be farcical. Anomalous as this may be, we like to think of this voting process as "consent," and most of us would probably resist even such a phrase as "the assent of the governed" on grounds of bad analysis as well as bad choice of words. We give our consent, as we say, so that this man might represent the people living on the plot of ground

[44] See, e.g., "Bank Proposal Backed," *New York Times*, 5 March 1959, p. 27.

[45] IBRD, *The World Bank, op.cit.*, pp. 24, 74-75.

[46] *Ibid.*, p. 21; Kotschnig, in Asher, *The United Nations and Promotion . . .* , p. 76.

which is our state or district or whatever. Without most of our votes he is but a political suitor.

We consent as voters, and it is our consent to which this representative looks at fixed or varying intervals. Yet it is not these votes alone which he seeks, nor are our words, as voters, the only ones he hears or solicits. These other voices may begin before his candidacy; they do not cease with his election. The contemporary American political scientist has provided a vocabulary with which to talk about them. Their source is the "group," concrete or conceptual; their nature is "interest," their present posture "access" or "influence," superseding the "pressure" they exerted in an earlier muckrakerish day. These words seem a natural fit for contemporary phenomena. The relationships which they symbolize are manifold; only one aspect of this range will be singled out for brief examination here. It is on all counts an unobtrusive association, portrayable neither by quantitative evidence nor by vectorial diagram. "Tractability" this mystic bond may be called, for present purposes; by it we signify an official-client[47] relationship, personal or otherwise, which turns on an axis of shared reference points and complementary objectives. The lines of communication may have been laid in earlier days, perhaps before recruitment of the official.[48] They are grounded more firmly by frequent usage, in private as well as public life. Above all the transmission of signals is encouraged by a virtual necessity for the support or acquiescence of the client in achieving tasks defined by the cognizant official. For this reason, the official may be the active agent in their transmission.

In the IBRD annals, consent was the dominant mode of accountability during the formulation and ratification

[47] For purposes of this illustration, the official may have attained his post either by the consent of the voters or by appointment.

[48] Cf. Aaron Wildavsky, *Dixon-Yates: A Study in Power Politics* (New Haven: Yale University Press, 1962), p. 188 and n.2, with "What Faces New World Bank Chief," *Business Week*, 20 October 1962, p. 123.

of the Articles of Agreement. The consent of governments to paper instruments was underlined by that consent implicit in their subscriptions to the capital base of the new international organization. Tractability there must have been also, but it was the tractability of prior acquaintance rather than that of interdependency.

The fight and resignation of Eugene Meyer over the question of whether IBRD would be run by Directors or "the Bank" marked the beginning of a decline in active consent by member governments. The redoubt had been built, buttressed with weighted votes, and now the provisioning excursions began. This period witnessed "a phenomenal growth of public-relations activity. An impressive campaign was undertaken to familiarize the investment community with the bonds of the Bank. . . . More promotion went into the issuance of $250 millions of securities than into any comparable fund-raising in the history of American finance."[49] The early contacts were largely personal, the early bond issues "placed" rather than "floated." By about 1950 the market was opened sufficiently for a more impersonal nexus to become the mode of these transactions. And with these mounting obligations grew the Bank's accountability to a financial community of expanding scope.[50]

What are the implications of this accountability?

Probably there are instances where the Bank management has been affected in an important specific judgment by attitudes held within this private sector. For instance, it was reported earlier that the proposed IFC was initially met by opposition from some quarters in this country; there is some evidence that this attitude carried over into

[49] Charles P. Kindleberger, "Bretton Woods Reappraised," *International Organization*, V (February 1951), 43. See also the chronicle of this campaign as recorded in the Bank's successive press releases during this period.

[50] See "Financing Weighed by the World Bank," *New York Times*, 14 July 1949, p. 35. For a discussion of the international aspects of these operations see Chapter IV, above.

the Bank's deliberations and extended the period of the Bank's "studies" of the proposal. Harold Linder, then Assistant Secretary of State for Economic Affairs, testified before a House subcommittee in March 1953 that while his department was sympathetic to the proposal, he had to state candidly that part of the private banking community opposed it, and "since the International Bank goes to the banking and business community as one of the sources of its funds, through the sale of its own debentures, the management of the Bank cannot fail to take into account, and serious account . . . the attitude of that community with respect to this proposal. It is still before the Bank for consideration."[51]

But this relationship exercises a far more pervasive effect on Bank policy. The capital-market calculus in effect acts as a Procrustean bed to which the terms of Bank loans must be fitted.[52] Furthermore, the Bank is restrained from undertaking certain lines of action. Robert Garner succinctly portrayed the nature of this restraint on the occasion of his rejection of social and relief ventures on behalf of the Bank: "We wouldn't be able to raise any money out of the market if we did that."[53] During his IBRD Presidency, Eugene Black created "a meshwork of contacts—what the English call 'the old boy net'—with distinguished financiers in most countries of the West, through which many a gigantic project was first mooted and many a rash approach rebuffed from the start."[54]

[51] U.S. Congress, House of Representatives, *Hearings before the Sub-committee on Foreign Economic Policy of the Committee on Foreign Affairs, 83rd Congress, First Session*, p. 21, as quoted by Matecki, *op.cit.*, p. 76.

[52] Cf. IBRD, *Twelfth Annual Report, 1956-1957*, pp. 10-11; *The World Bank, op.cit.*, p. 73.

[53] "World Bank to Keep Present Loan Basis," *op.cit.*, p. 41. Cf. Black's rejoinder to criticism of Bank policy by members of the Economic and Social Council, as reported by A. M. Rosenthal, "World Bank Asked to Ease Standards," *New York Times*, 17 February 1950, p. 13.

[54] Morris, *op.cit.*, p. 59.

Black's achievement bequeaths both autonomy and accountability to his successors.

If this analysis is correct, it should illuminate certain other actions by the Bank. The rejection of a Philippines loan request "despite great pressure from the State Department," for instance, is more clearly seen in the light of the Bank's accountability than simply in terms of the Bank's relationship to U.S. governmental policy.[55] The appointment of major Bank Staff members may better be understood when viewed as subject to a passive veto by the Bank's financial constituency—now extended beyond these shores. And the pattern of Bank activities collateral to the lending process itself gains clarity when viewed from this perspective. This final point deserves more extended consideration.

In terms of most quantitative indices the Bank has made good prophets of the functionalists. Lending—surely the single most important quantitative index—has grown substantially over the years. Yet the expansion has not been entirely smooth. To choose perhaps the most striking example, the Bank extended loans for approximately $500 million in calendar year 1947; in 1948, the total dropped to $28 million.[56] The break occurred as the Bank extended its last major reconstruction loans. This was the period of the campaign to open a market for Bank securities. A further aspect of that campaign was the Bank's demonstration to potential bondholders that its lending standards were to be high, and that IBRD would carefully oversee the actual usage of disbursed funds to insure their productive application at the destination agreed upon at the time of the loan commitment. The "project basis" was to provide further assurance to the potential investor that the Bank's loans were soundly conceived.[57] The over-all

[55] The quotation is from Cater, *op.cit.*, p. 15.

[56] Kindleberger, *op.cit.*, p. 45.

[57] *Ibid.*, p. 43. Even so, the "specific project" criterion proved an inviolable rule neither in early nor later practice. Cf. the Bank staff's own statement, in *The World Bank*, pp. 41-42: "There are

effect of these developments, spurred largely by the Bank's desire to raise funds at a minimal cost, was to widen the gap between Bank lending standards, on the one hand, and the capabilities of would-be borrowers to provide blueprints of projects and warrants of "productivity," on the other. The newer wave of loan applications emanated from the underdeveloped sector of the Bank's membership.

Some measure of the anguish attendant upon this state of affairs has been indicated earlier, especially with reference to the underdeveloped members. Their feelings are perhaps adequately represented by the plea of Sir A. Ramaswami Mudaliar of India, who stated to Black before the Economic and Social Council in early 1950 that the Bank's requirements could not be met by those most needing loans, and urged "a little more sympathy, a little more heart, a little less of the logicality that is characteristic of bankers."[58]

The Bank's officials were not entirely happy with the gap. In his address presenting the Bank's Fourth Annual Report to the Board of Governors in September 1949, Black confessed that despite an increase for the Bank's year, he had to "say frankly that the volume of development loans granted to date has not come up to our earlier expectations." Several months later, in the exchange al-

---

special cases, of course, where detailed project investigations are neither necessary nor feasible. The early reconstruction loans to France, Denmark and the Netherlands, for example, were designed to meet emergency needs of those countries for foreign funds to finance a large variety of imports essential to the rehabilitation and continued operation of their industries. Because those needs affected so many different sectors of the economy, because it was so urgent to assist in meeting the needs in order to prevent a disastrous decline in production, and because the Bank had satisfied itself that the goods financed by the loans were to be used for essential and productive purposes, the Bank was willing to make the necessary financing available without detailed examination of the specific projects in connection with which the goods were to be employed." See also p. 136, above.

[58] Quoted by A. M. Rosenthal, "World Bank Asked to Ease Standards," op.cit., p. 13.

luded to in the previous paragraph, Black admitted to a feeling of "considerable frustration" over the "regrettably" limited number of loans, even while upholding the need for high banking standards. The limitation, said Black, was not a lack of Bank funds: it was "the lack of well-prepared and well-planned projects ready for immediate execution."[59]

Our contention is that the spanning of this chasm— achieved to the extent development loans have expanded over the years—was accomplished basically by initiatives undertaken by the Bank. The drive to bridge this gap helps to explain the Bank's survey missions, its technical assistance of various kinds, and some of its other activities.

Bank Staff members tell of an early loan request from an underdeveloped country which carried simply the written message "Please send money."[60] More generally, an IBRD publication has noted the common deficiencies which marked early project proposals.[61] Even before McCloy and Black publicly acknowledged the existence of a lag in the preparation of projects for the status of bankability, the International Bank had begun to move toward circumvention. In its First Annual Report the Bank showed its willingness to consider provisions of technical assistance in preparing loan applications. Recommendations of suitable engineering firms to assist in preparing projects were provided for member applicants.[62] The Bank sent its own staff to the field to investigate proposed projects, and these investigations involved more than recommendations for Bank approval or rejection of specific requests. The whole

[59] *Ibid.*, p. 13. John J. McCloy had pointed to much the same obstacle the year before. He stressed that the lag in consummating loans was due primarily to delays in "bringing projects from the concept stage to the bankable stage." Quoted in "The Role of the World Bank," *The Eastern Economist*, XII (4 February 1949), 192.

[60] Quoted by George A. Mooney, "World Bank Aims Pointed Up on Aid," *New York Times*, 3 November 1952, p. 45.

[61] *The World Bank*, *op.cit.*, p. 41.

[62] Asher, *The United Nations and Promotion* . . . , p. 318; "The Role of the World Bank," p. 192.

context of the project was surveyed. More recently one commentator has said that the Bank interprets its charter's admonition to loan "prudently" as requiring a "look into virtually every aspect, however peripheral, of a country's economic, political, and financial status."[63] But also these field investigations have suggested alternative projects. The Bank's inquiry "may reveal, first, that some projects which have not been submitted to the Bank and for which financing has not otherwise been arranged nevertheless merit a high priority; and, second, that a number of those submitted to the Bank are of relatively low priority. The Bank expresses its views accordingly in its discussions with the authorities of the country concerned, emphasizing its preference for financing the projects that seem most urgently required and advising postponement of those that appear less immediately important to the country's development."[64] Even the elaborate end-use checking system employed by the Bank provides a channel of communication through which borrowers "are able to discuss their plans for investment well in advance and to obtain an early indication of the Bank's opinion." The IBRD Staff adds that "this tends to facilitate subsequent financing from the Bank or from other sources."[65]

Thus did the International Bank go about "devising techniques by which it could put its experience at the service of other countries."[66] Black reported in 1949 that while in earlier days the delay in completion of loans was

[63] Frederick T. Moore, "The World Bank and Its Economic Missions," *The Review of Economics and Statistics,* XLII (February 1960), 82. See also Mooney, "World Bank Aims Pointed Up on Aid," p. 45; Sharp, *Field Administration in the United Nations System,* p. 30; *The World Bank,* pp. 37-61; Alec Cairncross, *The International Bank for Reconstruction and Development* (Princeton: International Finance Section of the Department of Economics and Sociology, 1959), p. 6.

[64] *The World Bank,* p. 42. Cf. Black, "The World Bank at Work," p. 409.

[65] *The World Bank,* p. 51.

[66] Cairncross, *op.cit.,* p. 6.

"about 75 percent our fault and 25 percent the borrower's," the percentages had since been reversed.[67]

As noted before, however, the lending rate had as yet risen very little. Even while abjuring a certain amount of responsibility, the Bank found and applied new techniques for aiding in the preparation of projects. Analysis of the economic setting of specific projects was systematized by using the general survey mission, the first of which was dispatched to Colombia in 1949. The Fifth Annual Report's prediction that these surveys would "certainly form a useful working basis for financial relations between the Bank and its member countries" seems to have been borne out by the record: since 1949, twenty-five loans totaling almost $400 million have been extended to Colombia, as borrower or guarantor.[68] The survey mission, general or otherwise, is only the most important of several devices which the Bank has used in bridging the gap between the lending standards pressed by its own financial clientele and the wishes of its less-developed members. Citing these devices in his annual remarks in 1961, Black underlined the ideal of a "well-conceived project" in a "sound development program," and stated that such "in fact . . . is the justification for our whole range of technical assistance projects."

v

The general argument thus far has been that the functionalist interpretation, by itself, is insufficient guidance to an understanding of the *why* of those general consequences successfully predicted. Emphasis was placed upon

[67] Quoted in "Financing Weighed By the World Bank," p. 35.
[68] Among its examples of "specific accomplishments [which] can be attributed in whole or in part to the work of Bank missions," IBRD's *Eleventh Annual Report* cites the highway programs in Colombia and Honduras. Up to that time the Bank had made three loans for highways totaling about $47 million to Colombia, and during the fiscal year covered by the report it extended a loan for $4.2 million to Honduras for highway construction. IBRD, *Eleventh Annual Report, 1955-1956,* pp. 24, 50-52, 54.

that range of developments which provides the functionalists, in the compass of the present study, with their best claim to the status of seers—IBRD's activities. This portion of the critique in effect acknowledged that functionalist guideposts can lead toward insights after considerable redefinition and reorientation of concepts and added specificity in application.

Beyond the insufficiency of the functionalist interpretation is a larger difficulty. It may be introduced by recounting some of the less successful functionalist prophecies.

In interpreting the vignettes of Chapter V, which provided glimpses of "attitude change" as manifested through shifts in position, the functionalist explanation afforded little assistance to understanding. We sought to fit out our perception with the provisional expectation of seeing functional activity as the training ground for cooperation. Yet in viewing these slices of functional life we perceived not so much habituation in agreement as the trappings of continuing conflict.

Similarly, there is a striking discontinuity between the magnitude of Bank operations and the solving of the problem of economic development. The "problem" almost seems to have grown with the expansion of Bank lending. Such a happenstance seems distinctly alien to the functionalist understanding. The community to be born of functional activities makes easier the solution of these problems. So goes the functionalist argument.

These perplexities cannot be fully explained, but in the final portion of this interpretative essay they will be explored.

Our theme is simple. The functionalists completely neglect the context of the activities they propose to explain, except as they take that context to be the ultimate beneficiary of functional endeavor. In the narrowness of its focus, the functional interpretation cuts off an understanding of the very dynamics which give rise to these activities and affect every aspect of their existence. To say "function" or "technical self-determination" is of itself to imply the overriding importance of a spontaneous motive and directive force which must be rejected, at least on the basis of this investigation.

These financing agencies are conceived and nurtured in a matrix pervaded by tensions. On the basis of the previous inquiry, this matrix of tensions would seem to have at least those dimensions which can be labeled intra-national, intra-alliance, and inter-bloc.[69] Chief among these, during the period surveyed, were the tensions subsumed under the rubric "Cold War"; though these order and inform the other tensional facets, they are far from constituting the sole driving or directive force behind the decisions witnessed in this study. As Chapters III and V suggest, it is impossible to understand IBRD, IFC, IDA, or the Special Fund without taking into account the impetus generated by friction between interest groups, political parties, government agencies, alliance partners, and alliances or UN voting coalitions themselves. The Bank's membership and its operations are hardly explicable without reference to the fashionable metaphor of a bipolar system with unattracted particles, resting tentatively upon a neutral field, which can and do remain "uncommitted" by dint of the offsetting forces emanating from the respective poles. IFC's pre-natal history abounds in the claims and counter-claims of interest groups in the United States, and gives evidence of a certain divergence between the U.S. Treasury and State Departments. We catch a glimpse of Executive-Congressional and Democratic-Republican maneuvering in regard to the IDA proposal. That agency's eventual espousal by the Eisenhower Administration is understandable both in terms of the quest for new swords to duel the Soviet economic offensive of the post-Stalin

[69] This discussion owes much to the suggestive formulation by Ernst B. Haas, in his "Regionalism, Functionalism, and Universal International Organization." For an interpretation of intra- and interregional "balancing" to the mid-fifties, see this article, in *World Politics*, VIII (January 1956), 238-63.

era and a desire to shift part of the burden of international financial assistance to those allies who were prospering even as confidence in the U.S. dollar weakened.[70] The Special Fund, child of a protracted series of antagonistic encounters, seems to owe its existence at least in part to the growing isolation of the United States, which was deserted in its opposition to SUNFED first by some of its own allies, and then, perhaps more significantly, by the Soviet Union and Czechoslovakia.

Governments of the developing countries have sought to direct this raw energy toward the creation of financing agencies. The intensity of their concern has helped make economic development a prime emphasis despite "the overwhelmingly security-oriented approach which the West seeks to give to the United Nations."[71] The persistence of their efforts to maintain the status of economic development as an ongoing agenda item has been exercised and extended through such devices as the reports of ad hoc experts' groups, subcommissions, UN and regional economic commission secretariats, and intergovernmental committees; by the two-pronged attack by which the staid Economic and Social Council is besieged with proposals for development efforts from both its underlings (such as the late subcommissions of the defunct Economic and Employment Commission) and the General Assembly; and by the process of drafting and negotiating the resolu-

[70] The annual meetings of the Boards of Governors have in recent years provided a forum within which the more affluent Bank members are subjected to pressure, exerted by the U.S. in the presence of the less-developed nations, to expand their long-term international investments. See, e.g., "Socialist Policy Upheld in Ghana," *op.cit.*, a report on the 1960 meeting which indicates that the inadequacy of German foreign aid programs was the object of critical comments; "Germany Sets Aid Loan," *New York Times*, 30 September 1960, p. 40; Edwin L. Dale, Jr., "Development Body [IDA] Will Require More Funds, Rich Nations Told," *New York Times*, 20 September 1961, pp. 37, 43; "Black's Appeal Scored [by Britain]," *New York Times*, 20 September 1961, p. 43.

[71] Haas, *op.cit.*, p. 250.

tions whose passage means little of itself. The brunt of this effort in recent years has been directed to the expansion of financing operations. Always the theme has been the discrepancy between stated ideals and evident practice, but more important to achievement has been the multi-level context of tensions, the role of the central UN organs, and the skillful practice of multilateral parliamentary diplomacy.

Furthermore, that "immense wave of hope" which Raymond Scheyven foresaw as a consequence of decisive UN action has been sustained, in the face of middling measures, by sporadic voices from within the major potential contributing state—voices not entirely discounted abroad despite their quasi-official character. Thus, the Gray Report, the Rockefeller Report, and Paul Hoffman's article in the *New York Times Magazine* each set off a ripple of speculation and helped buoy up expectations which might otherwise have flagged.[72] And it might be assumed that the proposal for a "UN Development Decade" put forward by the President of the United States will have the same effect, notwithstanding that proposal's emphasis on "rationalization" rather than expansion.[73]

In a sense it could be said that these are modern verifica-

[72] Besides Chapters III and V above, see Asher, *The United Nations and Promotion* . . . , pp. 629-30, on Gray Report.

[73] President John F. Kennedy, address before the General Assembly of 25 September 1961, reprinted as "Let Us Call a Truce to Terror" in the *United States Department of State Bulletin*, XLV (16 October 1961), 619; Philip M. Klutznick, U.S. Representative to the General Assembly, "A United Nations Development Decade," *idem*, XLV (4 December 1961), 939-47. Cf. the address by Secretary-General U Thant in Copenhagen on "The Decade of Development." *NB* especially the divergent assumptions between Klutznick's article and this portion of the Secretary-General's address: "I question whether men and women among the wealthier nations of mankind quite realize what abundance is at their disposal. . . . [While disarmament is to be desired,] I would stress with all the vigor at my command that we do not have to wait upon disarmament. Even with armaments, many economies now operate below capacity." *United Nations Review*, IX (June 1962), 38.

tions of the process which men like Elihu Root seemed to understand international institutions to follow in their development, a process called "in-principle gradualism" in Chapter I. The principles in the UN Charter, for instance, provide a kind of polestar which is often pointed toward in report and resolution, if somewhat less quickly followed in practice. But these principles, invoked as the leading-strings of action, do not issue into what Louis Hartz has called a Lockean consensus.[74] On the contrary, in focusing upon economic development as perhaps upon no other question, the United Nations often appears to be the scene of a " 'curious war in which everyone professes to be on the same side, marching under the same banner, toward the same goal.' "[75]

In such a setting it is not surprising that "needs" are better understood as demands, and their "satisfaction" becomes a question of the partial and temporary resolution of conflict through distinctly political procedures. The resultant consensus, shallow and ephemeral, scarcely supports agencies relevant to the functionalists' appellation. What emerges from this turmoil are not so much organs in a nascent world community as new instrumentalities born of the play of international politics. "Instrumentalities" is employed deliberately, for it would seem that IFC, IDA, and the Special Fund, whatever their differences, hold this characteristic in common: they are products of converging shifts in national policies without evidencing any fundamental change in position, much less "attitude." Along with IBRD, they may be aptly classed within that genus of the family *Gesellschaft* which Amitai Etzioni has labeled "utilitarian organizations" and described as those "in which remuneration is the major means of control over

[74] Louis Hartz, *The Liberal Tradition in America* (New York: Harcourt, Brace and Company, 1955), especially pp. 8-9, 59ff., 126, 129, 219, 232, 242f., 306.

[75] Isador Lubin and Robert E. Asher, "The Struggle for a Better Life," as quoted by Asher, *The United Nations and Promotion . . .* , p. 637.

lower participants and calculative involvement (i.e., mild alienation to mild commitment) characterizes the orientation of the large majority of lower participants."[76] The commitment to them, no less for donors than recipients of their substance, is of the order Mitrany implied in his phrase "limited liability associations"; but it is precisely because they are such that little attitude change has been necessary either to start them up or to keep them going. One paradox which appears among these utilitarian agencies sprouted from a consensual field of brambles is that the very instrumentality which has provided the largest output, IBRD, has also afforded minimal confrontation of participants and opponents within its chambers, whereas the Special Fund—blessed or cursed with maximum "membership" and eminent opportunity for confrontation—produces a slender output indeed.

Two qualifications must be imposed upon these generalizations. One aspect of the failure to "solve the problem" is undoubtedly the lack of a deep and abiding consensus on that problem's definition and its means of solution. Another aspect may indicate the *potency* of existing UN programs. There is some evidence that UN technical assistance has revealed additional possibilities for public as well as private investment, and thus in effect spurred new expressions of the magnitude of the "problem."[77] In this, at least, we are inclined to agree with the *Wall Street Journal's* appraisal of one implication of Paul Hoffman's

[76] Amitai Etzioni, A *Comparative Analysis of Complex Organizations*, p. 31. Etzioni, it should be noted, applies the term to "industries," his definition of which, while extending beyond the usual meaning, was presumably not formulated initially to encompass international organizations.

It hardly detracts from the Bank management's well-earned reputation for diplomatic trouble-shooting to observe that the Indus negotiations were aided by an offer of assistance contingent upon settlement. In Black's words: "Only when the prospect of development on both sides of the border was thrown on the scales was it possible to work out an agreement." "Newly Developing Nations . . . ," p. 36. See also "A Note on the World Bank," p. 71.

[77] Cf. Asher, *The United Nations and Promotion* . . . , p. 368.

"pre-investment": "What the . . . Special Fund is doing, with its studies and surveys, is . . . whetting the appetite of underdeveloped countries for an expected flood of capital from a massive U.N. aid program."[78] Perhaps one aspect of the problem is being "solved," in objective terms, even as the general problem gives the appearance of worsening. Truly, the functional teleology proceeds in wondrous and devious ways! But this is a foreboding of more controversiality, not less.

The more important possibility is that despite the churlishness of their parents and the quarrelsome atmosphere of their youth, these instrumentalities of international finance may yet prove to be significant contributors to a future estate. Should any such transformation occur, it would be much less apt to follow from the circumstances surrounding the actual input, deliberation, and output processes of these agencies than the ramifications of their operations from the points of impact in the field. As an operating unit, IBRD may do little to change the attitudes of participant financial interests and member governments in either the benefactor or beneficiary categories. It may seem to exacerbate the problem itself, if the volume of criticism is the sole index. But short-run discordancy may veil the emergence of patterns over the long haul, patterns beginning far from the scene of the immediate spectacle, about which we can presently do little more than guess. Such a handicap has saved us from neither venture nor misjudgment so far in this study, we suspect, and some further attention will be devoted to this question in the final chapter.

V I

The empirical confrontation of the functionalist argument has now been completed. We have contended that the argument, provocative though it be, is wanting in both

[78] "Why Grow Up?", p. 12.

the dimensions of specificity and context when employed as an interpretative device.

The former shortcoming we suggested might be remedied by grafting on additional variables—and by testing them in other, divergent studies so selected as to continue to satisfy the general conditions exacted by the original thesis. Thus, in the present inquiry we indicated that a certain disposition of factors only partially hinted at by the functionalist argument appears to contribute to the administrative discretion exercised by IBRD leadership. In exploring both the suggestiveness and the inadequacy of "technical self-determination," we took note of such elements as the necessary but passive role of the basic legal framework, of the constitutional-political "redoubt" conception which emphasizes the Bank's system of weighted votes, of the role of certain individuals in expanding the area of administrative autonomy and in utilizing a concatenation of norms to underwrite shifts and continuities of policy.

At the same time, we followed with anticipation and some reward certain suggestions by the functionalists in assaying IBRD's discretionary latitude. It was our hypothesis that the nature and logic of the Bank's "function" (as redefined) enhances the autonomy of its management. More important, we found that the autonomy of the International Bank seems to depend to a considerable extent upon a shift in the locus of its accountability from nation-state members toward the private sector, and upon the financial arrangements which are part and parcel of this latter relationship. We acknowledged a distant kinship between this international financial clientele and Mitrany's "functional assembly." But also we sought to imply that the potentiality for creative action inherent within this relationship bears with it a countervailing tendency.

This particular inquiry was pursued in order to better understand the actual conditions under which the most apparently successful of these "self-determined" multilateral financing agencies—IBRD—has exercised administrative discretion. In the course of the inquiry the functionalist thesis was helpful, but insufficient. Our basic quarrel with it on these points is not that it is "wrong," simply that it does not take us far enough.

The second shortcoming is a more serious hindrance to understanding. In its reluctance to embrace the dynamics constituting the matrix of these international financing programs, the functionalist argument is misleading indeed in pointing the way—the way toward an understanding of the present case, at any rate. To mention the most obvious example, the functionalist guidelines would lead us to expect a continuing, even an expanding atmosphere of non-controversiality; we found instead that the very impetus behind the origin and growth of these programs seems to be a pervasive, multilevel system of tensions which are sometimes—but only sometimes—ridden to their optimum point and then partially and temporarily capped or re-channeled by distinctly political activity.

While these findings can hardly be said to enthrone the functionalist thesis as an omnipotent interpretative device, they certainly do not lend unqualified support to more traditional modes of interpreting the activities of international organizations. We might, as a bench mark, take note of the general observations of two justly respected commentaries on the United Nations:

"The U.N. has been successful in conducting programmes designed to meet specific international problems not susceptible to national or regional action. It has collected funds for these internationally agreed objectives and in the social and economic fields has a long list of accomplishments to its credit. When the nations of the world recognize a common objective of a specific kind the U.N. provides a useful forum and administrative framework for the pursuit of this objective. Its capacity for constructive action of this type is a direct function of the willingness of individual governments to undertake such action together. In fact it is difficult for the United Nations to promote any successful action unless there is approximate unanimity on the issue amongst the members of the international community of nations. In all cases the basic limitation on the extent of international co-operation remains the degree to which individual states are willing to work with others and at times to submerge or adapt their own national interests in relation to the general international good. This principle applies to both the economic and the political field."[79]

"To understand and to evaluate fairly the work of the United Nations in the economic and social field, it is first necessary to recognize the nature and limits of what the General Assembly and other United Nations organs may and can do. Here it is especially important to realize that neither the Assembly, nor the Economic and Social Council which functions under its authority, has the power to take decisions with respect to matters of substance within the economic and social field that are binding upon Member states, least of all upon the citizens of those states. The powers of legislation and taxation which have in the past been the peculiar prerogatives of states in dealing with economic and social problems still remain so vested. No United Nations organ has these powers."[80]

Our findings would indicate that these more orthodox general interpretations of the activities of international organizations are only partially relevant to an understanding of the financing programs. The intellectual problem here is not the inaccuracy of these interpretations; it is their tendency in practice to function as question-stopping formulae. One may agree that "it is difficult . . . to promote any successful action unless there is approximate unanim-

[79] Hadwen and Kaufmann, op.cit., p. 56.
[80] Leland M. Goodrich, The United Nations (London: Stevens and Sons Ltd., 1959), p. 268.

ity on the issue amongst the members of the international community of nations," yet we have observed "successful action" by IBRD and concurrent disunity on related specific issues among the nations of the world. The observer may acquiesce in a judgment that the very nature of universal international organization leaves for it no power and few powers, yet we have seen how the lack of a capability for "legislation" and "taxation" has not altogether crippled the Bank in its action. In sum, the student of international organization must heed the general clues afforded by traditional wisdom, but he may well beware lest these ensnare him in the course of his specific search for understanding. The plea is not for the substitution of a new organon; it is for a continuing pursuit of questions which might otherwise be thought to have found an answer.

VII

Beyond Interpretation

I

THE SCIENCE of politics is inclined to justify itself by claims of predictive power. We have sought to measure the functionalist argument by this yardstick, among others, but the investigation's overtones may well betray a feeling which has grown stronger in the course of the undertaking. This is not the belief that foresight into emergent political trends is an unworthy objective. It is the judgment that prophetic insight lies somewhere *beyond* a series of strategic positions astride theory and empirical materials, rather than wrapped neatly at the end of any mechanical process. It may be that the quest for prescience is best aided by the systematic formulation of research guidelines and the rigorous working of data. Perhaps. But these procedures do not of themselves offer the kind of prediction sought by the political scientist. No automaticity has been discovered in the present scheme, at any rate.

Another, greater difficulty confronts the political scientist with a yen for prediction, but its consideration can be deferred for the moment while tentative projections are advanced and questions for further research efforts posed. What developments may be plotted within the radius of possibility of the programs assayed?

It seems likely that the Bank Group—IBRD, IFC, and IDA—will add depth and scope to its comprehensive service. No doubt technical assistance and training endeavors will be strengthened and extended. The field apparatus will continue to be nurtured. IBRD financing criteria will probably be broadened further in the directions indicated earlier. The Bank Group will almost certainly intensify its activities as promoter and organizer at international, national, and subnational levels. A third regional development bank has recently been mooted in the councils of the

UN Economic Commission for Asia and the Far East (ECAFE). New consortia may be fashioned, perhaps from present consultative groups in some cases; additional consultative groups probably will be formed. IBRD liaison with the Development Assistance Committee (DAC) of the Organization for Economic Cooperation and Development (OECD) is and will remain an important element in this and other undertakings. Private international syndicates will probably play a larger future role as financing participants.[1] It should be interesting to follow the new relationships between these various international arrangements and the multitudinous industrial and agricultural development companies throughout the southern tier. The International Bank triad will not be an idle onlooker at the shape of patterns to come.

[1] The role, immediate results, and byproducts of Bank Group activities in generating private international financing arrangements on both the borrowing and output sides of the Group's financing processes warrants study. ADELA (the Atlantic Community Development Group for Latin America), which participated in an IFC investment in Colombia in June 1964, appears to be institutionalizing. See Henry Kamm, "54 Concerns Form Latin Finance Unit," *New York Times*, 1 October 1964, pp. 45f.; "*Per ardua ad* . . . ?," *The Economist*, 20 February 1965, p. 804; Paul P. Kennedy, "Latin Financing Steps Forward," *New York Times*, 22 June 1965, p. 49.

One major conclusion of this study is the significance of IBRD's relationship to the private financial community, a relationship explored earlier in terms of the themes of autonomy and accountability. With the practice of corporate participation in investments now firmly set and widely understood in international private investment circles, as implied by the gross data in Chapter IV, a careful investigation might discern instances in which would-be participants have actually *initiated* certain Bank Group undertakings culminating in joint public-private investments. If so, this would suggest a further step in bridging the gap between investment standards imposed by IBRD's financial-market ties and the relatively raw status of investment possibilities: private international investors would in effect augment IBRD "technical assistance" (and, for that matter, SF pre-investment) as intelligence agents surveying potential IBRD-family investment opportunities. This finding would also serve as an interesting illustration of demands or articulated interests advanced

Newer tasks described in Chapter V may be expected to grow for much the same reason they were undertaken —determinations by a management attuned to the climate of international finance and international politics as well as "needs" in a narrower sense. Thus, IBRD President George D. Woods' offer "to join actively in the search for answers to the vexing question of how to stabilize income from commodity exports," along with the International Monetary Fund's creation of special drawing facilities for primary producers in temporarily dire straits on the world market, may ultimately prove to have been a major step toward coverage of the gap left by the aborted International Trade Organization. But in retrospect it may likewise be seen as an effort to deflect the determined charge of the southern tier representatives, assembled and banded together for the first time at the United Nations Conference on Trade and Development, where Woods was speaking. One may gain enlightenment from a contemporaneous remark by Thorkil Kristensen, Secretary-General of OECD. Kristensen advised his official constituents, who are prime governmental movers in the Bank Group, to cease "theological" arguments about whether commodity market organization is good or bad and take an active part in decisions which will be made in any case.[2]

IFC's authorization to borrow from IBRD may well turn recipient members' attention toward a similar authorization for IDA. An Israeli "interest equalization" proposal would direct funds to be borrowed from the international financial sector and lent at reduced rates to developing countries with repayment guarantees and grants covering the interest differential being extended by pillar state members of the Bank Group. Possibly these arrange-

by non-state actors receiving an authoritative stamp in the decision-making process of a quasi-universal international organization.

[2] Richard E. Mooney, "Big Powers Urged To Aid Poor Lands," *New York Times*, 31 October 1964, pp. 35, 43.

ments will be combined. IBRD might continue to raise funds from the financial market and allow IDA to borrow from it; the Association's Part I members would act as guarantors for these loans, if this safeguard were deemed wise, and pay interest charges to IBRD. This would not compromise the Bank's status vis-à-vis the international financial community; it would allow IDA to expand and retain control of no-interest loans to members. Furthermore, assuming governmental acquiescence, IBRD executive determination might be exercised in floating additional Bank securities within states not faced by balance of payments difficulties.[3] For these reasons IDA access to IBRD-raised funds must be reckoned a likely development.

The quest for a UN capital development fund (by whatever name) is not likely to cease. "Merger" of the Special Fund and EPTA will be upon the Nineteenth General Assembly's agenda. ECOSOC has proposed a single Governing Council at the intergovernmental level (to succeed the SF Governing Council and the Technical Assistance Committee), an Inter-Agency Consultative Board at the inter-agency level (to succeed the SF Consultative Board and the Technical Assistance Board); a single United Nations Development Programme administrator (to succeed the SF Managing Director and the TAB Executive Chairman) is apparently contemplated. This exercise in rationalization will perhaps nourish certain expectations that the UN has perfected its programs financing economic development; it may amplify other suggestions that the programs can be perfected through an additional streamlining step, by combining the "characteristics and operations of the two programmes as well as [the] two separate funds,"[4] thereby dropping the other shoe. But it

[3] But see "The World Bank Family," *The Economist*, 12 September 1964, pp. 1037-38, for intimations of possible French resistance.

[4] The words are from ECOSOC res. 1020 (XXXVII) of 11 August 1964, but they refer, in that resolution, to the conditions

will hardly stem the pressure for additional development funds. Representatives of developing states have served notice that they will support the "merger" only if it takes place without prejudice to General Assembly and UN Conference on Trade and Development (UNCTAD) resolutions looking toward Special Fund transformation into an agency for capital investment.

The UNCTAD era will bring new development-financing discussion arenas as well as new acronyms. A Trade and Development Board, Conference, subsidiary organs, and secretariat unit will offer additional sustenance to capital development fund protagonists. The UN-adopted aim for 1 percent of developed nations' incomes to go forth as international development assistance and capital will attain future prominence as a supplementary focus. UNCTAD's Final Act sharpens the principle by specifying 1 percent as the objective for *each* developed state, thereby affording a more discriminating standard for application in the "process of conciliation" foreseen for the Trade and Development mechanism by UNCTAD Secretary-General Raúl Prebisch and other Geneva participants.[5]

New UN financing agencies and the allocation of additional public resources to UN development programs may depend partly upon a continuation of Soviet and United States policies of mutual example (including the reduction of armaments, bases, and military personnel), along with collateral expectations which this process fans. But development finance increments from a U.S.-U.S.S.R. diplomacy of mutual example would perforce be due to factors other than the Cold War dynamic assayed earlier. More precarious is the projection of multilateral development

---

for "merger": preservation of special characteristics, operations, and separate funds.

[5] If the 55-member Trade and Development Board becomes a going concern, there will be ample justification for a reassessment of ECOSOC's role by students and practitioners of international organization alike.

financing programs into a changing global system which
may well unleash additional actors of consequence. The
pattern of tensions and political dynamics which affects
UN development financing in the newer system may not
be precisely the same as that encountered in the present
study, but it is our guess that after a phase initiated by
the expansion of new bilateral programs and marked by
the subsequent disappointment of rival donor governments
which find competitive political suitors in the field, dis-
gruntlement by the populace of benefactor nations, more
general charges of wastefulness, lack of coordination and
inefficiency of the several coexistent national programs,
and the constancy of UN program supporters, the latter
will gain in the newer system no less than the one which
appears to be passing. It may be that the United States and
the Soviet Union will see more advantages in some multilateral programs (though not necessarily the same ones)
as France, China, and others extend their own assistance
offerings.

What longer-term promises and forebodings do these
programs bear in terms of economic, social, and political
change emanating from their impact points? This question, an important but exceedingly difficult one, ranges far
beyond the confines of the present study. Here it is possible
only to sketch two general patterns and the evidence
which can be adduced to argue their respective probabili-
ties.

It is quite possible that these programs are helping to
sustain the age of nationalism by encouraging strong
foundations of central national planning and control. As
Ernst B. Haas has warned, the multilateral effort to
achieve economic development may rather unexpectedly
be creating "the kind of national environment in which
less [global] integration will take place a generation from
now. To the extent that the UN effort strengthens national economies and administrative structures it actually

may *reduce* the final integrative component."[6] This thesis can draw upon data regarding the relationship between financing agencies and political systems of recipient countries: multilateral demands for development programing and the correlative establishment of new national machinery to plan and direct these programs. Paradoxically, it might be said in support of the thesis, stringent loan criteria may enhance this possibility. The prospective IBRD security holder's support has been sought with assurances and substantial evidence that strong central governments are administering development plans in the borrowing countries. And strong central governmental control places developing countries "in a better position to live up to the ideological pressures associated with integral nationalism."[7] But this argument's authentication must await systematic investigation on a comparative basis, if not the passage of time.

On the other hand, these programs may be laying pluralistic economic underpinnings for quite different social and political patterns. This "pluralization" thesis can point to the built-in insulation for development projects demanded by the IBRD complex; it can take note of the record on creation and encouragement of local enterprise.[8] It can

[6] Ernst B. Haas, "International Integration: The European and the Universal Process," *International Organization*, XV (Summer 1961), 389-90. Emphasis in original. See also Haas, *Beyond the Nation-State* (Stanford: Stanford University Press, 1964), p. 494, with reference to Special Fund programing.

[7] Haas, *Beyond the Nation-State*, p. 494. Integral nationalism conceives of the nation as "an organic whole with a life of its own. . . . [and] tends to merge society, economy, and polity into one monolith. . . ." There are two variants, integral totalitarianism and integral corporatism. The latter embraces "political systems of an authoritarian nature" which espouse integral nationalism "as an official myth without being full-blown totalitarianisms." *Ibid.*, pp. 466, 467.

[8] Besides the Bank Group's role vis-à-vis local agricultural and industrial development companies, discussed in Chapter IV, its organization-and-management touch extends to utilities and transport authorities. Said IBRD President George D. Woods to the U.S. Investment Bankers Association on December 5, 1963: "Wherever and whenever we can, we try to make a loan proposal the occasion

stress the International Bank's insistence upon "adequate management," for which the Bank may "suggest that the borrowing country or the enterprise concerned look abroad."[9] Having exhausted its incontrovertible evidence, however, the pluralization thesis must leap from economic factors to configurations of social change and political "development." It may envisage intranational "communities of modernizers."[10] It will perhaps stress the prospect of emergent interests and the transmigration of some politicized intellectuals to leadership positions in an increasingly segmented economy.[11] It may suggest that multiple and

---

to create or improve institutions working at key points in the economy—whether they be planning bodies, public authorities or private companies. . . . In Latin America, for example, we often have been asked to make electric power loans where no proper electricity authority or company existed. In case after case . . . , the Bank has insisted on the creation of a proper power entity. . . . The Bank counts among its clients in Latin America 32 organizations created to provide electric power, to develop and operate ports or railways, or to perform some other particular economic function. Of these 32 entities, 28 were organized or brought into operation with the help of the Bank, and together, they have received some $900 million of Bank loans—almost half of all our lending in Latin America."

[9] *The World Bank*, pp. 44, 45; *The International Bank for Reconstruction and Development . . .* , p. 49. Cf. Paul Heffernan, "World Bank: New Look," *New York Times*, 30 September 1957, p. 41; Lyman C. White, "Non-Governmental Organizations and Democracy," p. 441; Eugene R. Black, "The New Industrial Revolution," *The Virginia Quarterly Review*, 35 (Summer 1959), pp. 358ff.; Michael L. Hoffman, "Development Needs the Business Man," *Lloyds Bank Review*, April 1963; address by Martin M. Rosen, Executive Vice President, International Finance Corporation, at the First International Meeting of Financial Institutions for Development, Caracas, Venezuela, 19 February 1964.

[10] The phrase is Lucian W. Pye's, from *Politics, Personality, and Nation-Building* (New Haven: Yale University Press, 1962), p. 296. Though Pye does not predict this, he calls for it: "We have established many successful programs for training individuals but we have not done as much toward building environments in which these individuals can associate with each other and thus create the communities of modernizers that can serve as islands of stability in the nation-building process."

[11] At this point the emphasis is on entrepreneurial elements or a

diverse interests will yield balance which in turn will promote conciliatory modes and democratic ways. It tends to lean heavily upon a premise of the progressive evolution of modern (if not Western) man.

This line of argument may posit as its terminal point a world of transnationally empathic, pluralistic nation-states thriving in an amicable global system.[12] More likely, it will go on to suggest that the same dynamism accentuates the quest for larger territorial units[13] or more consequential universal special-purpose arrangements. Certainly this is a far more difficult thesis to substantiate than the other, although its exponents and proponents perhaps enjoy the compensatory advantage of contending that even

---

"middle sector" rather than on a new urban proletariat. See, e.g., John J. Johnson, *Political Change in Latin America* (Stanford: Stanford University Press, 1958); John H. Kautsky (ed.), *Political Change in Underdeveloped Countries* (New York: John Wiley & Sons, Inc., 1962), pp. 22-29, 112-19; William J. Foltz, "Building the Newest Nations: Short-Run Strategies and Long-Run Problems," in Karl W. Deutsch and William J. Foltz (eds.), *Nation-Building* (New York: Atherton Press, 1963), pp. 124-31; Myron Weiner, *The Politics of Scarcity* (Chicago: University of Chicago Press, 1962). But cf. Zbigniew Brzezinski and Samuel P. Huntington, *Political Power: USA/USSR* (New York: The Viking Press, 1964), pp. 420ff.

[12] However, to reach this point the thesis must also explain how simultaneously generated suspicions of "neo-imperialism," "neo-colonialism," and "collective colonialism" will be laid to rest. For an exposition of "collective colonialism," see Rubinstein, *The Soviets in International Organizations*, pp. 345ff.

[13] The role of regional development banks may provide a sensitive indicator of the regional impulse. What criteria will be employed, for instance, in the African Development Bank's allocation of financial resources? Will economic calculations such as physical resources and markets predominate in locating industries? Will priority indeed be given to projects which concern several members and which enhance economic complementarity, as pledged by the Khartoum agreement signatories? If so, the African Development Bank may prove an instrument as well as an indicator of integration. Or will decisions rather turn upon "geographic" criteria applied through and because of an essentially intergovernmental decision-making process?

short-run national strength with politically restrained pluralism means longer-run international amity.[14]

We might hypothesize that the ratio between social mobilization and accession rates induced by development programs will bear upon the extent of immediate dislocation and the character of subsequent social and political configurations.[15] Furthermore, the instrumentality of accession may affect national patterns: accession by and through a dominant political party or movement may encourage or strengthen integral nationalism, accession via an economic and social system already in the process of specialization

[14] There is a great opportunity for serious studies of the role of non-governmental organizations (NGOs). One focus suggested by the "pluralization" thesis would be to investigate the nature, extent, and incidence of international NGO member recruitment from the southern tier nations, and the effect of NGO membership and participation upon the skills, attitudes, and behavioral patterns of these members. See Murray Seeger, "Unions Seek Shift in World Group," *New York Times*, 30 May 1965, p. 22, for a report on a related controversy in the International Confederation of Free Trade Unions (ICFTU). It will be necessary to probe beneath the NGO ideology in this assessment.

[15] For a discussion of the attributes and indicators of social mobilization, see the pioneering work of Karl W. Deutsch, e.g. *Nationalism and Social Communication* (New York: John Wiley & Sons, Inc., 1953), especially pp. 100ff., and "Social Mobilization and Political Development," *American Political Science Review*, LV (September 1961), 493-514. "Accession" here means the process or decisions by which socially mobilized population increments attain and acknowledge membership and participant status within their territorial unit's economy, society, *and* polity. Deutsch's concept of assimilation is obviously closely related; see *Nationalism and Social Communication*, especially pp. 99-100. However, assimilation could take place without accession. For related notions, cf. Ernst B. Haas, *Beyond the Nation-State*, pp. 469 ("the successful absorption of the mobilized into the existing structure of society"), 482-83; Seymour Martin Lipset, *Political Man* (Garden City: Doubleday & Co., Inc., 1963), pp. 66ff.; Gabriel A. Almond, in *The Politics of the Developing Areas* (Princeton: Princeton University Press, 1960), pp. 26ff.
A challenging but potentially significant investigation might seek to ascertain the mobilization/accession ratios induced by various UN system programs or by types of project. Even an assessment of specific cases would be valuable at this point.

and differentiation may increase the chances of transnationally empathic pluralism, leading toward amicable relationships among relatively autonomous nation-states, new or more efficacious regional and/or special-purpose international arrangements, or international community. But the direction no doubt will depend largely upon the character of existing development-impacted political systems.[16]

Either pattern would serve as presumptive evidence of significant consequences emanating from functional projects. The latter would, of course, be more compatible with the functionalist argument. If realized, this pattern would go a long way toward substantiating a claim that the functional approach had facilitated pacific international relations and perhaps even international community. Our criticisms of the failure to solve problems or permanently modify attitudes would then have to give way to far more important developments.

These are long-term possibilities; they are not the only alternatives. Rupert Emerson writes that "If economic development really takes hold, it cannot but operate as a profoundly revolutionary force. . . ."[17] Any conjectural pattern will probably prove, in retrospect, to have been overly simple. Finally, but not least in consequence as a caveat for prophecy, policy is an intervening variable.

[16] Cf. William Kornhauser, *The Politics of Mass Society* (Glencoe: The Free Press, 1959), pp. 230-32. For suggestive typologies of existing and emergent polities, see David E. Apter, "System, Process and the Politics of Economic Development," in Bert F. Hoselitz and Wilbert E. Moore (eds.), *Industrialization and Society* (UNESCO, 1963), pp. 139ff.; Ernst B. Haas, *Beyond the Nation-State*, pp. 464ff.; James S. Coleman, in *The Politics of the Developing Areas*, pp. 532ff.; Edward Shils, *Political Development in the New States* (75-Gravenhage: Mouton & Co., 1962), Part III.

[17] Rupert Emerson, *From Empire to Nation* (Cambridge: Harvard University Press, 1960), p. 413. Cf. Hadwen and Kaufmann, *op.cit.*, p. 80.

I I

In fitting out the functionalist argument for assessment as an analytical and interpretative device the focus was narrowed to an application of functionalist guidelines and explanations to the multilateral programs selected for study. With this confrontation behind us, the return to a more general level of discourse will help to set these findings into the perspective afforded by the broader functionalist claims.

The functionalist argument bases its contentions regarding world peace upon a claim that functional activity creates peace-bearing community. Community is analogized to a natural organism. The functionalists then derive their admonition: so act as to achieve performance of the functions which constitute this community.[18] What does our inquiry suggest with regard to the actual advancement of the process?

If the specific structural indices applied previously are an apt indication, the functional approach to creation of an organic complex for the financing of economic development has burgeoned in the years since Bretton Woods. But this generalization must be qualified by several additional observations. First of all, the functionalists seem to be right for the wrong reasons, even with respect to these structural indices. To a considerable extent functionalism seems to be a dependent variable—dependent, that is, on the pervasive factor which is of preeminent importance at the conception of these agencies, in their growth, and indeed as the vital element in their lives. For example, little has been observed which would justify a functionalist

---

[18] It will be recalled that David Mitrany draws upon L. T. Hobhouse in order to define community as " 'the sum of the functions performed by its members.' " Mitrany further suggests that each functional activity would contribute to "peaceful life," and together these activities "would create the living body of a true world community, . . . a community within which the absence of war would be as natural as it now is within each of our own countries."

contention that the UN financing programs have reoriented the purpose of international society or diverted its efforts from financial emphasis on the "security function." Yet certain political settlements might well lead to augmented IDA or Special Fund resources and quite possibly beget a capital development fund.

Furthermore, the structurally expanded financing function must be questioned in its role as preventer or eliminator of friction sources within a nascent world community. It has not been possible to assess this claim adequately in the present study; such an inquiry should include investigations in the field. The consideration of problem-solving by analysis of the financing agencies and their activities leaves us wary. On the other hand there is reason to suspect that not all the returns are in yet.

Even with these qualifications, structural expansion in the UN financing programs lends some credence to the functionalist argument. Given the single purpose which seemingly has provided a common thread of meaning for these activities throughout the period (that is, enhancement of the private investment capital flow), the "function" has undergone an extraordinary series of structural elaborations. These in turn exemplify one principle near the heart of the functionalist argument: the development of consequences unforeseen by international participants at the initiation of a given program. In order to validate this functionalist contention we need only recall the "spill-over" from task to task as the IBRD leadership sought and instituted new structural means toward the attainment of its elusive objective.[19]

[19] Ernst B. Haas has defined "spill-over" as a "political process which results in the accretion of new powers and tasks to a central institutional structure, based on changing demands and expectations on the part of such political actors as interest groups, political parties and bureaucracies. It refers to the specific process which originates in one functional context, initially separate from other political concerns, and then expands into related activities as it becomes clear to the chief political actors that the achievement of

There are limits to this spill-over process. On the basis of this study it seems that these limits are set less by legal framework than the purpose to which functional endeavor is actually attuned, along with the nature and extent of participant commitment which this operative purpose evokes. The present inquiry shows both the continuity of a single essential purpose and the absence of any significant redirection of energy toward other purposes. This tends to deny the existence of a dynamism within the logic of functionalism which is sufficient to transform basic participant intentions, but it does not, we trust, exclude the possibility of changes emanating from outside the functional subsystem.

The embryonic community of functions must be further considered. When Mitrany and others argue for a functional approach to international organization, they ordinarily offer examples of quite specific functions. Functional units for the satisfaction of specific needs are most easily set up in the first place. They best lend themselves to isolation from political contagion, and they are capable of a relatively autonomous generation of new tasks and structure to meet emergent related needs or to fulfill the original one, if unforeseen complexities should arise. On the other hand, when the functionalists draw out the ultimate consequences of their proposed efforts, they portray a Great Community in which every function has its place and every man realizes himself—in part, at least—by his membership and participation in the functional firmament.[20]

The distance between initiation and realization seems

the initial aims cannot take place without such expansion." Haas, unpublished MS.

[20] Cf. Émile Durkheim's exhortation: "we . . . see perfection in the man seeking, not to be complete, but to produce. . . . In one of its aspects, the categorical imperative of the moral conscience [assumes] the following form: Make yourself usefully fulfill a determinate function." From *Division of Labor*; quoted by Sheldon S. Wolin, *Politics and Vision* (Boston: Little, Brown and Company, 1960), p. 387.

vast indeed when the two are juxtaposed. This juxtaposition suggests a question critical in evaluating the functionalist argument. Are all "functions" in the economic, social, and humanitarian sectors equal in their propensity to create community? Does the functionalist argument not require restatement in terms of priorities *within* these sectors? To state the question more specifically and in relation to this study: Which seems to have contributed more to the building of world community—the functional approach to international organization or the financing of economic development?

Perhaps the problem is purely semantic. Still, it would seem that the semantic difficulty hides certain important research possibilities. When Mitrany stresses the individuality of functional dimensions, powers, and so on, he implies in effect that the consequences of these functions may similarly be distinctive. As an argument prepared for pamphlet presentation, Mitrany's plea is restricted to an emphasis on those *procedural* benefits which are to accrue to functional participants, for only in terms of procedure may these functions be collectively acclaimed. It is perhaps for this reason that Mitrany has become enmeshed in his own efforts to cast forth a general term suitable to encompass the substantive results of his entire functional congeries. "Problem-solving" is his attempt and, in our judgment, the weakest link in his argument.

What we propose is further exploration of the differential effects of international organizations in terms of the substance of their programs. A systematic comparison of administrative discretion was suggested in Chapter VI, with the substance of the output of international agencies as a guiding principle in selecting an adequate sample. The comparative assessment of differential feedback patterns might be undertaken at the same time.

There exists a reservoir of hypotheses which might prove fruitful in this undertaking. The more general functionalist tradition has in recent years produced a number of lists under the rubric "functional requisites" (or prerequisites) which purport to capture and state those conditions necessary to the existence of any society.[21] It might be supposed that international organizations, as potential organs in a world community, could with imagination plus careful empirical investigation be evaluated in terms of their respective contributions to the performance of prerequisite functions. For instance, several lists of functions include the category "allocation of resources," or its equivalent. To what extent has the UN complex of financing programs come to function in the allocation of values as part of an evolving global order?

This question is posed as an illustration. But the question also leads to a second facet of community implied by the functionalist argument which must now draw our attention in the effort to set these findings within a broader perspective.

The functionalist community envisaged as a necessary and sufficient condition for peace manifests certain characteristics which raise squarely the question of obligation.[22]

[21] See, e.g., D. F. Aberle, A. K. Cohen, K. Davis, M. J. Levy, Jr. and F. X. Sutton, "The Functional Prerequisites of a Society," *Ethics*, LX (January 1950), pp. 100-11, reprinted in part in Roy C. Macridis and Bernard E. Brown (eds.), *Comparative Politics* (rev. ed.; Homewood, Ill.: The Dorsey Press, 1964), pp. 77-89; Talcott Parsons, *The Social System* (Glencoe: The Free Press, 1951), especially Chapter II; Marion J. Levy, Jr., *The Structure of Society* (Princeton: Princeton University Press, 1952); Parsons, *Structure and Process in Modern Society* (Glencoe: The Free Press, 1960); Don Martindale, "The Formation and Destruction of Communities," Alvin Boskoff, "Functional Analysis as a Source of a Theoretical Repertory and Research Tasks in the Study of Social Change," and David Lockwood, "Social Integration and System Integration," in George K. Zollschan and Walter Hirsch (eds.), *Explorations in Social Change* (New York: Houghton Mifflin Company, 1964); Gabriel A. Almond, "A Developmental Approach to Political Systems," *World Politics*, 17 (January 1965), 197.

[22] See above, Chapter II, especially Mitrany's statement that "the functional way . . . leaves the individual free to enter into a variety of relationships—religious, political and professional, social and

What inferences does our empirical inquiry yield regarding the modification of obligation's bases and manifestations?

In his fine little essay, Joseph Tussman utilizes the voluntary association, somewhat embellished, as model for the body politic. "Saving the best for last," he writes after a survey of two alternate models,

"I come now to the notion of 'agreement' as expressing the core of political relatedness. A body politic, on this view, is a group of persons related by a system of agreements; to be a member of a body politic is to be a party to a system of agreements. The model is obviously the voluntary group or organization. A voluntary group is composed of a number of individuals who, in pursuit of a common purpose, agree to act in concert, putting themselves under a common discipline, authority, and obligation."[23]

And at later points in his discourse Tussman seeks to broaden his model's relevance as he adds that the United Nations,

"while lacking some of the necessary conditions of being a body politic, has some of its features. . . . It is of no special significance that the units involved are themselves states. The problem is that of creating a system of agreements, to which states are voluntary parties, with decision-making tribunals authorized to deal effectively with the problems whose existence makes the organization necessary. In this area we still move entirely within the basic analysis and concepts of social contract theory. . . . [T]he compact theory of the state is the great contribution of the Western secular mind to the hope for world peace. In a world of diverse creeds it provides the bedrock of [a] universally intelligible moral and political conception upon

---

cultural, and so on—each of which may take him into different directions and dimensions. . . ."

[23] Tussman, *Obligation and the Body Politic*, p. 7.

which, if we escape disaster, the world community will erect its saving political institutions."[24]

Tussman's conception is related to that view of international organization earlier labeled "apocalypticism." But his argument, unlike the approach which Clarence Streit is wont to defend with the aphorism that "the most dangerous way to cross a chasm is one step at a time," seems to allow for a piecemeal development of the foundation of agreements necessary to undergird a new world order. It should be emphasized that Tussman's logical structure is quite different from that of the functionalists; in particular, his stress on *knowing* consent to obligations runs counter to the functionalist insistence that propitious conditions will yield consequences which were unforeseen by participants at the outset.[25] But if the form may be extracted from the substance of Tussman's argument, it may serve to launch an evaluation of the obligation-creating process by UN development financing programs.

Viewed in quantitative terms, it can hardly be denied that a vast international network of agreements has been woven among various public and private entities in the course of the financing programs reviewed. We surveyed the widening circle of member states willfully agreeing to those compacts which were addressed above by their more specific designations—the Articles of Agreement of

[24] *Ibid.*, pp. 33, 57.

[25] *Ibid.*, pp. 36ff. Tussman founds his philosophy of political education upon this base. His endeavor may be viewed as an effort to provide direction to the political participant more than the political spectator. But he has difficulty in resolving the thorny question of the relationship between knowing consent to agreements and their subsequent "interpretation" by public tribunals.

A. Lawrence Lowell's thought provides a contrast strikingly near the functionalist thesis: "men, like animals, may attain a self-consistent and harmonious system of conducting their affairs by a process of striving for immediate intentional objects, if the conditions happen to be such as to lead to a system of that kind; and this although the actors themselves do not contemplate it, or even if the result is quite contrary to their preconceived ideas."

IBRD, IFC, IDA. We followed the emerging configurations traced by loan, investment, and Special Fund agreements. We noted the broadening pattern outlined by those contracts elsewhere referred to as International Bank bonds or obligations.

But we saw that there are rather definite limits to this web of agreements. Soviet and East European states do not belong to IBRD, IFC, or IDA, and their permanent official status vis-à-vis SF is due to membership in the UN family rather than explicit adherence to any separate contract including the provision for payment of a specified capital subscription.

This network of agreements indicates the outer bounds of financing program community-building, but it hardly confirms the intensity of obligation *within* these bounds. It may be argued that the high degree of actual adherence to specific decisions made by the financing agencies demonstrates a clear acceptance of obligations assumed by becoming a party to the contract. But there remains a very real question as to both the depth of any commitment signified by these agreements and their collective significance as harbingers of an international community.

What is the depth of commitment toward the financing programs by the developed nations? What, in particular, is the foundation of obligation beneath the governments of these states? What attitudes are held toward the several financing programs by relevant elites within these developed states? Our findings would suggest that there is, at this level, a rather conditional commitment which is apt to become even more tenuous with the shift in emphasis toward programs which demand public financing as a condition or an indirect consequence of their operations —IDA and the Special Fund. We have noted the growing feeling in certain quarters in the United States that public and private investment are competitors rather than partners, that public funds—which of themselves represent a tax burden—drive or keep the "good money" out of international investment channels by way of a kind of Gresham's law. The law's impact in this particular instance is seen as the devious decree of an assemblage of irresponsible governments. "Mingled with the moneys of other nations, [the U.S. dollar] is disbursed by 'multilateral' decision. . . . It's a system that almost defies examination by the American taxpayer. . . ."[26]

Furthermore, the present range of agreements involving private corporate entities based in the developed countries would seem to constitute an element of dubious strength in a framework of international obligation. Here we refer not to the long-term consequences of these agreements but to their direct role as part and parcel of the framework of obligation. In regard to this more immediate consideration, the question may perhaps be posed in rhetorical fashion. What is the nature of that commitment shouldered by the corporation which participates in a project financed by IBRD, or purchases the securities issued by an IFC-financed enterprise? What is the sense of obligation assumed by the bank which buys and holds IBRD obligations?

Commitment by developing countries to the obligations they have assumed has not as yet undergone the test of fire. As the previous chapter suggested, adherence to a gamut of compacts running from membership in financing agencies to local Special Fund counterpart expenditures rests to a considerable extent upon the expectation that more of the same benefits will follow. Fulfillment of contract seems to be viewed in much the sense that honesty is sometimes acclaimed the best policy—as a means to further business. On the basis of the prior analysis, furthermore, it would hardly be appropriate to claim that junior member obligation is generated by the decision-making process within the councils of the IBRD com-

[26] Philip Geyelin, "Re-Channeling Aid: U.S. Plans to Route More of Its Foreign Aid Through the U.N.," *Wall Street Journal*, 23 September 1960, p. 1.

plex. On the other hand, it may be contended that the universally acknowledged high competence of Bank officials is an important factor in gaining and holding the commitment of less developed members.[27] Even so, the last point is but an augmentation of the first—expertise and moderate resources have thus far made for a sense of progress, if not a full-fledged "solution" to the problem of economic development, and despite some chafing there have been few resignations from the effort. To phrase it differently, the commitment by developing countries appears to be eminently result-oriented: that which produces is worthy of concurrent support. In this sense and to this degree the utilitarian strand within the functionalist theory of obligation has actually been realized in these programs. Reports Philip Shabecoff on the reception accorded President George D. Woods' UNCTAD announcements of IBRD subventions to IDA and refinancing arrangements: "Mr. Woods's proposals were the first mention of hard cash at the trade conference. His speech was warmly applauded."[28]

This commitment bears its own standard, but there are other limits in addition to the utilitarian calculus. There is afoot a certain spirit of abandon which has been variously analogized—to youthful exuberance, to adolescent irresponsibility. This spirit may be fed by neo-Marxist theories of a new economic colonialism, but basically it is the far more visceral response to a new status within a fragmented world lashed by competing values. The status is that of Melville's Ahab, "proud as a Greek god, and yet standing debtor," and it is the spirit of Ahab, too: "Cursed be that mortal inter-debtedness which will not do away with ledgers. I would be free as air; and I'm down in the whole world's books."

[27] But see "Latin Nations Seeking to Block [IBRD] Unit for Expropriation Disputes," *New York Times,* 10 September 1964, pp. 47f.; "The World Bank Family," p. 1038.

[28] Shabecoff, "World Bank Head Urges Debt Shift," *New York Times,* 26 March 1964, p. 49.

To raise these questions is not to predict the collapse of the entire framework of obligation, but it does illustrate the fragility of a web of agreements. Of themselves, these ties hardly bespeak the existence of a war-resistant community. To the question "How many small agreements make an agreement of genuine significance?" the present situation as well as the history of the first half of this century suggests a sombre answer indeed.

It might be contended that the focus on written agreements is precisely what the functionalists eschew. The functionalist emphasis, after all, is on more substantial consequences than the signing of paper contracts.

One answer to this justifiable contention is that even the functionalists acknowledge the necessity of these agreements in order to initiate the functional process. But this answer does not quite meet its mark. It is necessary to look more closely at the relationship between agreements and the functionalist conception of community if we would understand the limitations of the functionalist argument when taken as a normative directive for nurturing a peaceful world order.

An earlier theme is the backdrop for this discussion. Chapter II stated that the functionalist argument offers a new meaning for the traditional concept of "peaceful change" in international relations. Further, it was suggested that the non-territorial substance of this functionalist version of peaceful change implies more than the argument itself makes explicit. The actual existence of some elements implied by the functionalist peaceful change would indeed go far toward signaling the growth of international community. Here we return to an aspect of peaceful change with special relevance to the empirical analysis—the reallocation of scarce resources. This time, however, we approach it not as a potential operating unit within a community of functions, but from the perspective of obligation.

The argument is simple. Community formation by independent political units involves ascendance from the plane where interests intersect to a more permanent juncture of commonly accepted responsibilities. Analysis of UN programs which finance economic development shows that insofar as the reallocation of scarce resources adequately represents this step, little advance has occurred. Furthermore, the functionalist argument itself takes no account of the necessary shift in levels.

Our argument distinguishes interest from obligation. The distinction is an important one and demands reaffirmation in this day and place. Sheldon Wolin vigorously contends that interest has come to play the same role in social and political thought that conscience once played in religion;[29] the shift from sacred to secular values would thus suggest that conscience has been virtually displaced by interest. We see men or groups acting in various political arenas according to the dictates of their interests—if indeed we do not see them *as* interests. No modern man can know his neighbor's interest, yet he knows his own through reflections from his socio-economic environment: What loftier justification for democracy? What better explanation of individualism, the privatist predicament— alienation? No *group* can know the "interest" of those other groups which are perforce its adversaries, though it knows its own mainly through their vectorial tergiversations: What grander justification for multiple access points in the decision-making process by which values are authoritatively allocated? What better explanation of the lack of responsibility for resultant patterns in that allocation? Without a pause to consider logical or definitional difficulties in working upward from a base so atomistic, we extend these principles to the level of *national* "interests": What more glorious justification for self-determination and sovereignty? What better explanation of the poignant, backward-and-inward looking quest

[29] Wolin, *Politics and Vision*, pp. 331-42, especially p. 338.

for "national purpose" in a milieu which generates threatening stimuli and pointedly rejects solipsism?

Presented only with the proposition that interests are personal and uncommunicable as his introduction, the visitor from Mars might well expect to witness, at his first game of politics, a knock-down-drag-out played within a Hobbesian state of nature. Based on this meager description of the players, our friend might envisage a struggle guided by a single principle: to the survivor goes the spoils.

His query shows his ignorance of earthly ways, and we quickly clarify. Not all interests are vital, the struggle is mitigated by automatic compensatory devices including the countervailing or balancing of power and, anyway, the game has some rules, like majority rule and minority rights.

We may be asked why these rules are followed, there being no officials apparent at the moment in this particular arena, and we come up with an elaboration on an earlier point: some interests are not vital because those individuals who hold them are members of more than one group, and thus it is relatively painless to compromise, as the game played under these conditions demands. The interest lost or alienated to one sector of a man is the benefit added by another sector of his being. We may suggest that interests or their bearers abide by the rules because they know that a present loss will be followed by a future gain. We may even break away from the confines of gamesmanship altogether to invoke Mary Parker Follett's conception of integration through constructive conflict, using her words to explain that "when two desires are integrated, that means . . . a solution has been found in which both desires have found a place, that neither side has had to sacrifice anything."[30]

Much as we would wish to favor the last response, it is

[30] Henry C. Metcalf and L. Urwick (eds.), *Dynamic Administration: The Collected Papers of Mary Parker Follett* (London: Sir Isaac Pitman and Sons Ltd., 1941), pp. 32-33. Emphasis omitted.

our firm conviction that none of these replies adequately explains processes in a pluralistic community. Each perhaps contributes; all together do not suffice. A pluralistic community reduced to the play of interests, however those interests were mediated and channeled, would rapidly tear itself to shreds. It cannot be denied that there are pluralistic communities at the national level which approach pure interest politics. But such a state of affairs is dependent upon more pervasive factors than those outlined above. Interest politics implies the existence of something beyond interests.

We are aware of that specter called "public interest" and its suspect status. Half-brother to "national interest," the former is the more introspective of the pair, and by all odds the less favored in respectable academic circles. Often hunted down and slain by political theorist and political empiricist, public interest has as often been revived by those with other sensibilities.

We shall not try to restore the public interest here; our objective is far more modest. The concept is drawn into the discussion only to note that its persistent reappearance must signify a deeper underlying reality of sorts, even if that reality is not easily validated by modern methods. The notions of procedural consensus, political culture, and loyalty all reach beyond the play of interests in quest of this elusive aspect of reality. Shortly we shall follow a *substantive* clue toward it.

Interest politics demands a mechanistic model as its symbolic representation, and physics has been the source of more than one figure of speech for the modern student of politics. These ideas hardly sustain obligation by the political actor to public decisions which restrain or deprive him of his interests, except as indicated above. Accordingly he would, if a grocery jobber, accept the directive that he append to his produce a label stating that it has been sprayed with a specified insecticide only because he is also a consumer of other similar products, or perhaps because he expects to get the order rescinded before next season.[31]

This conception goes ill with reality, for like impositions occur constantly. We accept them almost without question, if not, indeed, without thought. Chapter II suggested that obligation may be viewed as the acceptance, by a societal segment, of the strictures imposed upon it by decision of that society's agent or agents, insofar as the acceptance is a matter of choice. Here we would add or reemphasize that one crucial test of community is the common acceptance of responsibilities which may in their specific manifestations demand more of some participant units than others.

Our example hardly begins to exhaust the vast range of strictures upon interests imposed through the modern state mechanism. Far less is it pressed forward as an adequate representation of the responsibilities shared within communities everywhere in all ages. But the graduated income tax is, we submit, a particularly fitting illustration, for it lends quantitative expression to the process by which the chief accounting unit of interest in the modern polity is treated by public decision. We witness here the primary phase in a continuing reallocation of scarce resources.

If world community is to precede a global power structure, there must at the very least be a substantial development of obligation in terms of commonly shared responsibilities. The present study reveals little of such an evolution on the universal level. Those financing arrangements which do manifest certain asymmetrical features are driven largely by the dynamics of world politics in a Cold War era. "Consciously or unconsciously, every action of the rich nations towards the poor ones is in some degree inspired by the struggle between the East and the West, a struggle in which the underdeveloped countries are at

[31] We put aside the role of enforcement and deterrence. Obviously they are relevant considerations, but they are not germane to obligation as defined earlier. See Chapter II, especially pp. 45ff.

once the prize and the judge."[32] Agreements are balanced —perhaps tenuously balanced—upon the common interests of donor and recipient, whether these interests be material or otherwise.[33]

What, then, would serve as evidence of an advance toward community along this line? M. Pierre Moussa argues that "only the creation of [a world organization financing actual development] will prove that the rich nations of the world have given up an exclusive concern with themselves, with pride and avarice as their only companions. . . . if it is to act on a scale equal to the need, . . . it will have to [employ] an international tax based on each nation's *per capita* income."[34]

Less spectacular but of considerable significance as an indication of obligation jointly shouldered would be a decision-capped consensus to finance the "merged" SF-EPTA undertakings as regular assessed expenses of the United Nations. To presume consensus is of course to make the rest easy; consensus more than its conse-

[32] Pierre Moussa, *The Underprivileged Nations*, translated by Alan Braley (London: Sidgwick & Jackson, 1959), p. 179. Moussa adds (p. 186) that the "young and poor nations are in danger of entering upon the stage of history with the mental paraphernalia of prostitutes, and the Big Powers are to blame for this."

[33] "At length, two great parties were formed . . . which pursued distinct objects with systematic arrangement. The one struggled with unabated zeal for the exact observance of public and private engagements. By those belonging to it, the faith of a nation or of a private man was deemed a sacred pledge, the violation of which was equally forbidden by the principles of moral justice and of sound policy. The distresses of individuals were, they thought, to be alleviated only by industry and frugality, not by a relaxation of the laws or by a sacrifice of the rights of others. . . . The other party marked out for themselves a more indulgent course. Viewing with extreme tenderness the case of the debtor, their efforts were unceasingly directed to his relief. To exact a faithful compliance with contracts was, in their opinion, a harsh measure which the people would not bear." John Marshall, *The Life of Washington*, Vol. II, as quoted by Charles A. Beard, *An Economic Interpretation of the Constitution of the United States* (New York: The Macmillan Co., 1961), pp. 297-98.

[34] Moussa, *op.cit.*, pp. 189, 188.

quences would endow the step with significance.[35] Structural and financial foundations for more effective programs would be a probable result, especially since a consensus to make SF-EPTA financial support obligatory would presuppose specific decisions regarding burden-sharing criteria and their application.

The International Court of Justice advisory opinion of July 20, 1962, regarding the scope of "expenses of the Organization within the meaning of Article 17, paragraph 2 of the Charter of the United Nations" and pressures to fashion SF into a proper development fund help make assessment a live option if not a lively question. Reticence to partake of this most hypothetical consensus by the affluent West need hardly be elaborated upon at this point in the study.[36] The United States would probably find that its present self-imposed ceiling of 40 percent of total *voluntary* contributions to SF-EPTA had not shrunk, following a general *obligation* for financing, to the present theoretical 32.02 percent of the regular UN assessment. Actual amounts might be expected to rise for all Western member states. However, the consensus, the decision, and the consequences would also signify concessions by others of an order sufficient to establish this as a step toward *commonly* shared obligations rather than unilateralism. The Soviet Union and some East European member states would probably find their assessed shares increased by the General Assembly or a designated sub-

[35] A critical commentary on abandonment of the voluntary principle may be found in Stoessinger, *Financing the United Nations System*, p. 211.

[36] Writing a separate majority opinion in the badly fragmented ICJ decision mentioned just above, Judge Sir Gerald Fitzmaurice (United Kingdom) sought to restrict the ambit of obligatory expenses to those of a peace-keeping nature rather than leaving open all purposes of the UN stated in Article 1 of the Charter. Otherwise, "the Assembly could vote enormous expenditures, and thereby place a heavy financial burden even on dissenting States, and as a matter of obligation even in the case of *non-essential* activities." Emphasis added.

sidiary organ.[37] Furthermore, assessment could make more difficult if not impossible predestined or tied contributions. Even the developing states might find additional international guidance and controls upon the direction and rate of unpremeditated social change, with all that implies, as a condition for expanded SF-EPTA operations.[38] A budget with more than token assessed resources for economic and social purposes might be expected to invigorate central UN processes as questions of direction as well as assessment are deliberated. Thus would dawn an era of more UN politics, not less. But it would also represent a step upward toward international community: universal community, human community.

How dissimilar the present! The 1964 SF-EPTA pledging conference opened with Secretary General U Thant's judgment that "the United Nations work of peace-building, through activities that promote economic and social progress, is no less important and pressing than diplomatic, political and constabulary activities aimed at peace-keeping." Shortly afterwards Nikolai T. Fedorenko pledged the Soviet Union's usual equivalent of $3 million in tied, nonconvertible rubles, and Franklin H. Williams confirmed an earlier announcement that the United States would withhold its entire pledge "in view of circumstances with which members are familiar." Six days later a report on Richard N. Gardner's book, *In Pursuit of World Order*, quoted the U.S. Deputy Assistant Secretary of State as arguing with regard to the peace-keeping assessment issue that the financial basis of *both* UN peace-keeping *and* development operations "would be eroded if members

[37] It may be recalled that the voluntary Soviet contribution to SF decreased from 4.5% to 1.6% of the total between 1959 and 1963.

[38] Cf. Ernst B. Haas, "Toward Controlling International Change: A Personal Plea," *World Politics*, XVII (October 1964), 9, 11. A panel of experts to *advise* upon the potential social mobilization/accession ratio of UN development programs and related matters might be envisaged as one condition. See above, note 15.

could deny their financial obligations with impunity."[39]

The perversity of reality turns us again to the functionalist argument. By what process does it anticipate an elevation from the level of converging ad hoc interests of independent political units to one characterized by a foundation of obligation? We must conclude that it hardly confronts the question.

In A *Working Peace System*, Mitrany urges initiation of the functional process by "natural selection" of "those interests which are common, where they are common, and to the extent they are common."[40] This is the beginning. But the culmination—insofar as we are allowed a glimpse of an order which would "have to come about functionally"[41]—looks very much like an expanded version of this initial pattern, garnished by its perceived attendant values for humanity.

"The problem of our generation, put very broadly [writes Mitrany], is how to weld together the common interests of all without interfering unduly with the particular ways of each. It is a parallel problem to that which faces us in national society, and which in both spheres challenges us to find an alternative to the totalitarian pattern. A measure of centralized planning and control, for both production and distribution, is no longer to be avoided, no matter what the form of the state or the doctrine of its constitution. Through all that variety of political forms there is a growing approximation in the working of government, with differences merely of degree and of detail. Liberal democracy needs a redefinition of the public and private spheres of action. But as the line of separation is

[39] Sam Pope Brewer, "U.S. Will Withhold A U.N. Fund Pledge In Arrears Dispute," *New York Times,* 7 November 1964, pp. 1f.; Thomas J. Hamilton, "U.S. Tells U.N. It Is Withholding Aid but Hopes to Make Donation Later," *New York Times,* 17 November 1964, p. 15; John W. Finney, "U.S. Aide Depicts 'Crisis' In The U.N.," *New York Times,* 23 November 1964, p. 5.

[40] Mitrany, A *Working Peace System,* p. 32.

[41] *Ibid.,* p. 35.

always shifting, under the pressure of fresh social needs and demands, it must be left free to move with those needs and demands and cannot be fixed through any constitutional restatement. The only possible principle of democratic confirmation is that public action should be undertaken only where and when and in so far as the need for common action becomes evident and is accepted, for the sake of the common good. In that way controlled democracy could yet be made the golden mean whereby social needs might be satisfied as largely and justly as possible, while still leaving as wide a residue as possible for the free choice of the individual.

"That is fully as true for the international sphere. It is indeed the only way to combine as well as may be international organization with national freedom."[42]

With all his organismic metaphor and talk of central planning, Mitrany's projected world commonwealth bears the earmarks of the Liberal state writ large. More precisely, the Mitranian vision seems to elevate to an international level that pluralist dream analyzed by Wolin:

"The assumption prevailing among most groupists has been that the perpetuation of society requires the performance of a certain number of functions. These functions, in turn, are the complement to a determinate number of human needs. The next step in this chain of reasoning calls for listing the number of these functions that are being satisfactorily discharged by non-political associations or groups, such as trade unions, churches, corporations, and other private or voluntary groupings. The sum of group functions is then subtracted from the totality of socially necessary functions, and the precious little that remains is allowed to be the province of the political order. And more often than not the remainder turns out to involve mainly administrative functions. In this way the

[42] *Ibid.*, pp. 31-32.

political order comes to occupy the status of residuary legatee, shouldering those tasks which other groups or organizations are unwilling or unable to perform."[43]

But there is an important distinction. Mitrany begins without a ready-made framework provided by state or community; so do we. If the building of a world community is our goal, the task would seem to entail far more than binding together common international interests, laudable as that objective is. Admittedly the view afforded by the present investigation is sharply limited by the narrowness of its single empirical vantage-point and a relatively short lapse of time since the UN financing programs began. But given these limitations, our findings suggest that the functionalist argument has purchased non-controversiality at too dear a price.

I I I

What the London *Observer* once said of the International Bank for Reconstruction and Development might with almost equal pertinence be said of the functionalist argument itself: "a fascinatingly ambivalent blend of the revolutionary and the conventional, bold but tentative in conception, a little vague, a little self-contradictory even, but also flexible. . . ."[44] The functionalist thesis deserves critical examination, but I hope this treatment does not hide my respect for what it seeks to accomplish. It is difficult to take exception with the essence of the functionalist argument—the simple plea for a little more international cooperation in doing things which need to be done very badly, the guileless plea for greater reluctance to infuse these undertakings with the spirit of power politics. Sir Arthur Salter succinctly pins down both its attraction and its weakness as a more systematic doctrine with his

[43] Wolin, *op.cit.*, p. 431. Emphasis omitted. Cf. the quotation from Herbert Spencer's *Essays*, *ibid.*, p. 350.

[44] Quoted by Cater, *op.cit.*, p. 13.

mature judgment: "It is tempting, when the creation of a world political government seems so difficult, to imagine that separate functional bodies—a Bank, an organization to deal with transport or economics or finance—will add up to a total of all that is needed; but if there is no political heart there will be no life in the limbs."[45]

My own critique can be reduced to two themes. The first is commitment. It is a manifestation of that activist impulse which the functionalist argument appears to encourage and yet, paradoxically, tends to subvert. There is an element of sacrifice within commitment, but it appears as sacrifice only to the uncommitted. To elaborate would be redundant.

The second theme is purpose—that which provides for commitment a longer and higher view, and thus informs its striving with a sense of direction. Without commitment, purpose becomes either manipulation or empty sloganeering; without purpose, commitment dies for want of vision. Mary Parker Follett's words frame the thought: "Our contribution is of no value unless it is effectively related to the contributions of all the others concerned. This is a problem which needs the best efforts of our best organization engineers. For the 'will to integrate' . . . is not enough. Integrative unity willed with ardour will not unfold itself before our eyes. By willing ends we do not automatically will means. The success of organization engineering depends on its treatment of the problem of participation, of functional relating. To draw out the capacities of all and then to fit these together is our problem."[46]

There is a role here for the statesman. "Organization engineering" in an international context is high politics, nothing less, and its achievements involve a creative union of commitment and purpose.

---

[45] Sir Arthur Salter, *Personality in Politics* (London: Faber & Faber, 1947), p. 129.
[46] Metcalf and Urwick, *op.cit.*, p. 229.

In one respect the student of politics is relegated to a subservient position, though it may be a joyful or an unknowing subservience. For the statesman is ultimate guardian of the scholar's title as prophet. A single Point Four can make or break his claim, and may very well shape his subsequent research efforts, as well.

In another respect the student of politics pursues his own course. He can seek and strive to communicate the meaning of human life, including the changing modes of man's life with other men, and in his exploration may possibly come upon some of the perplexities which have troubled me, and trouble me yet. There is the question of how to check or avert the chilling prospect suggested by one side of Robert Redfield's dichotomy:

"Technical order and moral order name two contrasting aspects of all human societies. The phrases stand for two distinguishable ways in which all activities of men are coordinated. . . . [As used here,] 'the moral order' refers to . . . the binding together of men through implicit convictions as to what is right, through explicit ideals, or through similarities of conscience. The moral order is therefore always based on what is peculiarly human—sentiments, morality, conscience—and in the first place arises in the groups where people are intimately associated with one another. . . .

"[A]ll the other forms of co-ordination of activity which appear in human societies may be brought together and contrasted with the moral order under the phrase 'the technical order.' The bonds that co-ordinate the activities of men in the technical order do not rest on convictions as to the good life; they are not characterized by a foundation in human sentiments; they can exist even without the knowledge of those bound together that they are bound together. The technical order is that order which results from mutual usefulness, from deliberate coercion, or from the mere utilization of the same means. In the technical order men are bound by things, or are themselves things. They are organized by necessity or expediency."[47]

And there is the unanswered question suggested by Wolin's plea for a return to the quest for "that form of knowledge which deals with what is general and integrative to men, a life of common involvements."[48] What can fulfill the integrative role of the space-bound and territorially oriented "citizenship" while at the same time taking account of newer relationships between modern man, his several territorial domains and his involuted social universe, to which the functionalists draw our attention?

I offer no answers to these questions, for I have none. But if that fusion of reason and energy which William Blake symbolized as the marriage of Heaven and Hell is to be brought about, it will be necessary to look to the good life as well as the living organism, to design as well as evolution, to vision as well as activity. Function gains its impetus from commitment. It finds its human meaning as purpose.

[47] Robert Redfield, *The Primitive World and Its Transformations* (Ithaca: Cornell University Press, 1953), pp. 20, 21. Cf. Karl Polanyi, "Our Obsolete Market Mentality," *Commentary*, III (1947), 109-17; Erich Kahler, *The Tower and the Abyss* (New York: George Braziller, Inc., 1957), especially pp. 22f., 227, 261, 293, 294ff.

[48] Wolin, *op.cit.*, p. 434.

Bibliography of Selected Items

The scholar who wishes to follow inquiries pursued in this study will not find here a compilation of the sources used. He will find (or has found) this information in the footnotes. Lists of selected readings concerning functionalism, as defined at the outset, and financing economic development through the United Nations complex may be helpful to the person who wishes to read further on either topic. The first category has been heavily weighted toward David Mitrany's writings. In the second I have included a few works which emphasize institutional aspects of the financing agencies much more than could be done in this study.

FUNCTIONALISM

Claude, Inis L., Jr. *Swords Into Plowshares: The Problems and Progress of International Organization.* Revised edition; New York: Random House, 1964, Chapter 17.

Engle, Harold E. "A Critical Study of the Functional Approach to International Organization," unpublished Ph.D. dissertation, Department of Public Law and Government, Columbia University, 1957.

"Functional Approach to International Co-operation," *Nature*, CLIV (22 July 1944), 97-100.

Haas, Ernst B. *Beyond the Nation-State: Functionalism and International Organization.* Stanford: Stanford University Press, 1964.

———. "International Integration: The European and the Universal Process," *International Organization*, XV (Summer 1961), 366-392.

———. "Regionalism, Functionalism, and Universal International Organization," *World Politics*, VIII (January 1956), 238-263.

Joyce, James A. (editor). *World Organization: Federal or Functional?* London: L. A. Watts and Company, Ltd., 1945.

Martin, Curtis W. "The History and Theory of the Functional Approach to International Organization," unpublished Ph.D. dissertation, Department of Government, Harvard University, 1950.

Mitrany, David. Address to International Congress on Mental Health, in *Proceedings of the International Conference on Mental Hygiene*. London: H. K. Lewis and Company, Ltd., 1948. Volume IV, pp. 71-85.

———. "An Advance in Democratic Representation," *International Associations*, VI (March 1954), 136-138.

———. "The Functional Approach to World Organization," *International Affairs*, XXIV (July 1948), 350-363.

———. "A General Commentary," in *The United Nations Charter: The Text and a Commentary*. London: National Peace Council, 1945.

———. "International Consequences of National Planning," *Yale Review*, XXXVII (September 1947), 18-31.

———. "International Cooperation in Action," *International Associations*, XI (September 1959), 644-648.

———. "Problems of International Administration," *Public Administration*, XXIII (Spring 1945), 2-12.

———. *The Progress of International Government*. New Haven: Yale University Press, 1933.

———. *The Road to Security*. London: National Peace Council, 1944.

———. *A Working Peace System: An Argument for the Functional Development of International Organization*. First edition; London: Royal Institute for International Affairs, 1943.

———. *A Working Peace System: An Argument for the Functional Development of International Organization*. Fourth edition; London: National Peace Council, 1946.

Mitrany, David, and Maxwell Garnett. *World Unity and the Nations*. London: National Peace Council, n.d.

Potter, Pitman B. "Note on the Distinction Between Political and Technical Questions," *Political Science Quarterly*, L (June 1935), 264-271.

Rappard, William E. "The Evolution of the League of Nations," *The American Political Science Review*, XXI (November 1927), 792-826.

Reinsch, Paul S. *Public International Unions: Their Work and Organization: A Study in International Administrative Law*. Boston: Ginn and Company, 1911.

Salter, J. A. *Allied Shipping Control: An Experiment in International Administration*. Oxford: Clarendon Press, 1921.

Salter, Sir Arthur. "From Combined War Agencies to International Administration," *Public Administration Review*, IV (Winter 1944), 1-6.

White, Lyman C. "Peace By Pieces: The Role of Nongovernmental Organizations," *The Annals of the American Academy of Political and Social Science*, CCLXIV (July 1949), 87-97.

FINANCING ECONOMIC DEVELOPMENT

"A Developing Bank," *The Economist*, 27 June 1964, pp. 1492-1494.

Asher, Robert E., Walter M. Kotschnig, William Adams Brown, Jr., James Frederick Green, Emil J. Sady, and Associates. *The United Nations and Promotion of the General Welfare*. Washington: The Brookings Institution, 1957.

Basch, Antonín. *Financing Economic Development*. New York: The Macmillan Company, 1964.

Black, Eugene R. *The Diplomacy of Economic Development and Other Papers*. New York: Atheneum, 1963.

Cairncross, Alec. *The International Bank for Reconstruction and Development*. Princeton: International Finance Section, Department of Economics and Sociology, 1959.

Cater, Douglass. "Eugene Black, Banker to the World," *The Reporter*, XVI (4 April 1957), 13-16.

Cheever, Daniel, and H. Field Haviland, Jr. *Organizing for*

Peace: International Organization in World Affairs. Cambridge: Harvard University Press, 1954.

Gardner, Richard N. *Sterling-Dollar Diplomacy: Anglo-American Collaboration in the Reconstruction of Multilateral Trade.* Oxford: The Clarendon Press, 1956.

Hadwen, John G., and Johan Kaufmann. *How United Nations Decisions Are Made.* Revised edition; Leyden: A. W. Sythoff, 1962.

Hoffman, Paul G. *One Hundred Countries, One and One Quarter Billion People: How to Speed Their Economic Growth and Ours in the 1960's.* Washington, D.C.: Committee for International Economic Growth, 1960.

International Bank for Reconstruction and Development Staff. *The International Bank for Reconstruction and Development, 1946-1953.* Baltimore: The Johns Hopkins Press, 1954.

————. *The World Bank, IFC and IDA: Policies and Operations.* Washington, D.C.: IBRD, April 1962.

Jacobson, Harold Karan. *The USSR and the UN's Economic and Social Activities.* Notre Dame: University of Notre Dame Press, 1963.

Kindleberger, Charles P. "Bretton Woods Reappraised," *International Organization,* V (February 1951), 32-47.

Knorr, Klaus. "The Bretton Woods Institutions in Transition," *International Organization,* II (February 1948), 19-38.

Matecki, B. E. *Establishment of the International Finance Corporation and United States Policy: A Case Study in International Organization.* New York: Frederick A. Praeger, 1957.

Mikesell, Raymond F. "The World Bank in a Changing World," *Challenge,* XI (February 1963), 14-17.

Morris, James. *The Road to Huddersfield: A Journey to Five Continents.* New York: Pantheon Books, 1963.

Moussa, Pierre. *The Underprivileged Nations.* Translated by Alan Braley. London: Sidgwick and Jackson, 1959.

Rubinstein, Alvin Z. *The Soviets in International Organi-*

zations: Changing Policy Toward Developing Countries,
1953-1963. Princeton: Princeton University Press, 1964.

Seers, Dudley. "International Aid: The Next Steps," *The Journal of Modern African Studies,* II (December 1964), 471-489.

Sharp, Walter R. *Field Administration in the United Nations System: The Conduct of International Economic and Social Programs.* New York: Frederick A. Praeger, 1961.

————. "Trends in United Nations Administration," *International Organization,* XV (Summer 1961), 393-407.

Shonfield, Andrew. *The Attack on World Poverty.* New York: Vintage Books, 1962.

Stoessinger, John G., and Associates. *Financing the United Nations System.* Washington, D.C.: The Brookings Institution, 1964.

Thant, U. "The Decade of Development," *United Nations Review,* IX (June 1962), 36-39.

United Nations. *Target: An Expanding World Economy; A United Nations Special Fund Report, 1963.* UN Publication Sales No. 63.I.7.

Finally, several periodic sources might be indicated. They proved valuable in my research, and would no doubt aid future quests along similar lines. *International Organization,* a quarterly journal published by the World Peace Foundation, carries writings by practitioners and scholars, summaries of the activities of both quasi-universal and particularist international organizations, and a running bibliography. *The American Political Science Review,* quarterly journal of The American Political Science Association, also contains a running bibliography of selected articles and documents under the editorship of Richard L. Merritt. *International Conciliation,* edited by Anne Winslow and published five times yearly by the Carnegie Endowment for International Peace, presents as one of these numbers a preview of issues before the United Nations General Assembly. The *UN Monthly Chronicle*, published by the United Nations Office of Public Information, summarizes the work of the principal United Nations organs and related bodies. The *Yearbook of the United Nations*, also prepared by the Office of Public Information, offers more comprehensive if somewhat belated coverage of these activities. In the *Annual Review of United Nations Affairs*, edited by Richard N. Swift and published by New York University Press, international officials, non-governmental organization personages, and scholars strive to analyze and evaluate the major fields of United Nations activity.

Index